AF872311

# Modernizing SAP Business Warehouse

## A Strategic Guidance to Migrating to SAP Business Data Cloud (SAP Datasphere and SAP Analytics Cloud)

**Sourav Banerjee**

Apress®

***Modernizing SAP Business Warehouse: A Strategic Guidance to Migrating to SAP Business Data Cloud (SAP Datasphere and SAP Analytics Cloud)***

Sourav Banerjee
Kolkata, West Bengal, India

ISBN-13 (pbk): 979-8-8688-2191-2
ISBN-13 (electronic): 979-8-8688-2192-9
https://doi.org/10.1007/979-8-8688-2192-9

Copyright © 2025 by Sourav Banerjee

This work is subject to copyright. All rights are reserved by the Publisher, whether the whole or part of the material is concerned, specifically the rights of translation, reprinting, reuse of illustrations, recitation, broadcasting, reproduction on microfilms or in any other physical way, and transmission or information storage and retrieval, electronic adaptation, computer software, or by similar or dissimilar methodology now known or hereafter developed.

Trademarked names, logos, and images may appear in this book. Rather than use a trademark symbol with every occurrence of a trademarked name, logo, or image we use the names, logos, and images only in an editorial fashion and to the benefit of the trademark owner, with no intention of infringement of the trademark.

The use in this publication of trade names, trademarks, service marks, and similar terms, even if they are not identified as such, is not to be taken as an expression of opinion as to whether or not they are subject to proprietary rights.

While the advice and information in this book are believed to be true and accurate at the date of publication, neither the authors nor the editors nor the publisher can accept any legal responsibility for any errors or omissions that may be made. The publisher makes no warranty, express or implied, with respect to the material contained herein.

Managing Director, Apress Media LLC: Welmoed Spahr
Acquisitions Editor: Aditee Mirashi
Editorial Assistant: Gryffin Winkler

Cover designed by eStudioCalamar

Distributed to the book trade worldwide by Springer Science+Business Media New York, 1 New York Plaza, New York, NY 10004. Phone 1-800-SPRINGER, fax (201) 348-4505, e-mail orders-ny@springer-sbm.com, or visit www.springeronline.com. Apress Media, LLC is a Delaware LLC and the sole member (owner) is Springer Science + Business Media Finance Inc (SSBM Finance Inc). SSBM Finance Inc is a **Delaware** corporation.

For information on translations, please e-mail booktranslations@springernature.com; for reprint, paperback, or audio rights, please e-mail bookpermissions@springernature.com.

Apress titles may be purchased in bulk for academic, corporate, or promotional use. eBook versions and licenses are also available for most titles. For more information, reference our Print and eBook Bulk Sales web page at http://www.apress.com/bulk-sales.

Any source code or other supplementary material referenced by the author in this book is available to readers on GitHub. For more detailed information, please visit https://www.apress.com/gp/services/source-code.

If disposing of this product, please recycle the paper

*This book is dedicated to my wonderful wife Ishita who constantly supported me throughout my journey and my lovely daughter Evana without whom my family was never complete.*
*May God bless both in this life and beyond!*

# Table of Contents

# About the Author

**Sourav Banerjee** is a certified SAP BDC architect and Black Belt expert with more than 18 years of experience in different SAP Analytics products. He has worked as a solution architect and pre-sales lead for many Europe/UK/US-based customers. He has delivered many complex implementations and led the design of complicated analytics ecosystems. He has a keen interest in preparing technical documentation and diving into new product roadmaps/functionalities. Although he has been involved in technical design and coding, he has a strategic mindset to see a holistic picture of the entire landscape. His focus area is deep consulting and solution preparation for customer demonstrations in SAP BDC, Datasphere, and SAC. Technically he is expert in SAP BW/4 HANA, Enterprise HANA modeling, S/4 HANA Analytics, SAP BDC, SAP Analytics Cloud, SAP Datasphere, SLT, and Business Objects.

# About the Technical Reviewer

**Ameya Mirashi** is a senior consultant. He specializes in developing ETL solutions for databases using ORACLE PL/SQL and other similar products such as Informatica and SAP Datasphere. He has more than a decade of experience in the tech industry and has worked on projects that enhance user experience and data security. He is also interested in AI, data quality, and data governance. In his free time, he enjoys reading, playing outdoor games, and spending time with his family.

# Acknowledgments

I would like to acknowledge my mentors, colleagues, SAP help documentation, and SAP learning hub for enhancing my knowledge when writing this book.

I would like to thank Aditee Mirashi for giving me this opportunity to write and echo my voice to the world. Special thanks to Shobana Srinivasan for the timely help and guidance during the editing process. Last but not least, Thanks to the entire team at Apress for believing in me and helping me get my first book published.

# Preface

In the modern IT landscape, one strategy is to move to cloud-based products to avoid infrastructure-related efforts and costs. This is important also because most innovations within different products are applied to the cloud versions of those products.

SAP is no exception. Whether it is used for enterprise resource planning, supply chain, modern analytical capability, or predictive models, the focus is completely on cloud.

In this book, you will learn on how to plan for the modernization journey to SAP *Business Data Cloud.* Developers will benefit by understanding the product architecture, while business leaders can use this book to help them make strategic decisions.

It takes enormous amounts of time, research, and training to propose a plan of action for modernizing existing business warehouse solutions. This book will help potential customers and service providers to arrive at a sensible plan as to when and how the migration can be performed.

# Introduction

In today's world, most of the organizations on SAP ERP have already adopted SAP Business Warehouse (BW) for their warehousing and analytics solution in some shape or form. SAP BW has been a wonderful solution for more than two decades because it solves analytics, ETL, and planning needs and seamlessly integrates with SAP ERP solutions (namely ECC). But with the evolution of cloud-based solutions over the past few years, organizations are being forced to relook at their analytics landscape.

**Reasons for a Modernization Mindset**

There are several reasons for this. Mainly, the landscape components are very old, and no new innovations are planned by SAP in the on-premise products. To remain up-to-date, migration is needed.

For those who are using SAP BW, the need to integrate most of the BTP-based solutions that SAP provides today was inevitable. SAP BW has limited capability in that area. Some organizations are using the power of HANA modeling over BW modeling, which addresses some of their needs. However, there has always been a need for a robust data platform, with data that is reliable and available without delay.

Additionally, the need of artificial intelligence and machine learning use cases becomes a blocker with the old setup. It also becomes a tedious job to maintain (server monitoring, patching, upgrade, etc.) the SAP BW or HANA server.

Typically, customers start their cloud journey with ERP (namely, S/4 HANA) and then move the analytics solution to the cloud as well. This makes customers focus only on the solution without worrying about maintaining the server. This saves cost and makes the solution highly scalable and reliable.

**SAP and Legacy Together**

Some organizations adopt a mix of SAP and non-SAP products for their analytics. In some cases, this is based on their own design principles, but for the majority of instances this is because some specialized products are not available in SAP (for example, ADP is commonly used for the payroll purpose), and some integration is easier to perform using Microsoft products.

The following were other reasons:

- No SAP product deals with AI/ML scenarios.
- Microsoft or Oracle products were already adopted before SAP ERP was adopted.
- Some of the key stakeholders are from non-SAP backgrounds and prefer Microsoft/Oracle products over SAP products.
- The different licensing can be complex or transparent.
- There are outbound services in non-SAP environments.
- Tools like Power BI are being used as reporting solutions.
- Microsoft products have a robust data lake solution.

During a customer's modernization process, the key question is how the SAP cloud-based analytics solution will fit into the overall ecosystem. Given that the ecosystem consists of a mix of SAP and non-SAP products, it can be difficult to assess which components will be replaced and which components will co-exist along with the SAP cloud solution.

The best solution for the customers who are on SAP BW and willing to move to an SAP cloud-based solution for analytics, planning, and reporting is SAP Business Data Cloud (BDC).

For those who are adopting Business Data Cloud as a solution, it is imperative to know that the product BDC is not a single product by itself. It consists of a data warehouse layer (SAP BW on-premise or Private Cloud Edition aka PCE) for those who would like to retain their existing investment in BW, a data platform (SAP Datasphere previously known as Data Warehouse Cloud), a planning and/or reporting platform (SAP Analytics Cloud), and a ML/AI platform (SAP Databricks).

In Chapter 1, you will learn more about the innovations and evolution of SAP BW over time, including the planning capabilities. You will also learn how the design guidelines changed for BW/4 HANA and what SAP's strategic move on this product is.

CHAPTER 1

# SAP BW and HANA Evolution

SAP Business Warehouse launched in 1998 with version BIW 1.2 A. Over a period of time, several innovations happened in this space. BIW was replaced by BI followed by BW on HANA DB (on HANA), and then finally BW/4 HANA version was released with an add-on for FIORI. The application improved a lot over two decades, as shown in Table 1-1.

***Table 1-1.*** *BW Functionalities in Chronological Order*

| Order of Events | Innovation |
|---|---|
| 1 | GUI-based design with reporting on Infoset and multiproviders |
| 2 | Operational data storage replaced with data store object; multiproviders for reporting |
| 3 | Expert routine and BADI-based exits introduced |
| 4 | Cube replaced by advanced DSO |
| 5 | Multiprovider replaced by composite providers |
| 6 | Concept of Dataflow |
| 7 | LSA++ design came into effect |
| 8 | ABAP-based coding replaced by ABAP-managed database procedure |
| 9 | Eclipse-based development environment launched |
| 10 | BW/4 HANA launched |

(*continued*)



© Sourav Banerjee 2025
S. Banerjee, *Modernizing SAP Business Warehouse*, https://doi.org/10.1007/979-8-8688-2192-9_1

***Table 1-1.*** *(continued)*

| Order of Events | Innovation |
|---|---|
| **11** | Mixed modeling scenario (BW4 and HANA) established; HDI and HDA became preferred integration process |
| **12** | Bex query replaced by BW query |
| **13** | UI-based maintenance is introduced |
| **14** | Integration with SAC became seamless |

In a nutshell, BW/4 HANA and Enterprise HANA modeling became a preferred data warehousing platform for existing BW customers. This became increasingly significant when SAP launched S/4 HANA as an on-premise solution.

# 1.1 A Journey Through Time

Support for BW/4 HANA is guaranteed until 2040; however, SAP has confirmed there will be no more major innovations for BW/4 HANA. The main idea is to push product management to the SAP side rather than at customer side. This is exactly why organizations should eventually move toward a cloud-based solution.

There are two options: organizations can either move the existing business warehouse solution to Datasphere partially/fully or go for a greenfield implementation where you can mimic the BW artifacts with Datasphere native objects. This gives you an opportunity to get rid of the large set of objects that are no longer in use and start as a clean slate.

The migration process from BW to Datasphere can use either BW Bridge or BW PCE in which case the migration from BW to BW PCE is a prerequisite. If BW Bridge is selected as the solution, then first move the BW system to the cloud using the BW Bridge solution; then consume the BW bridge objects within Datasphere using Semantic Onboarding process. If BW PCE is used, then move the BW system to the cloud using BW PCE and then consume the data products in the Datasphere component of SAP Business Data Cloud.

BW Bridge is a cloud-based solution that is required to import the objects in Datasphere. It is hosted on the cloud and contains limited functionalities as compared to traditional BW. The BW Private Cloud Edition (BW PCE), on the other hand, has more features than BW Bridge and is required as part of the Business Data Cloud implementation. The details of these components are given the subsequent sections.

## 1.2 New Functionalities

BW/4 HANA launched with a lot of new functionalities that did not exist in the previous versions. Some of the previous versions of BW were not helpful with modern techniques and integration needs. SAP continued to perform innovations on the products by generating new versions along with releasing the migration guidelines.

**New Functionalities in Extraction Methods**

Extraction is one of the first points of interest in data warehousing techniques. BW on Oracle and other databases were suffering from large data loading and virtualization issues. This was largely resolved by using the Operational Data Provisioning (ODP) framework. Using the ODP framework, the extracted data is stored in a compressed format and therefore improves the response time and space requirements. The delta loading mechanism is also altered by implementing the subscription-based loading. This is useful for handling incremental data loading to multiple targets while the source remains the same. Earlier BW versions were creating only one delta point, and the information spreading to multiple targets was handled in the target while the source was clueless about where the data was flowing to. The exported datasources previously were designed to pull data from own BW systems. It was replaced by the ODP-based datasources in BW/4 HANA, which improved the data loading time and made administration easier.

ODP also leveraged the integration of BW/4 objects with the native HANA models by using ODP datasources. A variety of third-party applications could also be accessed (virtually and through replication) using remote sources from HANA. This specific data access method was possible due to the inclusion of HANA Smart Data Integration (SDI) and Smart Data Access (SDA) methods. As a prerequisite, you needed to install the required adapters.

**New Functionalities in Transformation and Loading Methods**

Major developments happened in the way the data used to store in BW as first-level storage. This created duplicate data in the target and allowed users to overwrite the source data before loading into the reporting layer. Many organizations did not trust the data that they saw in the reports due to this reason. The issue was resolved by decommissioning PSA to remove any data persistence in the staging area. This also meant that the data has now a single source of truth.

There were also innovations in the way the custom business logic was incorporated during the transformation of the data. ABAP managed database procedures (AMDP) were used in place of conventional ABAP while using the HANA runtime as an execution engine. Here, a typical loop over a number of records to perform any operation was replaced by a more robust full table operation (similar to that of SQL coding). This process made use of HANA SQL scripts for developing the logic.

Organizations often required only a few years of data (typically the current year to the past two years) for day-to-day reporting purpose. This means that accessing data older than a specific period does not need to be as fast as accessing the current dataset. Sometimes they are not even accessed on a day-to-day basis. It is therefore useful to move older data into a low-cost database or to a low-cost storage mechanism. This was achieved by using the Data Tiering option within the Advanced DSO. Normally there are three different tiers available: Hot, Warm, and Cold. The Hot tier is the default storage, while the Warm tier is typically a HANA extension node that is less costly. Very old data that is not accessed at all but required for disaster recovery purposes or as a backup can be moved to the Cold tier. This requires an additional server capable of handling a large amount of data such as SAP IQ.

**New Functionalities in Modeling**

Modeling in BW/4 HANA generally defines the architecture of the overall project. With LSA++ as a preferred modeling guideline, it became easier to store, maintain, and report on the data. The hybrid modeling scenario, i.e., usage of BW artifacts along with native HANA models together with composite providers, is useful to bring the flavor of both type of objects together.

An introduction of the Eclipse-based modeling process made the interface more transparent and interactive. Additionally, the use of the FIORI application for the BW cockpit provides an one-stop solution for monitoring the data loading process, scheduling jobs, and administration.

Although there was significant effort made on the innovation for this product, soon it was realized by many that the push is to move things to the cloud because customers were no longer interested in maintaining the server in terms of patches and upgrades. Therefore, a more stable outcome would be to focus only on the product rather than on the infrastructure.

## 1.3 Integrated Planning

*Integrated planning* is a concept useful for the organization planning purposes. This will support the end-to-end planning process and integrate closely with BW. Although the product is very old and later replaced by BPC, SAP is pushing toward SAP Analytics Cloud as a planning platform for future architecture.

The SAC planning platform is the tool of choice to replace the BW-IP or BPC because it is a cloud-based SAP managed solution that can be integrated with the analytics solution to provide a more strategic solution from a business perspective. It also facilitates tight integration with Datasphere.

In any case, integrated planning has been used for planning for several years.

Several database changes are usually done as part of the planning processes including copy, reposting, revaluation, delete, combination creation, lock/unlock, forecasting, file upload, currency conversions, etc. These changes are usually executed using a Planning functions. If there is need to run multiple database change activities, you can use a Planning sequence to define the list of Planning functions that need to run one after another.

From a reporting perspective, typically for budget maintenance, an input-ready report is generally required, which allows the user to change the measures (values) for each cell. For example, a General Ledger report based on the Profit & Loss hierarchy can allow a user to enter the budget amount (and company code and any other granular dimensions) for a particular year using an input-ready report.

While most of the work can be done with the built-in features of the tool, organizations needed customizations based on their business processes. In such cases, you can use a Custom formula (also known as FOX). Custom formulas, however, have several restrictions and limited functionalities. For a more complex situation, you can go for a Custom Planning function, which allows you to write object-oriented ABAP coding where the source data can be read, manipulated, and enriched as per need.

For organizations that are willing to perform a BW migration and use integrated planning/BPC for their planning needs, SAP Analytics Cloud planning becomes a preferred alternative.

# 1.4 SAP Strategies

Over the past two decades SAP Business Warehouse has been the only platform available for warehousing and reporting needs. With the evolution of SAP Analytics Cloud, the reporting part has shifted toward cloud-based dashboards. Prior to that, Business Object was the tool of choice for creating reports and dashboards, and it had very tight integration with BW.

While the fate of BW is unclear, SAP is moving toward the cloud-based BW product, although it needs to be combined with a more user-friendly cloud solution like Business Data Cloud.

Datasphere has never been marketed as replacement for BW, but it can possibly the way to redesign the warehousing needs that organizations have. Until now, the products are fully managed by customers/service providers, but with the evolution of Business Data Cloud, the intention is to create SAP-managed data products that can be easily consumed for reporting purposes.

**HANA Server**

HANA was introduced as a database type to have column-based storage and use an in-memory architecture to provide a faster response to any query. With the evolution of HANA, virtual queries became increasingly important. SAP HANA was born in 2010.

In today's world, many SAP solutions are running on HANA server. Initially the on-premise version was launched, and it was later upgraded to HANA Cloud where most of the analytics and ERP solutions are running today. This again provides SAP with an option to manage the product directly from an infrastructure point of view.

Figure 1-1 shows the chronology of events related to the HANA server.

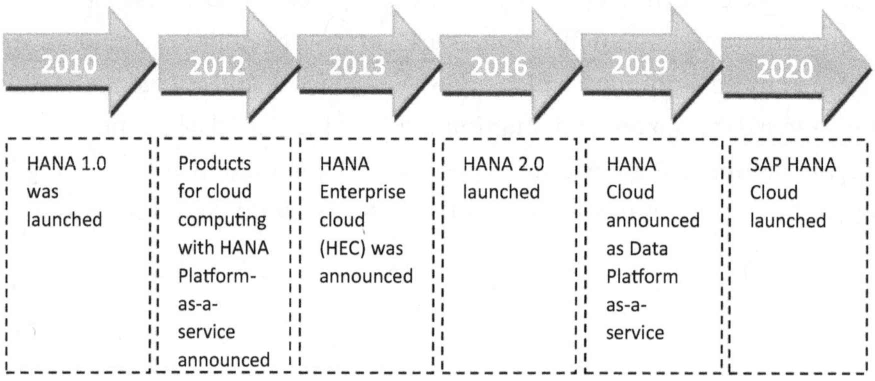


***Figure 1-1.** HANA innovations timeline*

## 1.5 Advantages of HANA

Currently all new SAP innovations are powered by HANA or HANA Cloud. This is a common server configuration, the usefulness of which is accepted already by all the active SAP customers and partners. The following are some of the advantages.

**In-Memory Database**

SAP HANA stores data on a high-speed memory platform that enables users to run queries faster than in traditional databases. The database stores intermediate results and the data in the computer's main memory instead of the disk storage. This makes the analytic engine run faster as a disk-level read usually takes longer.

**ACID Compliance**

Atomicity, consistency, isolation, and durability are maintained. Atomicity refers to the rollback of transactions that are partly executed; i.e., if one transaction fails, then the other related transactions won't get executed, and the entire statement will be rolled back, pushing the database to the previous state. Consistency means that the transactions will maintain the integrity of the database and follow all the constrains. Isolation means all transactions are independent, and the effect does not impact any other ongoing statements until the previous transaction was fully committed. Durability means that once the transaction is fully committed, the changes will be permanent even if there is a system failure.

**Multitier Column-Based Storage and Scalability**

Various temperatures are defined during the data storage: Hot, Warm, and Cold. This will significantly optimize the cost of space. The tiers are useful to define the way the data is stored and read. For example, the data in the warm tier can be required only a few times. This is generally older data, which has fewer reporting requirements. Therefore, the performance is not a major concern. It is therefore useful to store this data in an extension node that can be merged with the original dataset using union pruning.

*HANA* supports a very high volume of data with the capability to extend.

Column-based data storage makes it easier to show query results with a faster response time. This will also save a significant amount of space in the database compared to the traditional row-level storage.

In general, the HANA database becomes increasingly reliable, not only from the database design perspective but also from database management, application development, analytics, and virtualization perspectives.

The main solutions that are running today on the HANA database are the following:

- SAP S/4 HANA
- SAP Data Intelligence (Sunset planned)
- SAP Datasphere
- SAP Analytics cloud

## 1.6 Change in Coding Styles

The HANA database comes with its own database language called SQL script, which is an extension of the traditional SQL queries. The advantage of using SQL script over conventional ABAP is to move out of the concept of looping over the rows of a table and to run the operation on the entire table. This gives immense performance benefits, and the response time is faster. SQL script is a concept that is not only used within HANA for coding but also used using AMDP within BW/4 HANA object transformations and in the modern world within Datasphere as well. A typical ABAPer should change their mindset to table-level database operations to learn SQL script.

**Guidelines for SQL Scripts**

Here are some tips:

- Split complex statements into small parts. Do not write big SELECT statements that will lose readability and make troubleshooting difficult. If traditional SQL is used, a common table expression can be used.
- Select queries are mainly used to construct HANA SQL scripts. Scalar variables (tables) will be used to store the intermediate results (similar to ABAP internal tables).
- Joins must be performed carefully. Any WHERE statement can remove required data from the output. Wherever possible, use dynamic joins and join pruning and define cardinality.
- Avoid SELECT * at any cost. Always mention the field names in SELECT statements instead of writing * from a performance perspective.

- A declaration is generally not required for local tables within the script. You can directly name any table and assign data through SELECT statements.
- When appending data, if required, especially inside a loop, you can add an empty line to a table. Then append the output to another table using a union of the first and second tables. In each loop run, the first table is refreshed, while the second table retains the previous dataset. An example is given here:

```
While :lt_count < 4 DO
        Lt_temp = select "A","B" from "SAPHANA"."TABLE1"
        where "ROW" = :lt_count;
       Lt_final = select "A","B" from :Lt_final union select
       "A","B" from :LT_temp;
End While;
```

- A field sequence needs to be maintained to avoid incorrect mapping. While writing the final SELECT statement to return the data, the sequence of the target fields should be the same as the metadata definition; i.e., the position of the fields in the final SELECT statement is what you would get in the output.
- The **If-Else** decision block can't be used inside a SELECT statement. If a calculation is based on the conditions is required, then use case-when-end to assign a calculated field. An example is given here:

```
Lt_table = select case "CC"
 when 'GB01' then 'UK'
else 'US'
 end as "COMPANY" from "SAPHANA"."TEMP";
```

- Assigning a constant value to a field is a common requirement. If this is required, then it can be done by simply mentioning the value with the syntax: '*AS* <fieldname>'.

- Aggregation can be done by using clause, say SUM(<fieldname>), with an addition of group by <all the attributes separated by ‘,’>). An example is given here:

```
Lt_table = select sum("A"),"B","C" from "SAPHANA"."TEMP" group by
"B", "C"
```

- Identifying the first row for a condition is sometimes useful to determine duplicate entries for a particular selection. For instance, to find out the first row for a particular selection (say, the first item of every sales order), you need to use a partition statement with a specific order of fields. Here is an example:

```
Lt_table = select "A","B" from(select ROW_NUMBER() over
 (partition by "ORDER" order by "ORDER","ITEM" ascending)
as "ROW","A","B" from "SAPHANA"."SALESORDER" ) where "ROW" = 1;
```

- Input parameters, if defined, should be passed as a filter condition within the select statement and be treated like as a scalar variable (i.e., the name should start with ‘:’).

- The performance of the SQL scripts is always a debatable topic. Ideally script-based modeling/use cases must be written very carefully as it does not by default checks the performance of your code. A few tips would be to avoid nested statements, apply filters at the early stage, do not bring unnecessary data, and split complex joins into smaller pieces.

## 1.7 Test Your knowledge

Q1: What is the main reason to use Business Warehouse in any landscape?

a) As a middleware

b) As a data warehousing solution

c) As a reporting solution

d) For AI- and ML-related scenarios

Q2: Why is there a need to modernize BW?

a) Support is out to date
b) Need of pushing toward a cloud-based solution
c) Integration with other tools is not reliable or robust
d) All of the above

Q3: Which product is a potential replacement for integrated planning?

a) Datasphere
b) SAP BTP
c) Business Objects
d) SAP Analytics Cloud

Q4: Why is SAP's strategic vision to move to a cloud-based analytics solution?

a) To have customer-managed data products
b) To have SAP-managed data products
c) Both a and b
d) None of the above

Q5: What is the end of life for SAP Business Warehouse?

a) By the end of 2040
b) By the end of 2030
c) No date disclosed
d) None of the above

Q6: What is the full form of BW PCE?

a) Business Warehouse Public Cloud Enterprise
b) Business Warehouse Private Cloud Enterprise
c) Business Warehouse Public Cloud Edition
d) Business Warehouse Private Cloud Edition

Q7: Which one of the following is not an advantage of the HANA database?

a) In-memory architecture

b) Atomicity, consistency, isolation, and durability

c) High security firewall

d) None of the above

Q8: You should never write a SELECT on an intermediate table (scalar).

a) True

b) False

Q9: HANA always stores data in the disk memory.

a) True

b) False

Q10: Which of the following does not run on the HANA database?

a) SAP Datasphere

b) Business Object Data Services

c) SAP Analytical Cloud

d) All of the above

Q11: For conditional statements, IF-THEN-ELSE can be written within a SELECT statement.

a) True

b) False

Answer: b

Q12: HANA is always hosted on-premises.

a) True

b) False

Q13: The common function between SQL scripts and ABAP is that both can run operations on the entire table instead of running operations on each row.

a) True

b) False

# 1.8 Summary

In this chapter, you learned the history of SAP Business Warehouse and the innovations to it over two decades. Additionally, the chapter explained the first step of the cloud migration process along with the functionalities (reporting and planning) of SAP BW at a high level.

You also learned how the HANA database is internally organized and why it is more powerful than other databases. You also learned about SQL scripts and basic guidelines.

This chapter gave a clear historical and technical explanation of SAP BW and HANA, explaining their evolution from the early BIW versions to BW/4HANA. It effectively highlighted the innovations the platform has been through.

BW and HANA modeling have ruled the industry for quite some time. To make the landscape future-ready, it is inevitable to use Datasphere for modeling in a cloud-native environment.

In the next chapter, you will learn about Datasphere as a data solution for any organization.

# CHAPTER 2

# Datasphere

SAP Datasphere is a software-as-a-service (SaaS) product that was launched by SAP in 2019 originally named Data Warehouse Cloud (DWC). In 2023, DWC was rebranded as Datasphere and marketed as a trusted data platform managed by SAP. There is also a cloud-based product hosted on the HANA cloud. Datasphere delivers a Business Data Fabric architecture to access all the data and to create a uniform data access engine without losing the business semantics definition.

Business Data Fabric is meant to deliver all the organization's data without losing its context. This is required to integrate all the data from different business areas and access it seamlessly without changing the source of truth. It aims to centralize, connect, access, manage, and govern data across different applications. A data mesh, on the other hand, is an architectural concept that decentralizes the data so that the individual team can own their data. This is also known as *data autonomy*. The ownership is different in these two architectural concepts. Business Data Fabric is used to simplify complex software ecosystems while retaining the context of the data. This means that the usual loss of context during data extraction is not applicable in Business Data Fabric. The solution is scalable, simple, and semantically rich, and it is delivered using a single source of truth.

Data Builder is normally used by the developers to create and model scenarios with professional expertise, for example, writing scripts, associating hierarchies, advanced modeling with Python, etc. Business Builder is more business focused to make use of semantic data models that can be handled more easily by superusers as self-service.

## 2.1 Data Builder Artifacts

Data Builder in Datasphere delivers database artifacts that create the basic building blocks for the modeling. The following are the possible object lists:

> **Tables:** Tables are the structured definition of a data set often conceptually liked to a functional area for example: Sales Order



© Sourav Banerjee 2025
S. Banerjee, *Modernizing SAP Business Warehouse*, https://doi.org/10.1007/979-8-8688-2192-9_2

details or Employee details etc. This can be local (the metadata definition is within Datasphere) or remote (the metadata definition is in different source systems). A remote table is useful to connect with external systems such as S/4 HANA. A remote table can also be replicated/persisted within Datasphere. A local table, on the other hand, is created to fill results from other objects.

**Views:** Views are a combination of multiple tables or another view with a relationship defined in terms of joins.

*Graphical:* This view is defined using graphical display via a drag-and-drop feature. Usually, the intermediate results can be viewed for analysis purposes (for example, the outcome of an aggregation node can be viewed without running the entire view definition). This can be particularly useful for troubleshooting purposes.

*SQL:* This view is created when the logic is too complex to be achieved using a Graphical view. The code can be written either by writing SQL or by writing SQL scripts (table functions). Unlike Graphical view, in SQL view the intermediate results can't be displayed. The runtime check of syntax is possible only during the deployment process. Usually, the view outcome is written using the RETURN statement.

**Analytical models:** These are models used for analytics purposes. Currently this is the only Data Builder object that can be read from SAC. Here the relationship between facts and dimensions is defined along with the KPI (restricted and calculated) definitions. One can relate this to a BW query.

**Data flow and replication flow**: Both data flow and replication flow are used to bring data from different source systems. Replication flow is usually created to get the data (with delta capability) from other source systems into/outside Datasphere. This feature replaces the BW open hub concept. Dataflow, on the other hand, is mostly created to update tables within Datasphere (say local tables).

**Intelligent lookup**: The lookup functionality normally is based on the exact value of the conditions defined. However, the intelligent lookup allows you to find closest match through fuzzy search and to validate the data at runtime.

**Task chain**: This is like process chain in BW where multiple data loads will be added in one place for better control and scheduling purposes.

**Data access control:** This is related to the authorizations that can be implemented in the Datasphere objects.

## 2.2 Business Builder

Business Builder is used in Datasphere to create artifacts that are more aligned to the business and typically construct the business layer of your data. The entity and relationships of the objects can be easily created within Business Builder. In general, Business Builder does not work with raw datasets. Only when the context of the data, i.e., semantics, is re-created or retained, Business Builder can be used.

The following object types can be created in Business Builder:

- Facts
- Dimensions
- Fact models
- Consumption models
- Authorization scenarios

**Facts**

Facts are typically something that can be measured, for example, amount or quantity.

In the first screen, a data entity must be defined that requires an already created table or view within the data builder. Then the following needs to be defined:

*Measures*

- Source: Here three pieces of information are needed.

  ***Measure type***: This can be Aggregation (for normal measures) or Fixed value (a constant) or Calculated Measure (Calculation based on already available measure in the model) or Converted currency (where an existing measure needs to be selected with currency value)

***Source Measure*:** Only applicable for Aggregation or Converted currency. Here you need to specify the source measure name from the list of measures available in your data entity.

***Aggregation type*:** Only applicable to the models where measure type is selected as Aggregation. Possible options are SUM, Average, Count, Minimum, and Maximum.

- Exception Aggregation: Select one of the following options:

  ***Exception aggregation type***: Possible options are SUM, Minimum, Maximum, Count, Count excluding zero, Count excluding NULL and zero, Average or Average excluding NULL.

  ***Exception aggregation attribute***: Exception aggregation is not a generalized aggregation behavior. Therefore, an exception aggregation must be associated with a dimension. This makes sure that the aggregation behavior changes only when the specified dimension is also available in the display.

- Currency or Unit: Here you need to specify the currency (in case of amount) or unit (in case of quantity). You can use a fixed currency, or you can get the currency/unit from an existing field in your data entity.
- Auxiliary measure: This option is used when the measure is not needed in the final view and is used only for temporary purpose. For example, a calculated measure can use another measure for the calculation. In the outcome, only the calculated measure is needed. In that case, the checkbox Auxiliary measure needs to be checked when defining the second measure so that it will not be exposed in the consumption view.
- Replace Null with Zero: This option is used when there is chance of getting NULL records, which can create issues while performing aggregations. With this option, all NULL measures will be replaced by 0.

**Attributes**

- Source

  ***Attribute type*:** Here you can define the attribute that you are going to use. It can be either a source attribute (from the list of attributes available in your data entity) or calculated attributes (which requires a calculation to be created such as current date).

  ***Identifier Attribute***: Here you define the attribute required when the attribute type selected as "source attribute." You can choose from any available attributes.

- Auxiliary attributes: If this is selected, then the attribute will not be exposed to the consumption model.

*Input Parameters*: You can create an input parameter only when your data entity has at least one parameter defined. The property can be inherited, and values can be overwritten at runtime.

*Key Definitions*: In general, the primary keys are inherited from the data entity (there is also an option to start as a clean slate without the key definition copied). There is an option to define additional keys over and above the default keys.

*Hierarchy*: Hierarchies inside the fact can be inherited from an existing hierarchical data stored within Data Builder already. The exception is that Business Builder hierarchies are supported with only one key field.

*Association*: Associations can be created with another dimension or fact as a business entity. Once the business entity is specified, then the mapping of foreign keys needs to be defined.

*Authorization Scenario*: The authorization scenario can be applied to the fact along with the corresponding data restriction for the authorization.

**Dimension**

Dimensions are something that are navigable and produce a meaningful breakdown of the data. For example, the company code can be a dimension that when displayed in the report will show a breakdown of sales per company. It is also possible to display multiple dimensions together for a more detailed study of the data.

**Fact Models**

Fact models are used when you have repetitive definitions of measures and/or dimensions in several consumption models. In this case, the definition will be created only once but can be reused as many times as required.

Along with the definition of measures and dimensions, additionally dimension sources can be exposed to consumption models.

You can also define filters to restrict the amount of data and to extract only the records that are necessary. The filter is very basic, for example, filters based on a specific value or to exclude a constant from the selection. It does not support complex filters based on variable values or formulas.

**Consumption Models**

Consumption models are consumable models inside the Business Builder, which defines the facts, dimensions, hierarchies, and filters. Within the consumption model, you can define a perspective, which is a smaller set of the consumption model that can be used directly in SAP Analytics Cloud stories. These perspectives will need at least one measure and dimension from the fact view.

If you allow Public Data Access from the General tab, then the authorization scenario can't be maintained.

**Authorization Scenario**

The authorization scenario can be defined to control the data flow within and outside Datasphere. This requires a Data Access Control definition that will be used for defining the access. In the Permission table, you can add all required values that the user has access to.

The authorization scenario can be used within the Business Builder models and entities.

## 2.3 Currency Conversion

Currency conversion is an important and tricky topic in *Datasphere*. It is often required to report the data coming from different sources in a uniform currency, say, Group currency, which can provide output required to create, say, a P&L statement.

To perform currency conversion, it is required to understand various tables in the ECC/S4 HANA system that provides calculation blocks for the conversion:

TCURX: Decimal places for currencies

TCURV: Exchange rate types for currency conversions

TCURF: Conversion factors

TCURR: Exchange rates

TCURC: Currency codes

TCURN: Quotations

The standard way of doing currency conversions in Datasphere can be found within the Graphical views with the calculation node. A currency converted column must be defined where the reference of all six tables mentioned earlier must be defined. These tables can be remote table from the ERP system. To avoid errors, the tables need to be contained within separate Graphical views before they are referred to within this calculation. During the calculation, a conversion type (which typically defined how the conversion can happen, e.g., start of the year, YTD, monthly rates, etc.), source currency, target currency, and date using which the currency is converted need to be defined.

Once the details are filled, then based on the base measure available within the calculation, the conversion happens automatically. There are ways to define what happens if the conversion fails; i.e., the view won't show any data or skip the record or show 0 value or simply copy the source amount.

## 2.4 Command-Line Interface (CLI)

The command-line interface in Datasphere is used to perform several actions that are generally done in the Datasphere page. The CLI can be very useful in automating certain tasks from outside Datasphere, and it supports integration with Python.

**Installing CLI**

Before you install CLI, the following prerequisites must be met:

- The Node.js version should be between 18 and 22.
- The Npm version should be between 8 and 10.

The installation requires you run the following command:

```
npm install -g @sap/datasphere-cli
```

Once the installation is completed, you can log on to the CLI using the OAuth client.

An OAuth client can be created in the configuration window of Datasphere. Here a secret will be generated along with other details like client ID, token URL, and authorization URL.

The login can be done by running the following command:

```
Datasphere login
--Client ID <Specify client id>
--Client secret <Specify the secret>
--Authorization URL <Provide the authorization URL>
--token URL <Specify the token URL>
```

**CLI Applicability**

In general, the following tasks can be performed using the CLI:

**Configuration**: For the configuration, the following tasks can be performed (with users that have the role DW Administrator):

- List TLS Certificates

  Command:

  ```
  datasphere configuration certificates list
  ```

- Upload TLS Certificates

  Command:

  ```
  datasphere configuration certificates upload
  --description <description>
  --file-path<path> | --input <input>
  ```

- Delete TLS Certificates

  Command:

  ```
  datasphere configuration certificates delete
  --fingerprint <fingerprint>
  ```

**DB User:** Reset passwords for the DB users that have the DW Space Administrator role.

Command:

```
datasphere dbusers password reset
--space <id>
--databaseuser <id>
[--output <file>.json]
```

**Global Roles**: The following operations are possible (can be performed by users with the DW Administrator role):

- List global roles

  Command:

  ```
  datasphere global-roles list
      [--output <file>.json]
  ```

- List users in global roles

  Command:

  ```
  datasphere global-roles users list
  --role <ID>
   --output <file>.json
  ```

- Add users to global roles

  Command:

  ```
  datasphere global-roles users add
  role <ID>
  users <userID[,userID...]>
  ```

- Remove users from global roles

  Command:

  ```
  datasphere global-roles users remove
  --role <ID>
  --users <userID[,userID...]>
  ```

**Datasphere Marketplace**: The following operations are possible (by users with the DW Modeler role):

- List Marketplace providers

  Command:

  *datasphere marketplace providers list*

- Read Marketplace providers

  Command:

  *datasphere marketplace providers rea*

- Create Marketplace providers

  Command:

  *datasphere marketplace providers create*

- Overwrite Marketplace providers

  Command:

  *datasphere marketplace providers overwrite*

- Update Marketplace providers

  Command:

  *datasphere marketplace providers update*

- List Marketplace products

  Command:

  *datasphere marketplace products list*

- Read Marketplace products

  Command:

  *datasphere marketplace products read*

- Create Marketplace products

  Command:

  *datasphere marketplace products create*

- Overwrite Marketplace products

  Command:

  *datasphere marketplace products overwrite*

- Update Marketplace products

  Command:

  *datasphere marketplace products update*

- Install Marketplace products

  Command:

  *datasphere marketplace products install*

- Display change lifecycle status of Marketplace products

  Command:

  *datasphere marketplace products change-lifecycle-status*

- Delete Marketplace products

  Command:

  *datasphere marketplace products delete*

- List Marketplace products by provider

  Command:

  *datasphere marketplace products-by-provider list*

- Read Marketplace products by provider

  Command:

  *datasphere marketplace products-by-provider read*

- Create Marketplace products by provider

  Command:

  *datasphere marketplace products-by-provider create*

- Delete Marketplace products by provider

  Command:

  ```
  datasphere marketplace products-by-provider delete
  ```

- Overwrite Marketplace products by provider

  Command:

  ```
  datasphere marketplace products-by-provider overwrite
  ```

- Update Marketplace products by provider

  Command:

  ```
  datasphere marketplace products-by-provider update
  ```

- Display change lifecycle status of Marketplace products by provider

  Command:

  ```
  datasphere marketplace products-by-provider change-
  lifecycle-status
  ```

**Datasphere Objects**: The following operations are possible (by users with the DW Modeler role):

- List objects in space

  Command:

  ```
  datasphere objects <object-type> list
  --space <id>
  [--technical-names <name>[,...]]
  [--output <file>.json]
  [--select "<property[,...]>"]
  [--filter "<property operator value>[ and|or ...]"]
  [--top <n>]
  [--skip <n>]
  ```

- Read objects

  Command:

```
datasphere objects <object-type> read
--space <id>
--technical-name <name>
[--output <file>.json]
[--accept <format>]
```

- Create objects

  Command:

```
datasphere objects <object-type> create
--space <id>
--technical-name <name>
--file-path <name>.json|--input '<stringified-json>'
[--custom-validation-options <option[,option]>]   [ --save-anyway]
[--no-deploy]
```

- Update objects

  Command:

```
datasphere objects <object-type> update
--space <id>
--technical-name <name>
--file-path <name>.json|--input '<stringified-json>'
[--custom-validation-options <option[,option]>]
[--save-anyway]
[--no-deploy]
```

- Delete objects

  Command:

```
datasphere objects <object-type> delete
--space <id>
--technical-name <name>
[--delete-anyway]
[--force]
```

**Scoped roles**: The following operations are possible (by users with the DW Administrator role):

- List scoped roles

  Command:

  ```
  datasphere scoped-roles list
  [--output <file>.json]
  ```

- Read scoped roles

  Command:

  ```
  datasphere scoped-roles read
  --role <id>
  [--output <file>.json]
  ```

- Create scoped roles

  Command:

  ```
  datasphere scoped-roles create
  --file-path <file>.json|--input '<stringified-json>'
  ```

- Update scoped roles

  Command:

  ```
  datasphere scoped-roles update
  --role <ID>
  --file-path <file>.json|--input '<stringified-json>'
  ```

- Add spaces to scoped roles

  Command:

  ```
  datasphere scoped-roles scopes add
  --role <ID>
  --scopes <ID[,ID...]>
  ```

- Add users to scoped roles

Command:

```
datasphere scoped-roles users add
--role <ID>
--file-path <file>.json|--input '<stringified-json>'
```

- Remove users from scoped roles

  Command:

```
datasphere scoped-roles users remove
--role <ID>
--file-path <file>.json|--input '<stringified-json>'
```

- Remove scopes from scoped roles

  Command:

```
datasphere scoped-roles scopes remove
--role <ID>
--scopes <ID[,ID...]>
```

- Delete scoped roles

  Command:

```
datasphere scoped-roles delete
--role <ID>
[--force]
```

**Spaces**: The following operations are possible (by users with the DW SPACE ADMINISTRATOR ROLE for space administration and users with the DW INTEGRATOR ROLE for connection related changes):

- List Spaces

  Command:

```
datasphere spaces list
[--host "<url>"]
[--output <file>.json]
```

- Read space

  Command:

  ```
  datasphere spaces read
  --space <id>
  [--definitions [<obj1>,<obj2>]]
  [--no-space-definition]
  [--output <file>.json]
  ```

- Create or update space

  Command:

  ```
  datasphere spaces create
  --file-path <file>
  ```

- Delete a space

  Command:

  ```
  datasphere spaces delete
  --space <id>
  [--force]
  ```

- List connections in a space

  Command:

  ```
  datasphere spaces connections list
  --space <space>
  [--accept <accept>]
  [--details]
  [--name]
  [--features ]
  [--top <n>]
  [--skip <n>]
  [--output file.json]
  ```

– Read connection details

Command:

*datasphere spaces connections get*
*--space <space>*
*--name <name>*
*[--output file.json]*

- Create connections

Command:

*datasphere spaces connections create*
*--space <space>*
*--type-id <connection type id>*
*--file-path<path> | --input <input>*

- Validate connections

Command:

*datasphere spaces connections validate*
*--space <space>*
*--name <name>*

- Edit connections

Command:

*datasphere spaces connections edit*
*--space <space>*
*--name <name>*
*--file-path<path> | --input <input>*

- Delete connections

Command:

*datasphere spaces connections delete*
*--space <space>*
*--name <name>*
*[--force]*

**Workload**: The following operations are possible (by users with the DW Administrator role):

- List, read, update space priorities
- List, read, update statement limit for spaces

  Command:

```
datasphere workload list/update
[--host "url"]
[--output file.json]
```

**Task chains**: The following operations are possible (by users with the DW Integrator role):

- Run task chain

  Command:

```
datasphere tasks chains run
 --space <space-ID>
 --object <object>
```

- Get log

  Command:

```
datasphere tasks logs get
 --space <space-ID>
 --log-id <log-ID>
 [--info-level status | details]
```

**Users:** The following operations are possible (by users with the DW Administrator role):

- List users

  Command:

```
datasphere users list
[--accept <format>]
[--output file.json]
```

- Create users

  Command:

  ```
  datasphere users create
  --file-path <file>.json|--input '<stringified-json>'
  ```

- Update users

  Command:

  ```
  datasphere users update
  --file-path <file>.json|--input '<stringified-json>'
  ```

- Delete users

  Command:

  ```
  datasphere users delete
  --users <ID[,ID...]>
  [--force]
  ```

## 2.5 Integration with Other SAP Applications

SAP Datasphere is always branded as a trusted data platform for all the analytics need. This requires integration with other SAP applications. The following integrations can be made possible using Datasphere.

### 2.5.1 SAP S/4 HANA Cloud

S/4 HANA Cloud integration with Datasphere can be done by using a communication user. Normally, a communication user is created in the S/4 HANA system, and several communication scenarios are needed to be assigned to that user. A communication scenario enables the data exchange between the S/4 HANA system and outbound system. SAP provides several predefined communication scenarios that can be used for the data exchange. A communication user needs to have communication scenario SAP_COM_0722. This scenario enables the OData service for the CDS views that reside within the S/4 HANA system. Once the user is created, the connection in Datasphere can be established, and CDS views are exposed to Datasphere for data access.

## 2.5.2 SAP ARIBA

ARIBA is an application for vendor management by SAP. The connectivity with Datasphere is very tricky in nature. Normally ARIBA artifacts can be read via standard ARIBA APIs. To get the data into Datasphere, first a local table must be created within a new DB user schema under the working space. A new HDI container needs to be created that is associated with the same DB user. The rest of the configurations need to be done in the Business Technology platform. First the service instance for the HDI container should be created within BTP using the same DB user credentials. The extractor created using the service instance must be deployed via CLI using GITHUB.

Once the configuration is done, the extractor can be scheduled with a payload containing the name of the ARIBA view that can push data into the HANA Cloud DB table. Later this table can be consumed within a view in Datasphere for reporting purposes.

## 2.5.3 SAP Concur

Concur is an SAP application used for the travel maintenance purposes. The integration with Datasphere can be done through a local table within the DB user schema. The SAP-delivered Concur APIs can be read using a JDBC datasource created within an integration flow of the BTP integration suite. For the target table configuration, you must write a Groovy script powered by Apache. Once the data arrives at the local table in the HANA cloud DB, it can be consumed within Datasphere by creating a view.

## 2.5.4 SAP FIELDGLASS

SAP Fieldglass is an application used for vendor management where the external workforce can be managed efficiently. The integration with Datasphere is straightforward using a standard connector. To establish the connection, the Data Provisioning agent must be registered with a cloud data integration adapter.

## 2.5.5 SAP Integrated Business Planning (IBP)

The Integrated Business Planning is a product used in the supply chain that can perform sales and operation planning, forecasting and demand, response and supply, demand-driven replenishment, and inventory planning. It can predict demand using an advanced algorithm, perform multilevel supply planning, and integrate finance and operation planning. The integration with Datasphere is not straightforward. The integration requires an SAP cloud integrator as middleware, which is a cloud service in BTP. The communication with IBP can be made possible using a Web Socket RFC-based interface. Web Socket RFC works like a conventional remote function call with an added security layer. It enables a standardized transport layer where a VPN tunnel is not required. The fast serialization approach for Web Socket RFC enables a higher transmission speed, and all connections are TLS encrypted, which provides a higher level of security benefit. In BTP, the destination must be created using the IBP system's credentials. A JDBC datasource is then created to connect to the IBP system inside an integration flow in BTP. Finally, a Groovy script is written to push the data into the cloud HANA DB on which Datasphere is hosted.

## 2.6 BW Bridge

One important question for the customers who are already using SAP Business Warehouse with lots of complex processes: how do you ensure that the investments are retained after moving to the cloud? If the processes are quick to redevelop in Datasphere, then it is acceptable; otherwise, the complete replacement of the BW server becomes a very time-consuming and long process. This would risk losing some of the functionalities, which is very old and may not even have proper documentation. Before even starting this cloud journey of modernization, it becomes an important aspect to think of.

The landscape diagram for BW Bridge is as follows:

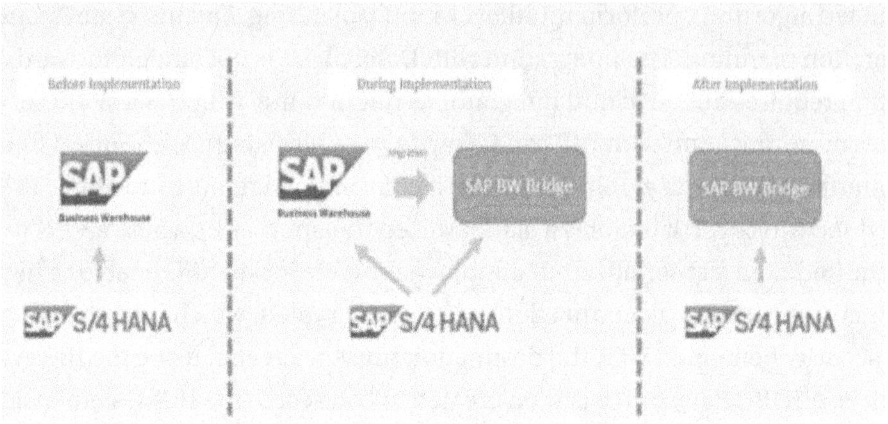


***Figure 2-1.*** *Landscape considerations BW Bridge*

Normally, the BW system is decommissioned after the migration and loading into the BW Bridge system. As soon as your BW Bridge is ready, then the data starts flowing from the source systems into the BW Bridge. At this point, technically there is no need to feed the data into the old BW system as BW Bridge will become the new source of truth for Datasphere.

## 2.6.1 Migration Process

The migration process of BW Bridge requires careful execution of all the relevant steps. When the migration is planned, the prerequisite is to procure the BW Bridge cloud environment and make the minimum configurations in the system to make it ready to accept migration. The following steps are required to be performed:

- *Pre-conversion:* Do a readiness check of your existing BW system by running the RS_B4HANA_RC program. Select a remote transfer to BW Bridge. Here you can see the potential errors that can occur during the conversion. Check for any code that is not compatible in HANA. Identify the sizing needs for the new environment. Create the communication scenarios in the BW Bridge cockpit.
- *During conversion:* The actual conversion of BW objects into Bridge is possible through scope transfer. Scope is an object (or objects) with all its dependencies captured within the tool for transfer. If a

shell transfer is selected, then only the objects will be created in the Bridge. In the case of a remote migration, the underlying data is also copied.

- *After conversion:* Once the conversion is done for a particular scope, the source system connection must be mirrored in the BW Bridge system. In the case of a shell transfer, the ODP-based datasources will have to be created from the original BW system to load the data in its own pace or the direct data loading will have to be performed using the ERP source system. In both cases, the delta pointers will have to set to allow loading the incremental data.

Usually, the migration happens step-by-step. It is not recommended to perform a system-wide migration in one shot. Instead, a smaller scope transfer can allow for better control over the overall migration process and avoid performance bottlenecks.

## 2.6.2 Import BW Bridge Objects to Datasphere

Once BW Bridge is completely ready after the migration, the next step is to move these objects into Datasphere. If you have used BW Bridge already, then a dedicated BW Bridge space will appear in your Datasphere tenant. All objects that exist in your BW Bridge tenant are available to import within the BW Bridge space. As soon as you import the tables, you can share the objects with other spaces to combine them with other sets of data. From this point onward, the data from BW Bridge is fully available inside your Datasphere models with continuous data availability.

With the current evolution of Business Data Cloud, it is no longer advised to use BW Bridge, although the functionality would continue to exist. A more reliable option is to use BW PCE. BW Bridge has several limitations, and it will not have all the features of SAP BW/4 HANA. Therefore, if you are not willing to let go or redesign some of your existing models in BW, then you should use BW PCE instead. The situation is different for every customer; it depends on their roadmap, development strategies, and drivers for the migration.

## 2.7 Seamless Integration with SAP Analytics Cloud

SAP Datasphere as a data platform has an added benefit with easy integration to expose and read items from SAP Analytics Cloud. Be it an analytics platform or planning platform, Datasphere provides seamless connection capability. Normally, SAP Analytics Cloud and Datasphere can be integrated using the Link Tenant with a live connection. This makes the connectivity so simple that one can navigate between Datasphere and SAC without leaving the screen. The option also enables storing the SAC planning model's data directly in Datasphere, which makes planning easier. There are several prerequisites to link the tenants:

- The role for Data Warehouse General is assigned.
- SYSTEM INFORMATION role should be assigned to view the administration settings.
- Only the system owner can perform the tenant linking.

Normally the analytical models created within Datasphere can be exposed and consumed by SAC directly if the tenants are linked. Now, the model should be created on top of a Fact view, which can have the dimension and texts linked using association. When the analytical model is created, it shows the data in a format that is readable for SAC directly. Please note that the analytical models created in Datasphere can't be edited in SAC; they will be used only in read-only mode. There are several restrictions of these models within SAC such as it can't be combined with another SAC model (although the linked dimension is possible within SAC).

Another use case for the connectivity is using the OData connection. This offers connectivity using the following parameter through OData 2.0 for interactive usage:

- Client ID
- Secret
- Authorization URL
- Token URL
- Data Service URL

Most of the above information can be obtained from Datasphere administration tab (create an OAuth client 2.0 for Interactive usage). The Data Service URL can be generated from the OData link within a Graphical/Analytical view. A sample link looks like this:

```
https://<tenant_url>.cloud.sap/dwaas-core/odata/v4/consumption/
relational/<Space_ID>/<view>
```

Once the OData connection is created, a data model can be created using the connection. This process is particularly useful for SAC planning when there is a need of uploading data from Datasphere into SAC.

If there is a need to read the SAC model's data in Datasphere, then a cloud connector can be used for this.

## 2.8 Test Your Knowledge

Q1: Which one of the following is not a valid integration process between SAC and Datasphere?

a) OData Connection

b) Link Tenant

c) Cloud Connector

d) None of the above

Q2: BW can be decommissioned after migrating to BW Bridge.

a) True

b) False

Q3: The DMIS add-on is used during the shell conversion to BW Bridge.

a) True

b) False

Q4: Delta pointers are automatically updated after remote conversion to BW Bridge.

a) True

b) False

Answer: a

Q5: Fuzzy logic can be used within a data flow in Datasphere.

a) True

b) False

Q6: Which table is not required for currency conversion in Datasphere from SAP ECC or S/4 HANA?

a) TCURR

b) TCURN

c) TCURP

d) TCURF

Q7: ARIBA integration with Datasphere requires writing Groovy Script.

a) True

b) False

Q8: BW Bridge contains all the functionalities that an on-premise BW system can provide.

a) True

b) False

## 2.9 Summary

In this chapter, you learned the core components of Datasphere, how to migrate to BW Bridge, how to connect SAP cloud applications with Datasphere, and the currency conversion process.

The chapter clearly explained the role of Datasphere in SAP. Data Builder, Business Builder, and Currency Conversion were also explained in detail.

Modeling with Datasphere can be useful to design the foundation of the data architecture. From a business user perspective, a more interactive and visually appealing interface would be required. The need of a visualization tool is therefore the need of the hour. Datasphere is well integrated with SAP Analytics Cloud for performing data visualization, reporting, and advanced scenarios like predictive models.

In the next chapter, you will learn about the main capabilities of SAP Analytics Cloud, development options, and connectivity with the Datasphere tenant.

CHAPTER 3

# SAP Analytics Cloud (SAC)

SAP Analytics Cloud is a SaaS product designed to support the analytics and planning needs of an organization. It enhances user experiences through smart visuals and interactive dashboards, harmonizes data by combining other SAP product's data, enables augmented analytics accessed via mobile applications, and supports seamless connectivity with SAP Datasphere as a trusted data platform. Along with the existing features like a digital boardroom (for presenting a story in leadership discussions), the Just Ask application enables Gen AI output. SAC also plans to be upgraded to be used with Joule (as part of Business Data Cloud to perform day-to-day operations through an AI agent) and Video story to present stories in the form of video. In short, SAP Analytics Cloud (SAC) has everything that organizations need in terms of planning and analytics. SAC can perform faster decision-making for organizations that have a large amount of data but lack a tool that can process and provide useful insight of the dataset in just a single click.

There are three types of SAC license:

**SAP Analytics Cloud for Business Intelligence, Predictive edition**: This license is typically for the user who does not need planning capabilities.

**SAP Analytics Cloud for Planning, Predictive standard edition**: This license is mainly used by the planners from a business point of view, which enables most of the planning functionalities.

**SAP Analytics Cloud for Planning, Predictive professional edition**: This license is for the developers who support the planning functions. This license is expensive and only a few need to be procured.



© Sourav Banerjee 2025
S. Banerjee, *Modernizing SAP Business Warehouse*, https://doi.org/10.1007/979-8-8688-2192-9_3

## 3.1 Features

SAP Analytics Cloud has many advanced features. In terms of analytics, the following are the main features:

- **Models:** Models in SAP Analytics Cloud can be related to either analytics or planning. An analytics model can be created with or without data and uses a connection to other DBs/files. The aim of creating a model is to serve as a foundation for stories. Once a data model is created, additional columns can be created with formulas and transformations. A model can have its own variable or can be imported from another system (for example, BW queries).
- **Stories:** Stories in SAC are created with single or multiple pages to support the visualization and planning requirements. Normally an optimized design experience should be chosen, while a classic design model will get phased out in the near future. A story can be created from a model or multiple models. Multiple models can also be combined using linked dimension features.
- **Widget:** A widget is a single component added to the story. It can be a plot, chart, button etc. Each widget will have its own property.
- **Charts:** A chart can be added as a widget using a model. The following types of charts are possible in SAC:

  *Bar/Column*: Could be Vertical/Horizontal. Requires at least one measure. See Figure 3-1.

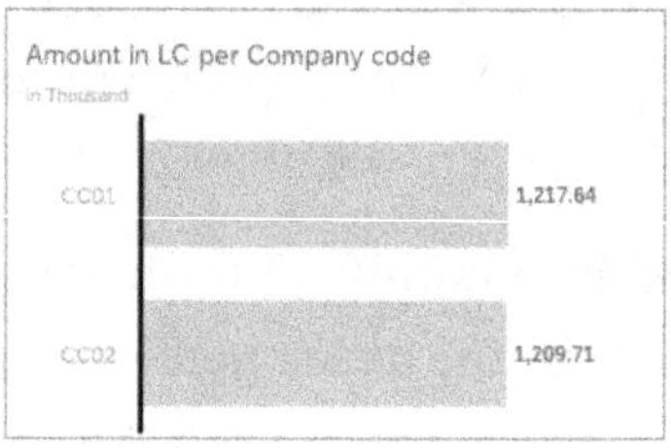


***Figure 3-1.*** *Bars/columns in charts*

*Line*: Left and right y-axis can be defined. At least one measure is required. See Figure 3-2.

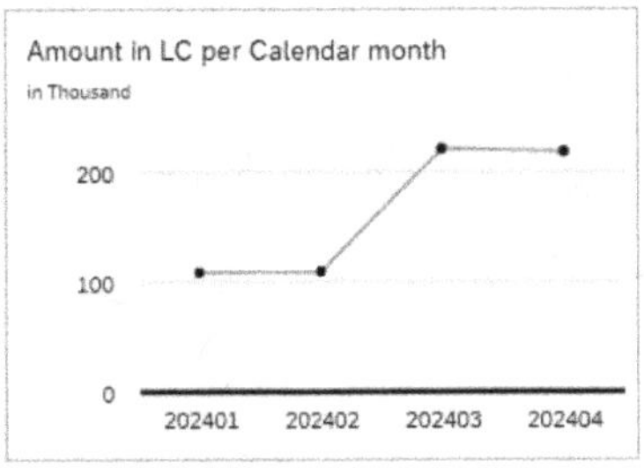


***Figure 3-2.*** *Line in charts*

*Numeric point*: A primary and a secondary measure needs to be defined.

*Combination column and line*: At least one dimension and one measure are required. Y-axis overlap is possible. See Figure 3-3.

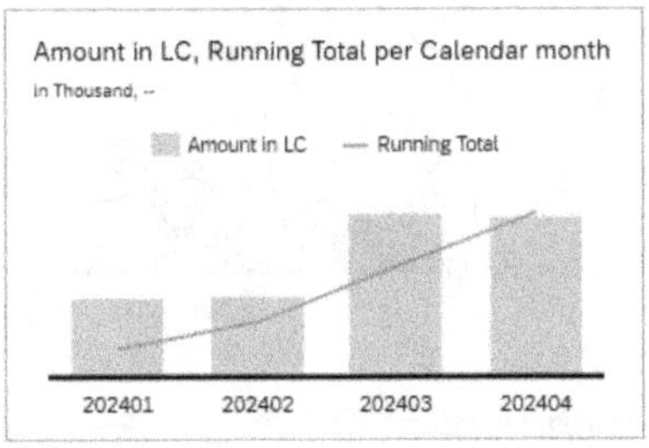


***Figure 3-3.*** *Combine column and line in charts*

*Stacked Bar*: At least one measure is required. Can be horizontal/ vertical.

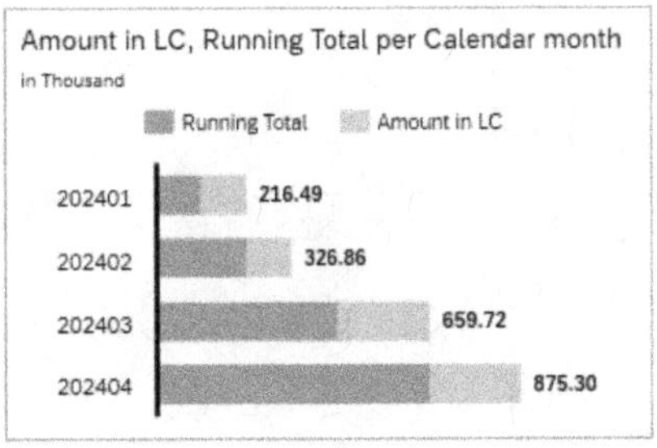


***Figure 3-4.*** *Stacked bar in charts*

*Combination stacked column and line*: At least one measure is required. For lines, additional measures should be defined. See Figure 3-5.

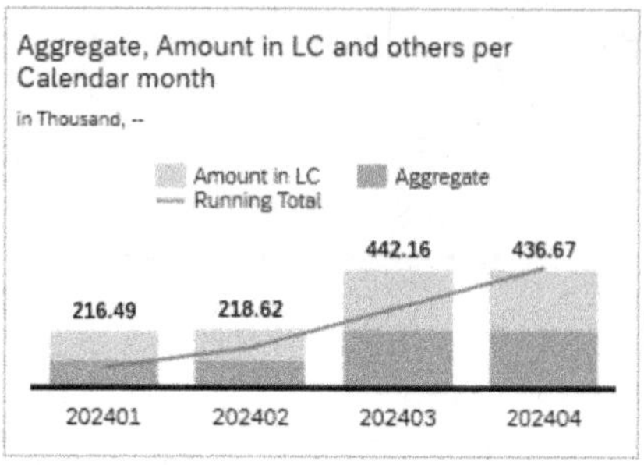


***Figure 3-5.*** *Combined stacked column and line in charts*

*Stacked area*: At least one measure is required. See Figure 3-6.

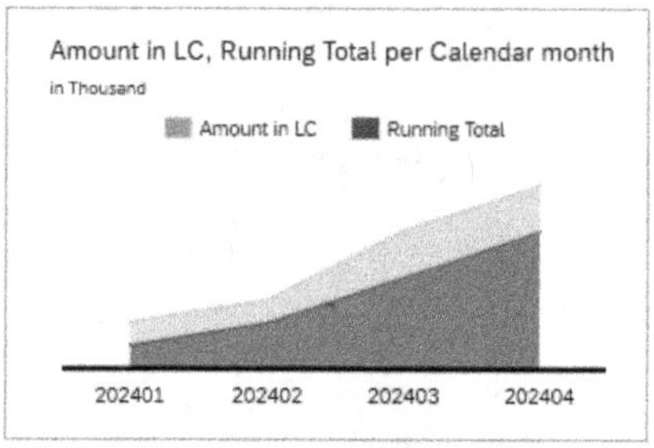


***Figure 3-6.*** *Stacked area in charts*

*Pie*: At least one measure and one color dimension required. See Figure 3-7.

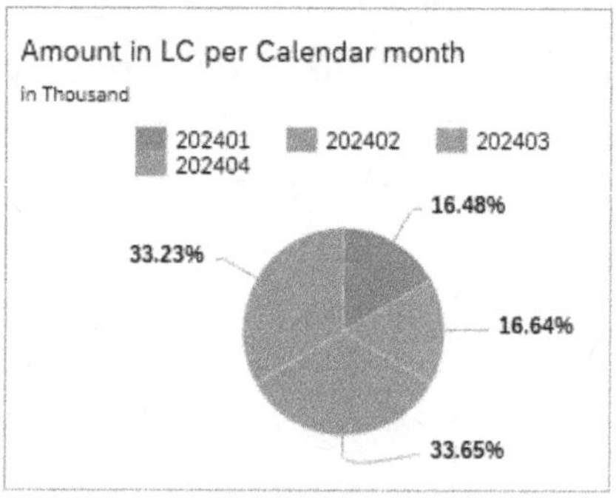


***Figure 3-7.*** *Pie charts*

*Donut*: At least one measure and one color dimension required. See Figure 3-8.

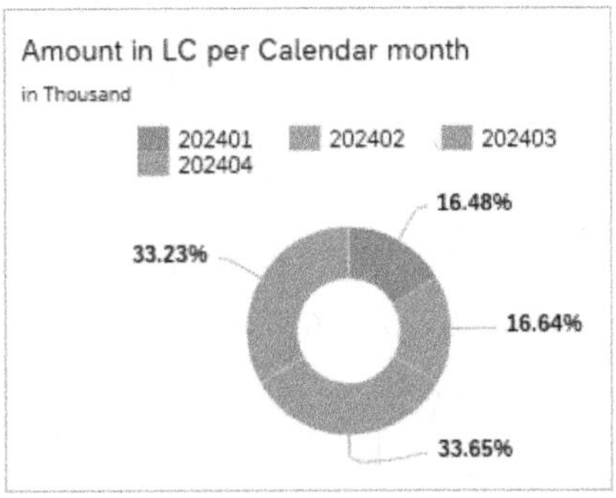


***Figure 3-8.*** *Donut charts*

*Bullet*: At least one measure is required. It is possible to define a threshold. See Figure 3-9.

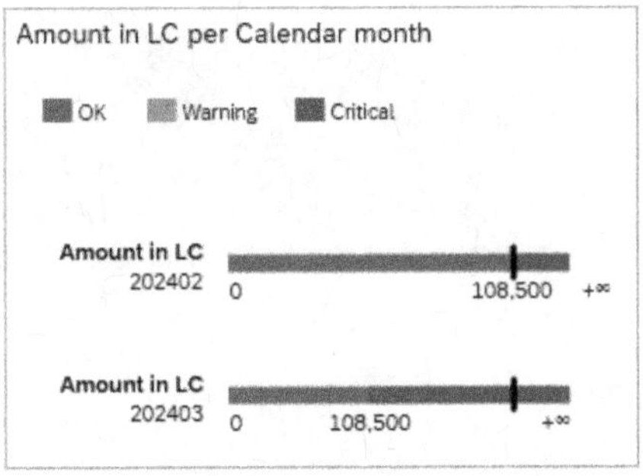


***Figure 3-9.*** *Bullet charts*

*Time series*: At least one measure and one time dimension are required. See Figure 3-10.

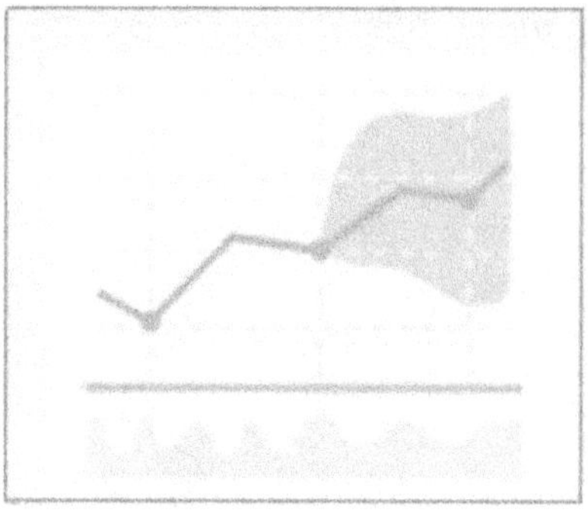

***Figure 3-10.*** *Time series in charts*

*Heat map*: One dimension and one color measure are required. See Figure 3-11.

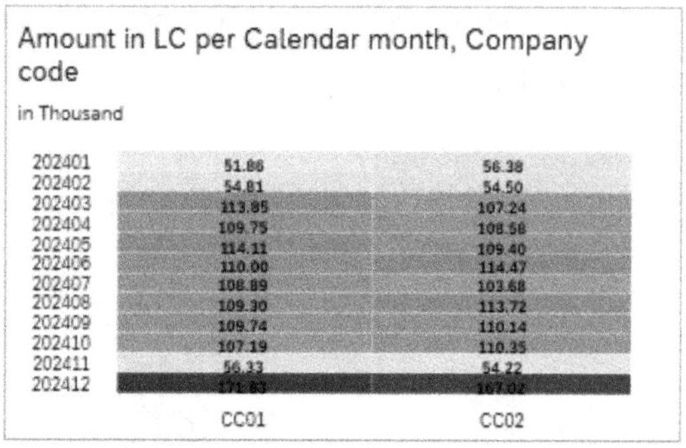


***Figure 3-11.*** *Heat map in charts*

*Waterfall*: Can be horizonal/vertical. At least one measure required. See Figure 3-12.

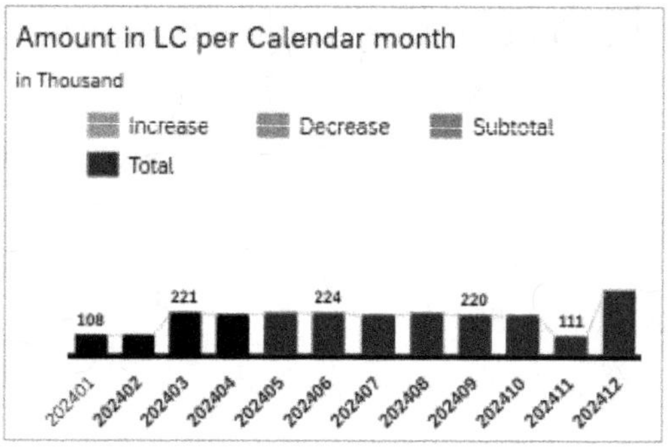


***Figure 3-12.*** *Waterfall charts*

*Tree Map*: At least one dimension and one size measure are required. See Figure 3-13.

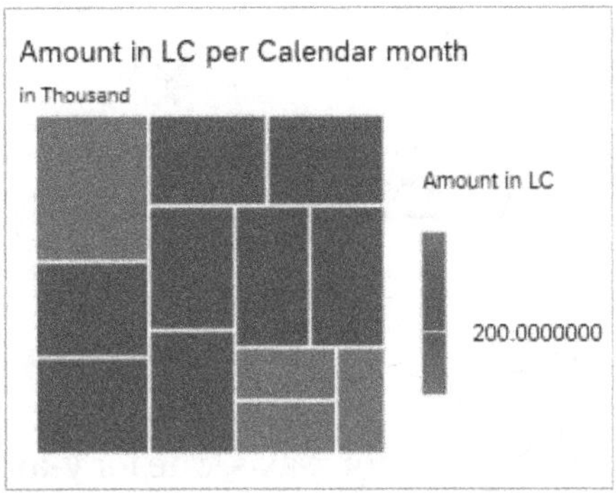


***Figure 3-13.*** *Tree map charts*

*Box plot*: Can be vertical/horizontal. At least one measure and one aggregation dimension are required. See Figure 3-14.

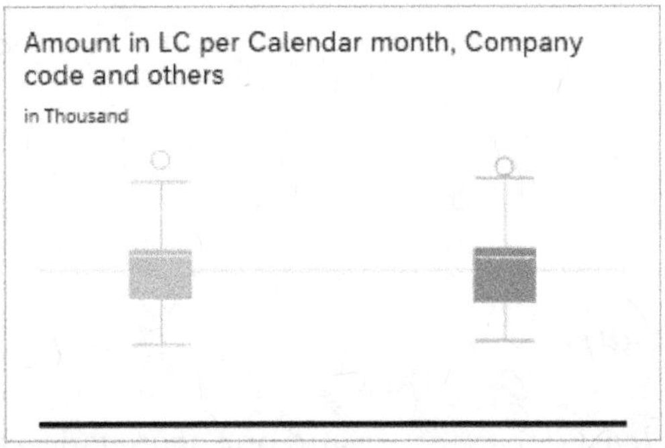


***Figure 3-14.*** *Box plot in charts*

*Marimekko*: One height measure and one dimension are required. See Figure 3-15.

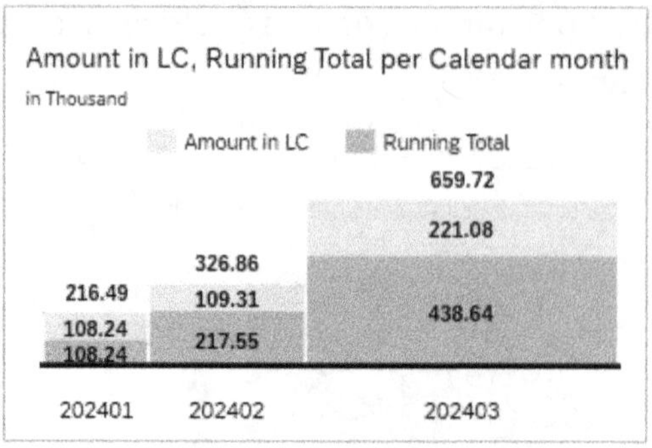


***Figure 3-15.*** *Marimekko charts*

*Bubble*: At least one measure for x-axis, one for y-axis, and one for size are required. One dimension and one color dimension/ measure are also required. See Figure 3-16.

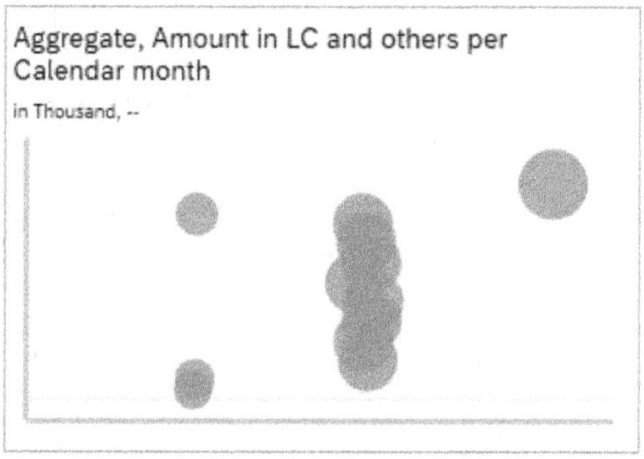


***Figure 3-16.*** *Bubble charts*

*Histogram*: At least one measure and one aggregation dimension are required. See Figure 3-17.

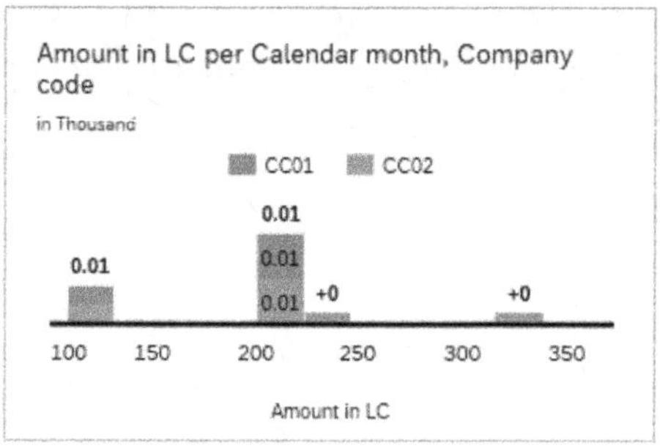


***Figure 3-17.*** *Histogram in charts*

*Scatterplot*: One x-axis and one y-axis measure are required along with one dimension and one color dimension. See Figure 3-18.

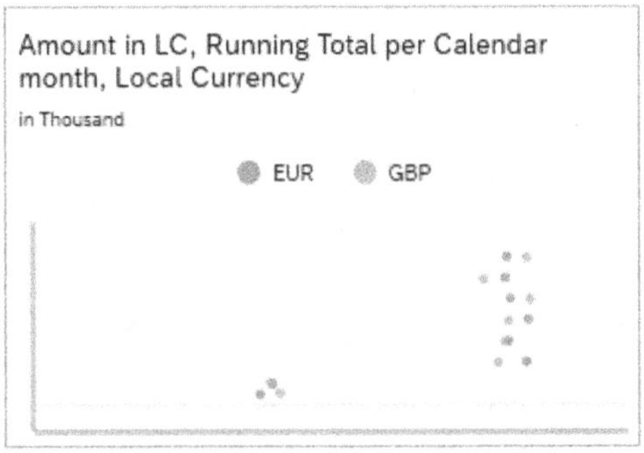


***Figure 3-18.*** *Scatterplot in charts*

*Cluster Bubble*: At least one measure, one dimension and one color dimension required. See Figure 3-19.

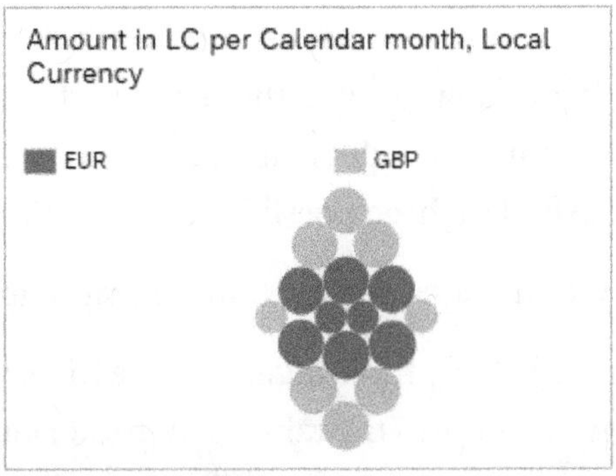


***Figure 3-19.*** *Cluster bubble in charts*

*Radar*: At least one measure, one dimension and one color dimension are required. See Figure 3-20.

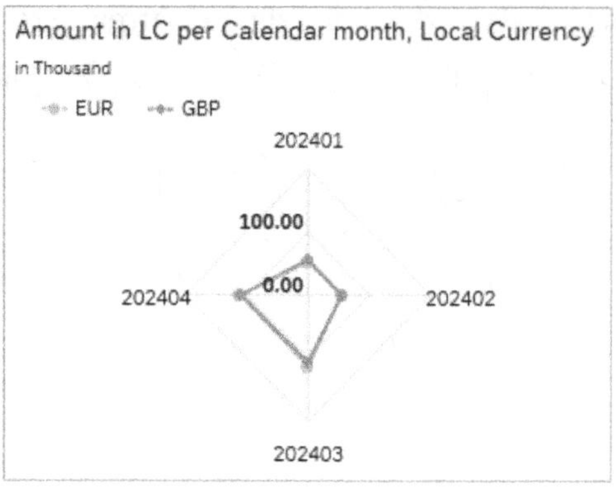


***Figure 3-20.*** *Radar in charts*

- **Table:** A table can be added from a model to display the data in simple tabular form. This requires at least one measure to be displayed. Columns can be zero suppressed to avoid showing a row where all measures are 0. Totals can be arranged both at the top or bottom of the table. In practical cases, the width of the column can't be predicted as it may change with the result of the execution. In such cases, an adaptive column width can be selected. The data in the table can be refreshed in three possible ways:

  *Always refresh*: When the table's content is always up-to-date.

  *Refresh Active widget*: Only the widget that is active, will be refreshed. This means if the visibility of the table is invisible; i.e., the table content is used only for some intermediate calculation that does not need to be shown to the user, then the content won't refresh every time. If required, they can be refreshed manually or through a script.

  *Always pause*: This option stops the data refresh of the table always including the refresh during the loading of the story.

- **Input Control:** This option creates a page filter, and all the dimensions and measures are automatically available to use a filter. This can create either static or dynamic filters. Filters can be a selection of members in the dimension or conditions (greater than, less than, etc., or text match).

- **Text:** This option allows adding either constant text or variable text. If a variable text is selected, it can be filled using a script or predefined values. The following options are available:

  *Story properties*: Current user (name of the current user), current date (system date), current time (current system time), last modified date (last date of modification), last modified time (last time of modification), last modifier (last modified by), creator (author of the story), tab number or page number (tab or page number from the story).

  *Dimensions*: Any dimension value available in the model

  *Input control (Selector tab for a dimension value)*

  *Calculation input control (Calculated value from input control)*

  *Measure input control (Measure from the input control)*

  *Structure member input control (Member of the structure from input control)*

  *Dimension Input control (Dimension selection from input control)*

  *Story Filters (Filters applied to the story)*

  *Tile filters or variables (Variable value)*

  *Model variable (Variable value defined for the model)*

  *Model Property (Property of the model)*

  *Team signature*

  *Script Variable (Value calculated for a script variable)*

- **Button:** A button is created to perform several actions within the story (for example, opening a new page). The script can be written in two places:

  *On Click*: This event will be triggered when the button is clicked.

  *On long press*: This event will be triggered when the button is pressed for long time.

- **Filters/control:** This option utilizes the filters in different ways. The following methods are possible:

  *Checkbox group:* This is useful when the possible options for filters are predefined. This will create a checkbox with these options. This can be members in the dimension or can be a constant option. If a constant option is selected, then the script has to be written to perform the filters on the tables/charts based on selection within the script. The code should be written under the event on_select. The checkbox filling method can be Manual or Script variable or Model variable or Tile filters/variable.

  *Dropdown:* A drop-down can be created in the same way as the Checkbox group. The Dropdown list can also be populated dynamically using a script.

  *Filter line:* This creates a line with the filter of choice. Filters can be extracted from the model/story,

  *List Box:* A list box can be defined with predefined values or dynamic values. In the case of text overflow, you can wrap or truncate text.

  *Radio button Group:* This creates a radio button group that can be selected at runtime. The value can be passed to a different widget using a script.

  *Range Slider:* This defines a range of values that can be used as a selection in the widget. This defines a range within a start and end value.

  *Slider:* Like range slider without the step calculation.

  *Switch:* This makes a functionality activated or deactivated within the story. The effect can be parsed through script.

- **Text Inputs:** This can be either a text input or a text area.

- **Containers:** Containers are small parts within your story to combine multiple widgets at a single place. The following are possible:

  *Flow layout:* You can make the area responsive by using a height/width ratio for each widget. This will help to reorganize your layout at runtime.

*Page Book:* Here you can add multiple pages.

*Panel:* This is an area where multiple widgets can co-exist.

*Tab Strip:* Multiple tabs can be included within your story page.

- **Starters:** This is relevant to different planning actions.
- **Geo Map:** You can use a location dimension to plot a bubble chart/heat map/choropleth/flow within a map. This application is mainly used for plotting data that has a location relevance, for example, sales in different cities of the United states.
- **Image:** An image can be imported and added to the story.
- **Shape:** Basic and advanced shapes can be added to the story.
- **Symbol:** Mainly required to show currencies in the story.
- **Comment:** Custom comments can be added to explain certain values from the models displayed as text.
- **RSS Reader:** Add the website URL that needs to feed the information.
- **R visualization:** R visualization can be added to perform certain actions. This requires a script to be written.
- **Value Driver:** A value driver tree can be defined using a measure from the model. You can also write a parent-child relationship.
- **Web page:** A web page can be added to the story by defining the URL.

## 3.2 Currency Conversion

Currency conversion in SAC is simple and like any other tool's currency conversion process. The prerequisite is to create a currency conversion table from the Modeler > Conversion tab. The conversion table structure would look like Figure 3-21.

| Source Currency | Target Currency | Valid From | Exchange Rate | Category | Rate Version | Rate Type |
|---|---|---|---|---|---|---|
| | | | | | | |
| | | | | | | |

***Figure 3-21.*** *Currency conversion sample table*

The conversion table contains three tabs.

- Conversion table
- Conversion errors
- Data management

Once the table is defined and data loaded into it, then the currency conversion can be enabled for the models from the Preference ➤ Conversion tab. Please note the model should have at least one date dimension to perform the conversion.

A measure in the model can be converted based on the selection of currencies in the details tab by selecting the unit, currency, and type of conversion (for example, average or closing).

If there is no data available for the conversion, the story will throw an error for the failure of the conversion.

## 3.3 A Guide for Scripting

In SAC, scripting should be done only when the functionalities can't be achieved using standard options. Each and every widget allows scripting to perform complex tasks.

**Common Guideline and Syntax**

The following are the guidelines that should be followed during the SAC scripting process:

> ***Events:*** Each script must be written inside an event. These events determine when the script will be triggered. In other words, it is the control mechanism for the scripts. *On Initialization* is an event that runs when the story is loaded for the first time or is refreshed manually. Any variable that needs to be prefilled or any dynamic story filter requirement must be added here. *On Select* is an event that runs when a particular widget area is selected (for example, a bar plot). *On result change* is useful when the script should run due to change in the widget data. *On after data entry process* runs the script when the data is entered in a planning relevant table. The *On Click* event runs when the widget is clicked (for example, a button). *On long press* runs a script when the widget is pressed for long time. For example, you need to get the months for a

particular selection and pass into the drop-down box. So, you write the script for getting the months in the On Initialize event. If you want to execute an action only after the planning users entered Budget values, then you typically write the script inside the event On Result Change of the input form.

***Lookup of data:*** If you need to look up the required data from another query/report, then the table needs to be added to the story and should be made invisible. Then the script should load the data of that table and apply required filters. It can then pull the required dataset by running a do..while loop based on the number of rows.

***Pass a message:*** It is possible to pass success, error, or warning messages through scripting. If you would like to pass a success message after the entire Data Action is completed, then you can use this method. SAC has its own default messages, but if you want to customize the text, then you can do it through scripting.

***Sequence of events:*** Please note that when multiple actions are performed by the script (refresh, filter, calculation, etc.) before displaying the result, then the user will see the effects one by one, which may not be visually appealing. Therefore, an ideal approach is to produce a busy indicator at the start of the script and keep it alive until the end of the operations. You can also add custom messages in the busy indicator such as "Please wait, data is getting refreshed."

***Initialization of variables:*** Normally the initialization of variables and widgets happens during story loading. If there are some variables whose data must be refreshed after certain operations within the story (for example, a planning input form changes the GL account value, which is rolled up to the Revenue figure that is shown in the main page), then once the planning input is done, the script should refresh that widget on the main page.

***Debugging:*** SAC does not provide the errors in the widget in a detailed manner; therefore, it is required to understand step-by-step how the script is behaving. To do this, add the Console.

log command to display the value of any intermediate variables. The value can be viewable in the developer page of the execution window and by selecting the console (right-click and then select Inspect ➤ Console).

***Case of the syntax:*** Please note that the SAC script is case sensitive, which means that the uppercase and lowercase keywords should be remembered well. For example, Application.showBusyIndicator() is correct and has a mix of upper- and lowercase letters. If you want to prevent user intervention when a data refresh is running or a filter for the checkboxes is running, then you can make the system busy through scrips. It is also possible to use a custom message while showing the busy indicator.

***Array of table:*** Each table or list of values can be referred to using an element number. For example, A[0] is the first element in the list. The text and key can be used by writing .description or .id after the array element, respectively. Let's say you want to make use of the amount against the January month from a table of data; you can find this by referring to the array element.

***Help for Syntax:*** At any point, you can get a help for the possible syntax by pressing Ctrl+space. Please note that only the first phrase of the syntax will be displayed. For example: Chart_1. And then Ctrl+space may show you getDataSource() as a possible syntax, whereas the complete syntax may be Chart_1. getDataSource().setDimensionFilter().

## 3.4 Test Your Knowledge

Q1: Tables created on planning relevant models can't be read-only.

a) True

b) False

Q2: A waterfall chart can only be vertical.

a) True

b) False

Q3: Which chart type can run without a dimension?

a) Waterfall

b) Bullet

c) Stacked area

d) Donut

Q4: A script in SAC is written in which language?

a) C++

b) SQL

c) JavaScript

d) Python

Q5: Which SAC event is triggered during the refresh of the story?

a) On Click

b) On Initialization

c) On Select

d) On Start

Q6: One story can have only one page.

a) True

b) False

Q7: Starter widgets are only used for the planning purposes.

a) True

b) False

Q7: A currency conversion table requires a time hierarchy in SAC.

a) True

b) False

## 3.5 Summary

In this chapter, you learned about the features of SAP Analytics Cloud and got a high-level scripting guide to address complex scenario and the currency conversion process.

SAC is used in many organizations for financial planning, and it is a tedious job to store and maintain all the data within SAC (as SAC is not an ideal data platform). A combination of Datasphere and SAC is the most accepted solution for making the planning process easier.

In the next chapter, you will learn how to integrate SAC and Datasphere from a financial planning perspective.

CHAPTER 4

# SAC Planning and Datasphere

SAP Analytics Cloud is a preferred planning and forecasting tool for many organizations. Those who are using IP/BPC can slowly move their planning artifacts into SAC. This not only provides planning capabilities but also supports integration with Datasphere. There are three types of scenarios in SAC planning in terms of data storage:

> **SAC stores the data**: Here the planning data is fully stored in the planning model inside SAC. To combine this data with the actual dataset, the data from the transactional system (say GL lines) is uploaded to the same planning model with the "actual" version. The load can be made recurring by scheduling the upload.
>
> **SAC and Datasphere both store data**: The source of the actual data is Datasphere, and the planning data is SAC model. Data in the SAC model is replicated/federated back to Datasphere where they are combined with the actual dataset. Later the combined data from Datasphere is exposed to SAC for analytics purposes.
>
> **Datasphere stores the data**: In this case, the tenants of SAC and Datasphere are linked, and the storage is selected as Datasphere. This means that the SAC planning model stores only the metadata definition, but the actual data is always pushed into the Datasphere table. This technique is called *seamless planning.*



© Sourav Banerjee 2025
S. Banerjee, *Modernizing SAP Business Warehouse*, https://doi.org/10.1007/979-8-8688-2192-9_4

Versioning of the data in the planning application is always of great importance. With the versioning of the data, it is possible to differentiate the data category. Amongst many versions that SAC can create, the major versions that are used widely:

**Public.Actual:** This is the actual from the ERP system.

**Public.Budget:** This is the budget data entered in the system.

In many cases, the foundation of the planning data is done through a data migration that creates the version for the year. When we create a planning model, Version and Date become mandatory dimensions in the model. A Date dimension can store both Date and Year as all the planning models are time relevant.

Planning models have the ability to write back and replace the entry in the database. Normally for finance planning, the data entry happens in local currencies, which are not useful for the reporting purposes as it is often required to show the final figure in terms of Group currency. Currency conversion is therefore an integral part of the planning process. It generally happens in two ways:

- Separate measures to be declared to store the converted data. It is not useful to make that measure input ready but should be calculated based on the local currency input amount.
- It is possible to introduce a new dimension that can store the currency type. For each type, a new line will be created with a different currency value.

# 4.1 Planning Using SAC

SAP Analytics Cloud can be used to create interactive dashboards to support the planning needs of an organization. Most of the planning application is possible using SAC planning models. Following are the features for planning:

**Data Action**

A data action is the instruction to create, change, or delete a particular dataset, which is often useful during the planning process. It can have the following components:

**Copy step**: A copy step copies a set of data into other versions or data for other filter restrictions to create a new dataset. A source filter to identify the dataset is required. The rules can identify the source and target dimension value with an option to append or overwrite. For example, at the beginning of the year, a published version of Budget from the current year can be copied to the Initial version of Budget for the next year. This can be executed for a single planning model in one step.

**Cross-model copy**: Here data from one model can be copied into another model. A filter to identify the source records and mapping for the target fields have to be defined.

**Allocation**: Here the value of a source measure is allocated to a target measure.

**Conversion step**: This step is useful for currency conversion where we can define the source and target measure for the conversion. We need to also define a Date for conversion and type of conversion (dynamic, rolling forecast, etc.).

**Advanced formula**: The formula written within a data action can be useful when none of the built-in steps meets the needs. It is written in Backus-Naur Form (BNF), a notation technique used to defined programming languages.

**Multi-Action**

A multi-action is a combination of multiple planning steps together that can run in series. The following are possible:

**Data action step**: A data action step adds an action that is created under the option of Data Action. Once you use a specific data action, you have the following options: Do not publish, Publish and fail in case of warning, or Publish in case of warning'. The option names are self-explanatory.

**Predictive step**: A predictive scenario can be added as one step in the multi-action. This requires the following information:

- Name of the predictive scenario
- Name of the predictive model
- Predictive actions such as train and forecast, only train, only apply
- Corresponding planning model

- The version of data where the forecast will be stored
- Save forecasted value in past period, which can be useful to compare the accuracy of the prediction; this is a time-consuming operation
- Save the prediction interval

**Version management:** This is useful when we copy the data to another version while publishing the data.

**Data locking**: It is a usual practice that multiple users are working on the same model. To avoid a conflict and manage the risk of possible data loss during the concurrent saving of the data, it is useful to lock the data of the planning model. There are three target states of the data:

> **Open:** This is useful when planning is possible and the model is open for change.
>
> **Restricted:** Data can be changed by someone who has ownership of locks for this combination of members.
>
> **Locked:** Value can't be changed.

As an example, let's assume that when planners are updating values, they submit the value to the reviewers. If reviewer approves, then only the data goes to the team for publishing. So, initially the lock is set as Open. Once the planners have submitted the change for review, then it is set as Restricted. If the reviewer approves the values, then the lock can be set as Locked so that no further changes to the data are possible.

**Import job**: Import jobs in SAC are created to perform data uploads to a model/dimension from another source. This source can be a file stored in a shared location or another server. Import jobs within the multi-action can serve two purposes:

> **Import model data:** This is used to update the planning model's content. This is mostly useful when you do not know when the data is updated in the source and is dependent from the previous action within the multi-action. For example,

if the data is stored in Datasphere using a copy function, the import job in the next step uploads that data into the SAC model.

**Import master data:** This option updates the master data (public dimension) using a similar process as importing model data. We can choose to select specific model or can select all models where this dimension is used, to cascade the updated information.

**API step:** The API step allows accessing APIs to fill the model. One earlier example is to use the data from Datasphere, which later was replaced by OData connection and cloud connectors.

**PaPM integration step:** PaPM is a product used for the profitability analysis and has a tight integration with Business Warehouse. A common scenario is to identify the route profitability of an airline industry.

## 4.2 Seamless Planning

Planning in SAP Analytics Cloud normally happens with a close Datasphere integration. Let's first identify what the possible options are using certain SAC planning models that can be connected with Datasphere (see Figure 4-1).

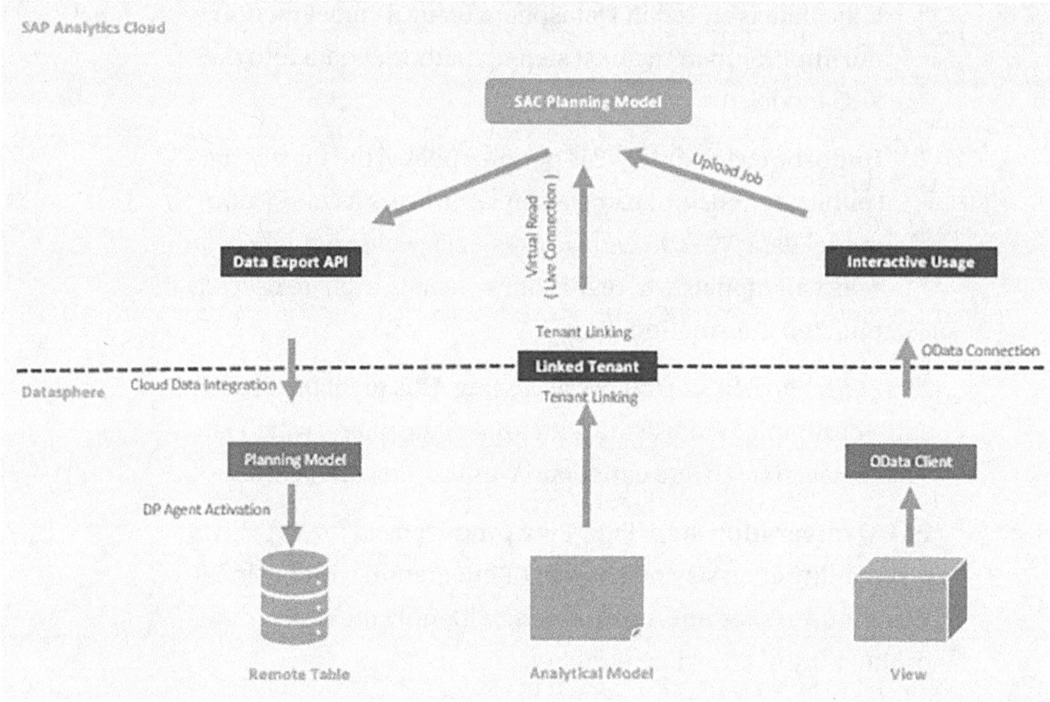


***Figure 4-1.** SAP Analytics Cloud and Datasphere connectivity*

**Cloud Data Integration**

Cloud data integration (CDI) is a technique to connect SAC with Datasphere. This will allow data exchange both remotely and through data flow (replication technique). This model works with a data export API given by SAP. The type of API connection is through ODATAV4. It generally requires three parameters: Token URL, OAuth Client ID, and a secret as part of the authentication. Step-by-step guidance is given here:

**Step 1:** Create a new OAuth client. This can be created by selecting Administration > App integration in SAC. The purpose should be Data Export Services. The Redirect URI should contain the same one from the Datasphere administration tab. Each token has a lifetime and should be added carefully.

**Step 2:** In Datasphere, from the connections, create a connection of type "Cloud data integration." The Data URL should be generated from the views in Datasphere by clicking the OData link. The authentication type should be selected as OAuth 2.0. The OAuth client ID should be taken from the SAC token previously created. Select the DP agent to allow remote table access.

**Step 3:** Once the connection is made, then the Import table option should be enabled. While importing any model from SAC into Datasphere, only the GUIDs can be found in the connection. The GUID can be matched against the GUID of the web URL of the planning model during execution. Please note that SAC supplies fact, master data, and dimension tables as separate tables in the model. To get the relevant planning data, select Fact Table. Once the remote table is created in Datasphere, it can be used within any view or data flow as the source.

CDI is used when you want to store the data to Datasphere. Let's assume you have a planning model but you require this data to be combined with some other data in Datasphere. In this case, you create a CDI connection that you can use to import your SAC model to Datasphere as a remote table. This can be combined with the other data within Datasphere.

**OData Connection**

OData connectivity in SAC is a preferred choice to bring Datasphere data into SAC. This connection has a performance limitation and therefore should not be used for a high volume of data. The following steps are considered:

**Step 1:** Identify the Datasphere object URL, which can be found by getting the OData link from the object. This, however, produces the URL in api/v1 format. A more reliable connection URL is to use OData/v4. The sample URL for this purpose is as follows:

```
https://datasphere-tenant.eu10.hcs.cloud.sap/dwaas-core/odata/v4/
consumption/relational/<space Name>/<name of the view>/<name of the view>
```

It is wise to run this URL in the browser first to see if the metadata of the view is displayed correctly. If this is an analytic view, then the term "Relational" should be removed.

**Step 2:** In SAC, create a new OData connection. Use the authorization type as OAuth 2.0 Authorization Code. Give the client ID, secret, Token URL, and Authorization URL from Datasphere administration.

**Step 3:** Create an OAuth client in Datasphere with a purpose of Interactive Usage. The redirect URI should be copied from SAC. Now the details about Secret, Client ID, etc., are copied from Datasphere into the OData connection in SAC. Please note that the secret for one client can be seen only once. So, please copy this once and use it afterwards. If you forgot to copy the secret in the first place, then it is not possible to see it again. A new client must be created. Also, when the connection is created, if you share this connection with others or someone else tries to use this connection in a new model, then the same secret must be passed again.

**Step 4:** Once the connection is established, if you create a new model from this data, first a new query should be created. This query can select the entire table, or it can add only a few fields from the table. In both cases, the data transfer is seamless.

Please note that there is no support for the delta load here.

The OData connection is typically required to upload data from Datasphere views into the SAC planning model. This is particularly useful when you are uploading the actual data in a planning model and would like to make the data up-to-date always. If Datasphere is a source of your data, then you can set up the upload using an import job, which utilizes the OData connection.

**Link Tenant**

Link tenant is a process that allows SAC and Datasphere tenant to be linked to perform a quick switch between the products. In general, the linked tenant option can be found under SYSTEM ➤ ADMINISTRATOR. On the product link tab, specify the URL for Datasphere. The following prerequisites must be met:

- The SAP Datasphere tenant must be hosted on the Cloud Foundry environment.
- Only the system owner can make this change.
- Only one Datasphere tenant can be linked from one SAC Tenant.
- Business Data Cloud Cockpit can also be linked.
- Linking to Neo Client is not possible.

Linking tenants is useful from a developer perspective. You can seamlessly toggle between Datasphere and SAC (and with BDC cockpit as well).

**Data Storage for Planning**

As part of the seamless planning process, it is possible to configure Datasphere as a physical storage of data from SAC planning models while the metadata definition will be available in SAC. In this case, SAP Analytics Cloud will be responsible for the visualization of data including the display of input-ready reports; once the data is changed, then the data will be automatically moved to Datasphere. This removes the overhead of manual data exchange with Datasphere in terms of the planning data. This process is completely based on data federation with no need to persist or replicate the data.

The following prerequisites must be met before this option is implemented:

- Datasphere and SAC tenants should be linked.
- The SAP Analytics Cloud tenant should run on HANA Cloud.
- Both Datasphere and SAC tenants should reside on the same data center.
- Both Datasphere and the SAC tenant must use the same identity providers.

If you want your Datasphere tenant to be your one and only data platform and a single source of truth, then you should set the Planning data storage option to Datasphere. In this way, SAC will work only to support the planning, but you do not have to worry about the storage part.

**Restriction for Using Datasphere for Planning Data Storage**

Please note that there are number of restrictions on the SAC side when this type of architecture is implemented:

- Delta is not possible for the Data export service. The SAC models will utilize the Datasphere data remotely. Therefore, it is not possible to capture the change timestamp.
- A public dimension in SAC can't transform data through an import job.
- Geo areas are not available in Geo Map. This is a product limitation.
- Geo points in the Choropleth layer of Geo Map are not available. This is a product limitation.
- Import package can't be re-pointed to a Datasphere space if they contain data analyzer.
- The exposure setting is unavailable during the transport of SAC models or during the import job execution. This is a product limitation.

## 4.3 Test Your Knowledge

Q1: Which one of the following is not a data exchange option between Datasphere and SAC?

a) CDI

b) OData Connection

c) Through Communication user

d) None of the above

Q2: Which dimension is mandatory to create a planning model?

a) Date

b) Year

c) Version

d) Both a and c

e) Both b and c

Q3: Which one is a prerequisite to enable planning data storage in Datasphere?

a) Both tenants use AWS.

b) Both tenants use MS Azure.

c) Datasphere has a minimum storage capacity of 200 GB.

d) Both Datasphere and SAC are using same identity provider.

Q4: A product switch is possible only from SAC and not from Datasphere.

a) True

b) False

Q5: Only a BI admin can do link tenant.

a) True

b) False

Q6: Data locking during planning can have the following states except which of the following?

a) Open

b) Restricted

c) Unlocked

d) Locked

# 4.4 Summary

In this chapter, you learned about the planning processes using SAP Analytics Cloud along with several connectivity options with Datasphere. You also learned about the seamless planning process.

When the needs of modeling, planning, and visualization are addressed, organizations must be ready to move toward Business Data Cloud (BDC), which can bundle all these products together for transparent licensing, ease of integration and to create machine learning models without physical data movement.

In the next chapter, you will learn about BDC including its core components, overall architecture, and data transfer methods.

## CHAPTER 5

# Business Data Cloud (BDC)

SAP Business Data Cloud (BDC) was launched in February 2025 as part of the Business Unleash event. BDC uses its integration capability to create a trusted data platform, uses the power of AI to automate many manual tasks along with forecasting scenarios, and performs the data visualization using a strong cloud-based reporting environment. It has everything that is needed to run a business operation with transparent licenses, strong data federation techniques, and business semantics at any level. Along with launching a new platform, SAP provides a long-term strategy to modernize the existing landscape by moving on-premise warehousing solutions to the cloud. It is a highly recommended product when an organization has a long-term cloud strategy and is on S/4 HANA or moving into S/4 HANA.

**SAP Business Warehouse/BW PCE**

Today many organizations are using SAP BW in some shape or form for their warehousing and reporting needs. With the evolution of Business Data Cloud, SAP provides a safe and reliable path to move to a similar cloud-based solution and eventually to a more SAP-managed data product within BDC called SAP BW Private Cloud Edition, also known as BW PCE. Although it is not a prerequisite to migrate to PCE to use BDC, it is a recommended path for gaining access to all of the BDC-relevant functionalities. BDC also provides an option to connect to existing on-premises BW systems, but the capability within BDC will be limited.

**Datasphere**

Datasphere can be procured as a single product. However, BDC provides an opportunity to rewire your existing Datasphere components with BDC. For all new customers, Datasphere can already be part of BDC to start with.

**SAP Analytics Cloud**

SAC is also available as a stand-alone version. It will possible, like with Datasphere, to rewire your environment to BDC in the future. As part of BDC-SAC, a new GenAI-based agent was introduced, called Joule. It uses advanced algorithms to perform certain



© Sourav Banerjee 2025
S. Banerjee, *Modernizing SAP Business Warehouse*, https://doi.org/10.1007/979-8-8688-2192-9_5

tasks, can retain the context of the questions for subsequent questions, and even can generate code for developers.

**SAP Databricks**

SAP Databricks was introduced to strengthen AI-related applications using data coming from SAP and non-SAP source systems. There is seamless integration with Datasphere so that the SAP data from different cloud applications can be consumed within SAP Databricks using the SAP-managed data products.

# 5.1 Architecture of Business Data Cloud

Figure 5-1 shows the main building blocks of Business Data Cloud.

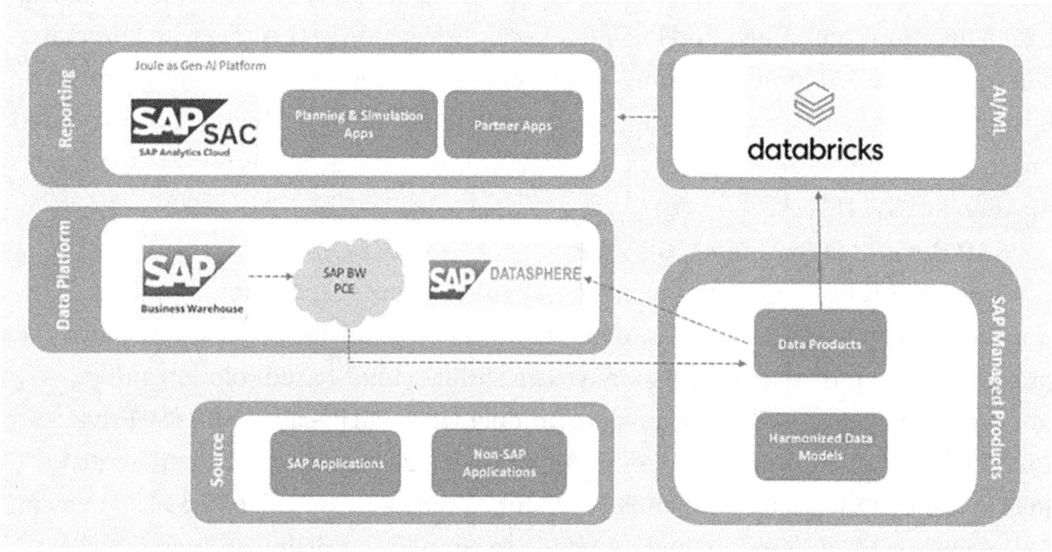


***Figure 5-1.** Business Data Cloud Architecture*

Business Data Cloud enables connecting with SAP and non-SAP sources, supports data blending, and creates the business data fabric with the semantic definition retained within Datasphere without a need to store the data. Other major components like Databricks will enable advanced AI- or ML-related implementations that include forecasting, predictions-, and what-if cases. As part of the reporting process, SAP Analytics Cloud enables interactive dashboard creation along with advanced Gen AI capabilities as part of Joule to allow the user to perform repetitive tasks, execute analysis in seconds, and even build a complete dashboard with advanced functionality. This is also helpful in terms of planning process executions. For a more industry-specific use case, Intelligent Apps are introduced to define business KPIs, dashboards, planning functionalities, etc.

**What is a Data Product?**

A data product is something that is a consumable entity within different BDC components. The push is toward creating more SAP-managed data products where customers can focus only on the business benefits while SAP takes care of the maintenance of them.

The customers, who are using SAP BW, will get an option to generate a data product from SAP. This functionality is called Data Product Generator.

**SAP Business Data Cloud Cockpit**

Business Data Cloud Cockpit is used for the following purposes:

- Entitlement management
- Installation of data products
- Security and governance

**Data Lake Files**

Data lake files in HANA Cloud provides a secured storage within the cloud for all types of data. This requires a data lake instance to be created. This is basically a container where the data can reside securely. The file container is a SAP-owned repository to store data on the cloud.

To read the data lake files, you would need data lake relational engine. This engine can perform bidirectional data exchange.

**Business Data Fabric**

First let's understand what Data Fabric is. Data Fabric is an architecture that allows you to manage and govern all the data of your organization in one place with a single source of truth. It is especially useful to make the data from a complex architecture with many technological components available for analytics and AI. A data mesh, on the other hand, is an approach that decentralizes the data by making the individual team own and govern the data. The Business Data Fabric is a data fabric process that retains the business context of the data that is otherwise often lost during multiple data transfers and data cleansing.

The key components of the Data Fabric architecture are as follows:

- Data connectors
- Data management (data integration, data governance and data security)
- Data modeling and semantic layer
- Data processing and analytics
- Data management automation

**SAP Knowledge Graph**

The knowledge graph is a new feature in SAP Datasphere as part of SAP BDC that automatically creates an ontology for the relationship of the data, including the context of the data. It is useful in order to draw a new context of the data as it shows the dependency of the data from difference sources, which is not possible to follow without this feature.

SAP Graph, on the other hand, provides a single unified API for developers to access business data across multiple SAP systems. This provides a 360-degree view of the data using a semantically connected graph of entities.

A HANA Cloud graph is a built-in graph engine that shows the graphical representation of all the HANA cloud data with all the relationships defined for further analysis of the data relations. This allows an algorithm to perform neighborhood search and pattern matching.

**SAP Joule**

SAP Joule is a built-in generative AI co-pilot within the SAP Analytics Cloud component of Business Data Cloud that allows a user to perform day-to-day activities, get answers to business questions out of the models, and execute planning relevant tasks with ease.

**Advantages**

Joule has the following advantages:

- Accelerates end-to-end business processes
- Drives productivity
- Performs development activities that are specific to your business scenario
- Retains the context of the questions asked in the subsequent questions

**Capabilities**

Joule agents are useful for performing deeper analysis on your business process. For example, starting with source-to-pay, you can navigate further into source to contract, then source product and service, and so on. This provides context for the data retained within that business process and performs meaningful decision-making by better using the data.

With help from Business Data Cloud, Joule will have access to all your organization's data without losing the context. This allows Joule to make fast, accurate decisions and create an action plan. Joule seamlessly connects with all the data products to perform such activity.

Joule also provides a seamless and secure way to perform business actions across the SAP business suite and non-SAP Applications.

Joule can combine and automate the activities performed by other AI agents to amplify the effectiveness of the automation. This includes collaboration with AI agents within the Joule ecosystem to understand the holistic picture and perform actions not in silo but in agreement with other dependent business processes in the organization.

Joule combines and assembles a team of trusted AI agents that work toward to simplify the complex business needs. It uses a knowledge graph at every step to determine the relationship of the data coming from different platforms and products. In general terms, it uses a team of virtual agents each of which are masters in their own business area so that the cascading impact is avoidable.

**Built-in Joule Agents**

Some of the built-in Joule agents are as follows:

- **Dispute solution agent:** Improves the cash position that can resolve disputes in seconds
- **Sourcing agent:** Makes better informed purchasing decisions that identify the best-fit suppliers
- **Account planning agent:** Transforms email requests into ready-to-send quotes thus improving sales effectiveness
- **Human resource agent:** Improves talent acquisition by identifying the best-matched talent to fit the job requirements
- **Supply chain agent:** Manages service orders efficiently by automating scheduling
- **Marketing and e-commerce agent:** Performs online purchasing with guided shopping experiences

Joule AI agents can be customized but must follow these steps:

**Step 1:** Define the purpose of the agent.

**Step 2:** Provide the business context.

**Step 3:** Define data connectivity.

**Step 4:** Assign skills.

**Step 5:** Enable collaboration with other agents.

**Step 6:** Deploy.

**Object Store**

Object stores in Datasphere provide a storage solution that is cost effective and at the same time detached with the computation engine so they yield a simplified solution connected through the delta share.

The data products are stored in the Object Store layer of Datasphere. At this stage, the data from, e.g., SAP BW is stored in a delta table. This table is used as input for the data product. The mechanism of data exchange through the data product is then used for further processing of data.

**Delta Share**

Delta sharing is an approach for secure data sharing, making it simple to share the data with other products. The source of the data for the delta share is always a delta lake table from which a bidirectional flow of data connects to the delta sharing server where the access permissions are checked. With this, customers can bring in live data in no time without any need to copy the physical data.

Delta sharing has the following advantages:

- **Open cross-platform sharing:** Easily share the existing data lake data to any platform.
- **Live data with no replication:** Share data across different data platforms without copying, and share using Cloudflare R2, which is an affordable cloud storage solution with zero egress fee.
- **Centralized governance:** Centrally manage the shared data in one platform.

- **Marketplace for data product:** Build AI models and datasets and share them to anywhere through an open marketplace.
- **Privacy:** Easily collaborate with your customers without compromising the data privacy.

Delta sharing uses Databrick's Unity Catalog, which is a unified and open data governance solution that provides the flexibility to maintain the data centrally within Databricks and share it with other organizations. This also allows collaborators to meet in a cloud environment that is private, agree on the scale of the shared data, and use it immediately without copying anything. The compute can be done in SQL or Python or R or Scala.

Databrick's Clean Room provides a secure way to collaborate with other collaborators on a different or similar cloud solution. This provides an opportunity to decide what type of data will be shared and in what form.

Clean Room provides the following advantages:

- **Any cloud, any platform:** Data always resides in the source. Sharing it allows you to build a data model on top of it only if all collaborators involved agree.
- **Any language, any workload:** An advanced implementation can include SQL, Python, R, and Scala.
- **Any scale, any level of trust:** Scale up a complex workload using built-in orchestration. Clean Room allows collaboration with multiple customers without any security compromises.

Let's assume your organization stores a large volume of data in your BW system. You would like to create a prediction based on your BW data without moving the data from that system. BW has a limited capability to perform such actions unless you are using a completely different product (with challenges to integrate the SAP data). You can then use BDC to get the data product from your BW system. You can first move your BW system to a private cloud, then generate a data product to Datasphere, and then share the product with the Databricks component of BDC. You can then apply ML rules to address your needs. Your data will still be in the BW system, but you can access it from Databricks to support the scenario you need.

# 5.2 Move BW to the Cloud

In many organizations, SAP Business Warehouse is the main data platform where the loading and cleansing of the data happens along with combining and transforming the data. Therefore, it is difficult to retire the application quickly based on the investments made in it. A wise decision is to combine the component with the other cloud-based applications within Business Data Cloud to start with. For example, an AI agent can be created using the BW data by converting it to a data product and consuming it within Databricks using delta sharing. This will allow you to control the data from BW but federate the require dataset to Databricks with a zero-copy approach.

This journey, however, is not simple and requires lots of prerequisites to be met. SAP recommends performing a cloud-based migration to BW Private Cloud Edition aka BW PCE as a first step to fully utilize the capabilities of the BDC environment. Although technically it is a lift and shift, it requires a predefined migration step to be followed.

The BW cloud makes the life of developers easy as the actual lift is done by SAP. This is like any other BW migration.

**Data Product Generator**

The Data Product Generator is a feature given in BW PCE that allows you to convert BW artifacts into an SAP-managed data product that can federate the data to Databricks and other platforms.

Please note the following points related to the Data Product Generator :

- Only Datasphere as part of the Business Data Cloud can be supported as the target for the Data Product Generator.
- Data Product Generator is available only for SAP BW 750 SP24 and newer versions. It is also available for BW4HANA 2021 SP04 and newer versions.
- Data Product Generator does not support the embedded BW system.
- A transport-based correction instruction (TCI) needs to be installed.

The following are the prerequisites for installing the TCI for Data Product Generator:

- The user should have SAP_OCS_STD and SAP_OCS_TCI_IMPORT roles to use the Support Pack Manager (SPAM).
- The minimum patch level for SPAM is 89.

- For BW4HANA 2021, all the notes mentioned within the note 3600085 must be implemented.
- For the installation itself, SAP note 3593519 must be implemented.

If you want to roll back the TCI from your BW system, please note the following points:

- If the attribute of TCI rollback if marked as "True," then it can't be rolled back. It is not possible to change this setting. The only option is to revert to a previous point from the system copy.
- The SPAM backup flag must be enabled.
- If any changes are made on the system manually or through transport after the TCI is installed, then it can't be rolled back.

**Embedded BW**

Embedded BW is a component that exists inside the ERP system. The embedded BW supports the BW functionalities along with BPC functionalities. The only version that supports an embedded version is SAP BW 7.5 on HANA.

In general, the following restrictions exist:

- Should not be used for EDW use cases.
- Persisted data in BW should not exceed 20% of the server capacity.
- BPC requires a separate license.
- S/4 HANA authorizations are not valid here. There could be a need to map the existing authorizations to the new embedded BW specific authorizations.
- A separate client is recommended for Embedded BW.

Data Product Generator is not available in the embedded BW option. Therefore, there is no direct migration path to Business Data Cloud.

Supplemental terms and conditions for BDC are available in Appendix C, which includes the capacity unit calculations, backup strategy, and incident response time.

## 5.3 AI with Databricks

In Business Data Cloud, one of the new features is the artificial intelligence use cases using SAP data. To achieve this, you must import the data product from Business Warehouse into Databricks (import means consumption in this context, i.e., without physical data movement). Figure 5-2 shows the architecture of the consumption.

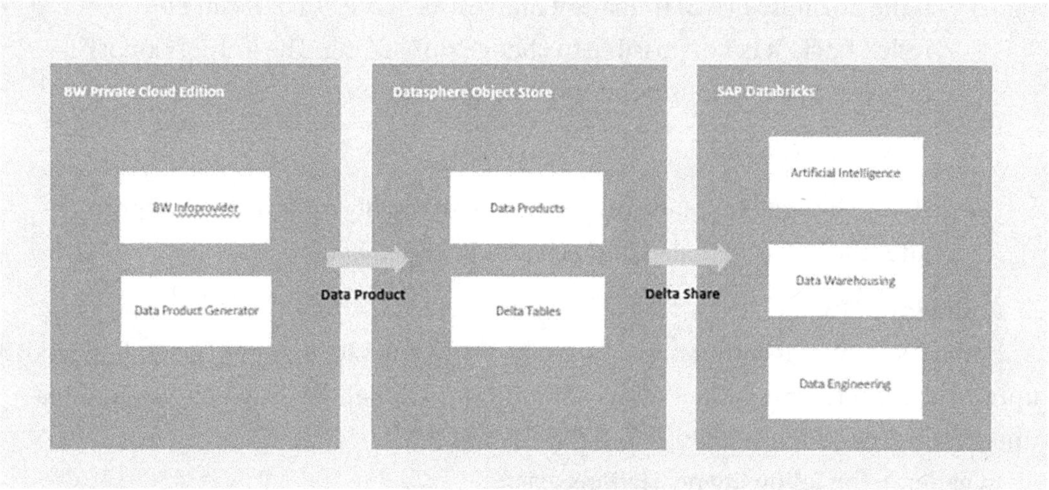


***Figure 5-2.*** *SAP Databricks Consumption architecture*

As shown, Databricks can consume the data products using delta sharing.

In the delta sharing mechanism, the following steps need to be executed:

**Step 1:** A new recipient needs to be created within Databricks delta sharing option. During the creation, a sharing identifier is required. A sharing identifier is required only when the recipient is also a Databricks provider. In all other cases, it must be left empty. In the case of other providers, an activation link will be generated and will contain important details on the user and other authentication parameters. The activation link can be opened in a browser, which will then prompt to download the credential document.

**Step 2:** Once the recipient is created, the next step is to create a share. Once the share is created, then the tables required to be shared can be added on the next screen. Please note that only the tables that are in the source connection will be visible for addition. At this stage, the recipient details need to be added to let Databricks know that is where the data is going to.

**Step 3:** In the delta sharing sections at the recipient side, there will be a section named "Shared with me" where the shared tables can be found. On the sender side, the section where the shared table is available will be named as "Shared by me."

**Step 4:** To read the shared data, a catalog needs to be created. Once the catalog is created, then the shared database will be visible within the catalog. Once the database is opened, you will be able to see the tables.

**Step 5:** Once the data is visible, it will allow governing the data by granting necessary access to the engineers working in the organization.

**Serverless Compute**

Usually, a physical server is required to run the web application. Databricks creates virtual servers on which these applications can run. This is called *serverless compute*. In this model, Databricks takes the responsibility to manage the infrastructure to host the applications while the developers can focus more on the content of what is being computed. This will reduce the operational overhead and speed up the development process.

Serverless essentially does not mean an absence of the server, but it means that the server is fully managed by the cloud service provider. The provider would make sure that the infrastructure is managed and scale up when necessary.

This solves the following:

- Managing the workload in a way that the correct compute type is determined and initialization is done seamlessly.
- The cost of the idle time when server is initialized or scaling up is significantly reduced.
- Sometimes the team ends up with unutilized server capacity and memory when they are not consumed. In such case, a serverless computing will help to reduce costs by consuming exactly what is needed.
- In some cases, server inefficiency can cause delay in the actual operation, for example, server unavailability, which leads to a delay in the overall process. With serverless computing, this situation is addressed with ease.

- With the autoscaling feature of serverless computing, developers will get the required space and memory when needed; thus, the operational overhead for server maintenance is no longer needed.
- Unplanned downtime will cause the business operation to impact significantly, which is addressed in the serverless computing process.

**Serverless Egress Control**

Serverless egress control allows organizations to control where the workload connects to outside the Databricks environment. This restriction applies to access to the destinations where the data is going. Only approved destinations will be able to access the data from Databricks.

The following benefits are realized:

- You can create an environment of trust where the full control is given to decide which organization will have access to the data.
- Administrators can create a policy that allows access to one or many predefined workspaces within Databricks.
- The access is always denied by default and can be overwritten by specifying the authorized destinations.
- Egress controls integrate tightly with the Unity Catalog of Databricks, which allows access to storage locations and connections within that catalog.
- A test environment is possible where the testing of the Egress Control can be done without deploying the centralized policy.

**Serverless SQL for Databricks**

Serverless Databricks SQL provides high performance and elastic compute. The general benefits of Serverless SQL compute are as follows:

- **Instant and elastic compute:** The environment is immediately available and scalable in nature. The idle time is reduced. The resources will dynamically change to support the load needed on the server to run the queries.
- **Lower cost:** The platform uses the advanced machine learning algorithm to provision and compute resources based on the needs.

- **No management overhead:** Since it is a fully managed service, the burden of capacity management, infrastructure management, patching, upgrade, etc., is no longer there.
- **Predictive I/O:** The machine learning models can make the data update faster than with normal SQL.
- **Cache:** The query cache response time is improved by using a local cache and a persistent remote cache.

**Anthropic Models**

Anthropic models are platforms where you can build, deploy and test AI agents. Anthropic's Claude Sonnet model is the first hybrid reasoning model available directly in Databricks on AWS, Azure, and Google platforms.

As AI agents are capable of addressing complex tasks, with a combination of Claude and Databricks, a customer can address powerful business cases with ease.

The advantages of having these models in Databricks are as follows:

- Building domain-specific models on enterprise data
- Integrating natively with data intelligence platform
- Unified governance

The Sonnet model balances internal and external use cases with enhanced capability for greater control over the implementation.

**Use Cases for AI Using Databricks**

The following use cases are widely accepted in many organizations:

**Retail**

Customer service, user preferences, pricing strategy, demand prediction, scheduling and tracking deliveries, in-store product finding assistance, virtual fitting rooms, etc.

**Energy**

Smart GRID management, drilling and exploration optimization, quality control, safety enhancement by determining potential hazards, etc.

**Finance**

Collecting data for regulatory compliance, fraud detection, trading management, financial crime detection, etc.

**Healthcare**

Collecting patient's data in real time, providing accurate diagnosis and treatment plan, transcribing medical notes, improving healthcare administration, etc.

**Manufacturing**

Identifying and resolving process bottlenecks, Co-pilot assistance to technicians

Autogenerating and adapting contracts, invoices, purchase orders, etc.

**Travel and hospitality**

Dynamic pricing, Baggage handling assistance, Facial recognition

Feedback analysis after travel, Integrated inventory and purchasing etc.

**Media and entertainment**

Customer engagement, operational efficiency, employee productivity, product performance etc.

**Cybersecurity**

Reducing risk, complexity, and cost; next-generation threat detection, proactive code security, etc.

**Federal government**

Leveraging AI for mission support, building constituent trust, improving national security, delivering innovation through operational efficiency, improving demand planning and resource allocation, etc.

**Gaming**

Player personalization, churn management, player segmentation, key player metrics, identify resolution, player journey, etc.

**Higher education**

Eliminating technical barriers to boost campus efficiency and data-driven innovations, optimizing campus operations for performance and cost efficiency, delivering personalized learning to improve student outcomes and engagements, advancing academic research, strengthening relationships, fundraising and sports performance, safeguarding sensitive information and ensure student safety, etc.

**Public sector**

Real-time ability to audit organizational data and prioritize outcomes that benefit citizens, optimize efficiency, and maximize impact to enhance services; enhancing safety and productivity by accessing real-time streaming data; applying predictability and precision to drive performance in every product and services; etc.

**Technology and software**

Reduced development time for building and deploying Gen AI applications, effective control on cost, security and governance, building ecosystem relationships, etc.

Within Business Data Cloud, the artificial intelligence in Databricks is handled by Mosaic AI, the data warehousing is handled by the Databricks SQL, and the data governance is handled by the Unity Catalog.

**Mosaic AI**

Mosaic AI is a platform within Databricks that helps developer deploy custom Gen AI applications. Mosaic AI uses retrieval-augmented generation (RAG) to output the result. RAG is a pattern-based AI application that searches for the data relevant to the question, and the outcome is used in LLMs to provide more accurate outcomes.

Mosaic AI is tightly integrated with the other Databricks components. Because of governance, the dirty responses can be avoided, and it complies with organization policies.

Mosaic AI also supports indexing of the data for virtual extraction. The vector search indexes the data and makes it available to the RAG applications quickly.

**Unity Catalog**

Unity Catalog in Databricks is a unified solution to govern all your data in a single place. It has the following features:

- Unified governance
- Open
- Built-in intelligence

# 5.4 Test Your Knowledge

Q1: Which of the following is not a component within Business Data Cloud?

a) SAP Databricks

b) BW Bridge

c) SAP Analytics Cloud

d) Datasphere

Q2: Anthropic Claude Sonnet model is which of the following?

a) Hybrid reasoning model

b) AI agent

c) Used within Datasphere

d) None of the above

Q3: Which of the following is not a capacity service in Business Data Cloud?

a) Object store request in SAP Databricks

b) Object Store request in Datasphere

c) Object store request in SAC

d) None of the above

Q4: A data product generator is available in SAP BW PCE and Embedded BW.

a) True

b) False

Q5: What is the production backup strategy for SAP BW PCE?

a) Daily with 60 days retention

b) Daily with 90 days retention

c) Daily with 2 weeks retention

d) Daily with 30 days retention

Q6: A data product generator can have which of the following targets?

a) SAP Datasphere

b) SAC Model

c) Databricks Unity Catalog

d) SAP Joule

Q7: One Joule agent can't collaborate with other AI agents.

a) True

b) False

# 5.5 Summary

In this chapter, you learned the architecture of SAP Business Data Cloud including all its components and AI use cases.

BDC not only allows the organizations to have a 360-degree view of data but also helps organizations anticipate future outcomes. This process is achieved using AI and ML models.

In the next chapter, you will learn more about the artificial intelligence mechanism and see more use cases. You will also learn more about different AI applications in SAP Analytics products.

# CHAPTER 6

# Evolution of Artificial Intelligence

Artificial intelligence is an ability to perform human-like tasks with an added thought process for accurate predictions based on experience.

It can perform the following tasks:

- Learning
- Reasoning
- Interacting with human with queries
- Problem solving
- Predictions
- Generating creative contents

While AI is a broader topic, it can be broken down into the following:

- *Machine learning:* Machine Learning process can find patterns in a high volume of datasets, learn and make accurate predictions based on events that have yet to occur. For example, you can train a model using the sales data of a company, and AI could predict whether the product is likely to see increasing sales during holidays.
- *Deep learning*: Deep learning involves advanced machine learning algorithms that use neural networks to process them through series of iterations to generate accurate predictions. As an example, if you want to identify whether an image shown is a flower, then you can use deep learning methods.



© Sourav Banerjee 2025
S. Banerjee, *Modernizing SAP Business Warehouse*, https://doi.org/10.1007/979-8-8688-2192-9_6

- *Generative AI*: This is an advanced deep learning mechanism processed using large language models (LLMs) for more random patterns. The applicability is not only limited to tabular data but also extends to video, images, and texts. An example is a chatbot that is the first point of contact for customer service. It can accept questions as text and then run the algorithm to find the best possible match. An advanced use case could be to request the AI to enhance the quality of an uploaded image.

Artificial intelligence was initially restricted to a smaller set of applications, but with the advancement of cloud-based technologies and products, it can be extended to the analytics area to acquire analytical and reporting capabilities from the enterprise data. It is also able to generate reports and dashboards, find issues within datasets, and make predictions to speed up the reporting and planning processes.

Artificial intelligence was first introduced to the world in 1956. The vision was to perform certain tasks that are time-consuming and require a high level of expertise. In today's world, most automation is done using AI.

An AI agent can be referred to as a *virtual agent* and stays behind the curtain to address all the needs. For example, a customer service agent can process queries of customers and output resolution steps based on the prior learning. This saves effort and manpower. This also provides customers with timely responses. Without Ai agent, customers had to wait in a queue for a physical agent to be available.

## 6.1 Introduction to AI in Analytics

As explained in the earlier section, the applicability of AI in the data and reporting area has become increasingly meaningful, especially when the data insight was done manually and requires specialized skills.

There are built-in features available in many analytics tools for introducing the AI agents. One classic example is SAP Joule embedded within SAP Analytics Cloud to help get report responses faster, perform planning-related tasks, perform a deep analysis of the data, and generate query ideas before a user enters one.

### AI-Based Applications Within SAP Analytics Cloud

SAP Analytics Cloud comes with three AI-based scenarios that don't require developing a virtual agent:

- Classification
- Regression
- Time series

### Classification

Classification is a statistical method to classify certain scenarios based on known datasets and for a particular time window. A driving factor will decide how the data must be classified. The smaller set will then need to be evaluated for a time window to understand the pattern within the data. This evaluation will help to perform the future predictions.

This is a supervised learning process, which means the model needs to be trained before performing the prediction.

*Types of statistical classification:* Classification can be divided into three categories:

- *Binary classification*: Binary classification is often most simple classification techniques as the number of outcomes is only two. As the name suggests, it is either true or false. It can, for example, identify whether the actual price of a particular product is higher than the estimated price or not. It therefore classifies the data into two distinct categories.
- *Multiclass classification*: This classification technique requires more than two categories to classify the data. Hence, the accuracy of the model is better than the binary category. An example would be to find the chair, sofa, and table from the input image. This requires identifying the volume, texture, and size of the product.
- *Multilevel classification*: In this technique, more than one outcome is possible when classifying a product. In simple words, one input can belong to multiple categories of different types at the same time. This requires many features to be matched before the classification is fully done.

Each classification technique requires the machine to learn based on the past dataset to understand the patterns inside the dataset. This learning helps the machine to decide on which category the incoming object belongs to. Based on this understanding, the machine can predict the classification for any future dataset.

Some of the classification-based algorithms are as follows:

- **Random forest**

  Random forest is a technique that involves creating multiple decision trees with various patterns and decides on the classification for each tree. These decisions from different trees are combined into the best possible outcomes. The process generally requires the following steps:

  - Create as many decision trees as possible.
  - Each tree should focus on random patterns and decision techniques. This will eliminate the biasness within the decisions.
  - All the trees will make its own decisions based on the prediction made.
  - Combine the decisions from different trees with majority voting. The best possible answer will be trustworthy.

  Random forest works well with a large dataset and does not need to be continuous. For example, if there is some missing data in the set, decision trees still produce an accurate outcome because of the randomness in the pattern.

- **Naïve Bayes**

  This algorithm relies on the Bayes theory, which assumes that the variables are not dependent on each other and therefore called "naïve." It uses the probability function to decide whether the variable belongs to a class. It's a repetitive process to generate the accuracy in the prediction.

  This algorithm is generally easy to implement and require less data for training. It works both with the continuous dataset and with random data.

  It is difficult to get a situation where the variables are not linked to each other. If there is a missing data for a specific class, this algorithm does not consider that class for assigning variables into it, which makes the prediction inaccurate.

- **K-nearest neighbors**

  The K-nearest neighbors is a technique in classification that finds the nearest match to the classes. This is a lazy learner algorithm because it does not need to be trained based on a historical dataset.

  The neighbor can be selected in one of the following methods:

  - Cross validation
  - Elbow method
  - Odd values to K

- **Gradient boosting**

  This method works by finding errors in the earlier predictions. It first trains the model in a sequential manner and performs a prediction in each model. Every model assesses the outcome of the predecessor model and finds any inaccuracy in the prediction. This method improves the accuracy in each iteration. Each model finds the weakness in the earlier model to minimize the gradient. The process is repeated until a predefined criterion is met.

  The model uses the following steps to perform the iterations:

  - Sequential learning process
  - Residual calculation
  - Shrinkage

- **Support vector machine (SVM)**

  SVM is particularly useful for binary classification techniques as it creates boundaries of the classes. The bigger the margin of the boundary, the better the model performs. The SVM technique can be performance intensive when using a large dataset for training the model.

  A margin in the SVM is the distance from the hyper plane to the data at both sides. The maximum possible distance leads to the best result. There are two distinct mechanisms for SVM algorithms:

  - Linear SVM
  - Nonlinear SVM

- **Logistics regression**

  Logistics regression is usually performed for the binary classifications where only two outcomes are possible. It uses the Sigmoid function (a probability function that can convert any input value into binary prediction using an S-shaped curve) to determine the outcome.

  The following are the types of logistics regression:

  *Binomial logistics regression*: The Sigmoid function is used for determining the outcome in the binary method (i.e., True or False).

  *Multinomial logistics regression*: The target variable can have more than two types in which case the Softmax function (which can perform probability distribution of the prediction scores) will be used for the prediction.

  *Ordinal logistics regression*: This uses the ranking of three of more variables to determine the categories as outcome.

**How It Works in SAP Analytics Cloud**

There are two major steps involved to perform classification in SAP Analytics Cloud:

1. Train the model.
2. Perform the prediction.

In general, only binary prediction is possible using this option. This means it allows predicting between two possible options only. Let's look at a hypothetical scenario to see how this option can be used.

First, a set of data needs to be prepared for the model to get trained. Please note that it requires a considerable volume of data for the model to get trained. The bigger the data volume and the more variety of the dataset, the stronger the prediction quality will be. The following fields need to be there as part of the training dataset:

*Influencers:* These fields are values that can influence the prediction. It can be a single field or group of fields that together influence the decisions.

*Predictive target*: This is the field that is the outcome of the prediction. In the training model, this field must exist so that during training, the model can understand how the influencer fields are steering the change in the target values. Only one field is possible to be defined as the target.

*Limit the influencer*: If there are many fields available that can be part of the influencer list but the user is not sure which field to select, then they can limit the influencer list. This will help decide which fields influence the most. In the case of five fields and three as a limit, it will first calculate the percent of influence on the target for each field and then apply the sorting to get the fields that influence most and ignore the others during the training exercise.

Prepare Your Dataset

Let's assume the training scenario is based on healthcare data. The data has three symptoms for every case, and it is deciding whether the diagnosis is flu or not. As it can provide only a Yes or No answer, it is therefore a binary classification. Figure 6-1 shows the dataset.

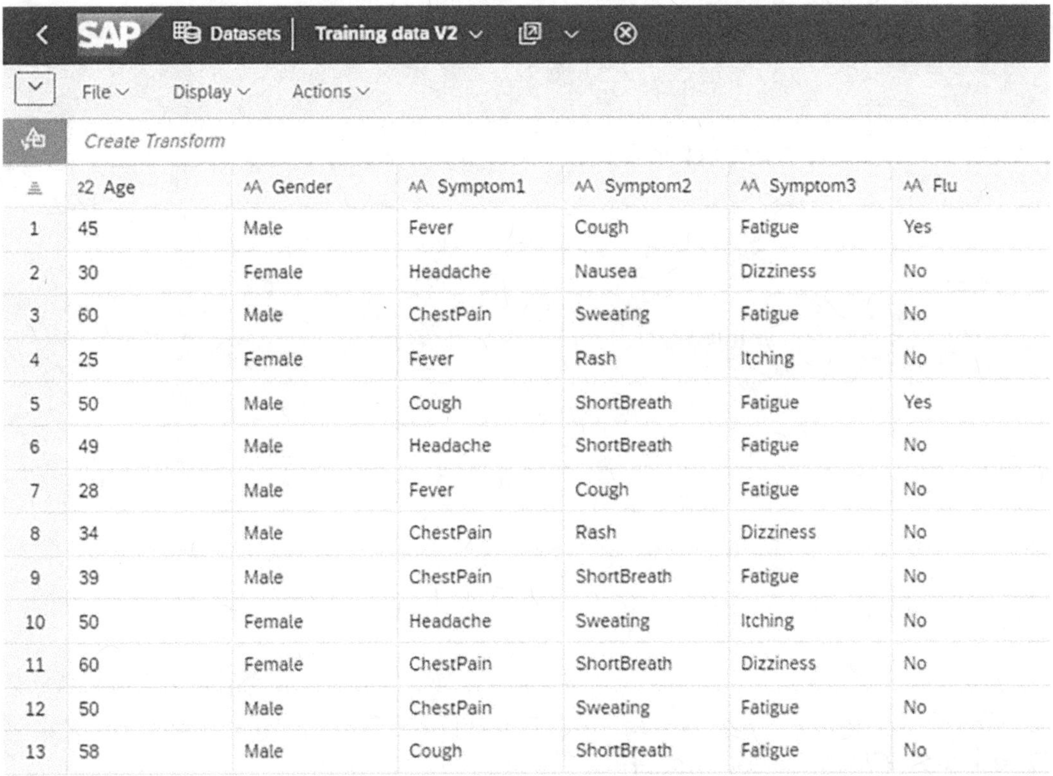


| | Age | Gender | Symptom1 | Symptom2 | Symptom3 | Flu |
|---|---|---|---|---|---|---|
| 1 | 45 | Male | Fever | Cough | Fatigue | Yes |
| 2 | 30 | Female | Headache | Nausea | Dizziness | No |
| 3 | 60 | Male | ChestPain | Sweating | Fatigue | No |
| 4 | 25 | Female | Fever | Rash | Itching | No |
| 5 | 50 | Male | Cough | ShortBreath | Fatigue | Yes |
| 6 | 49 | Male | Headache | ShortBreath | Fatigue | No |
| 7 | 28 | Male | Fever | Cough | Fatigue | No |
| 8 | 34 | Male | ChestPain | Rash | Dizziness | No |
| 9 | 39 | Male | ChestPain | ShortBreath | Fatigue | No |
| 10 | 50 | Female | Headache | Sweating | Itching | No |
| 11 | 60 | Female | ChestPain | ShortBreath | Dizziness | No |
| 12 | 50 | Male | ChestPain | Sweating | Fatigue | No |
| 13 | 58 | Male | Cough | ShortBreath | Fatigue | No |

***Figure 6-1.*** *Data preparation (classification)*

As shown, "Symptom1," "Symptom2," and "Symptom3" are the influencer fields. "Flu" is the target prediction field, which has possible values as "Yes" or "No."

Create a Classification Model in SAC

Create a prediction model of type Classification and select the dataset . Only the available dataset can be used for the training; no file/data source can be selected that is not available in SAC. In such cases, a dataset needs to be first prepared, and then the model needs to be created. See Figure 6-2.

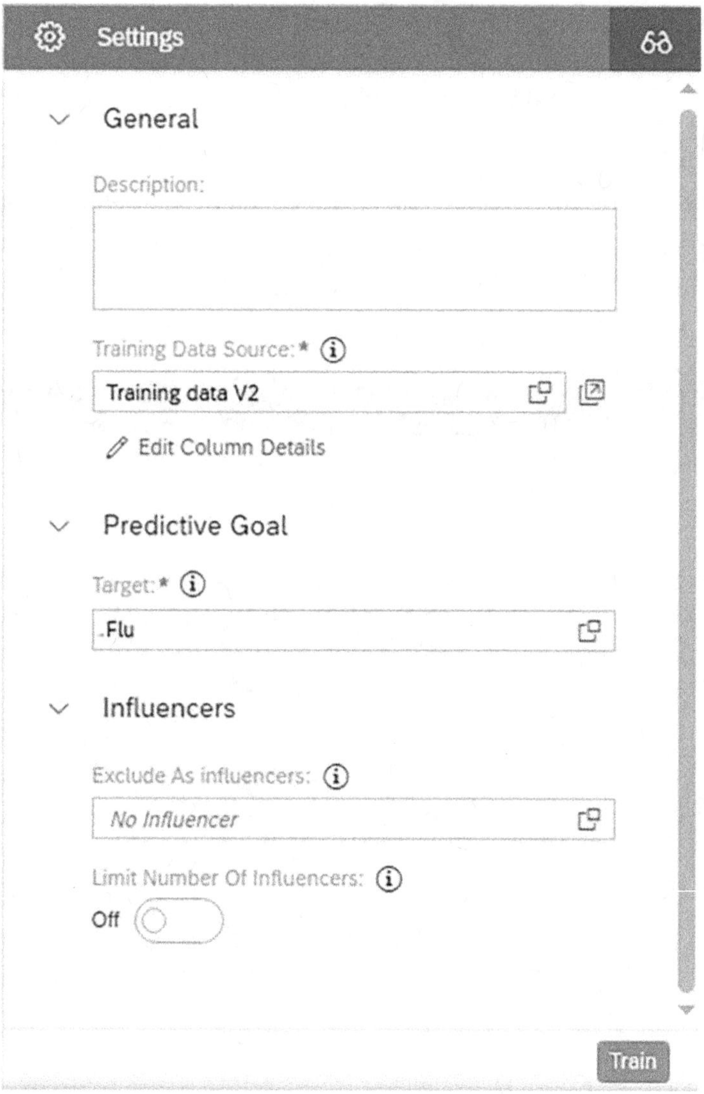


***Figure 6-2.** Classification model*

Training Data V2 is the name of the dataset that contains the data for training. In the section Predictive Goal, select the Target column, which is the outcome of the prediction. In our case, it is the field "Flu."

In the Influencer section, you can leave it empty because it is the exclusion list. Leaving it empty means all fields will be used as influencers. If a field is specified here, that would not be considered during the training.

Select "Limit number of influencers" if many influencer fields are available and you are not sure which fields to select as influencers. The system will define that according to the limit specified and by assessing the training data.

Once all these fields are updated, select Train. This will trigger the training process and will output several KPIs to determine the strength of your training model. See Figure 6-3.

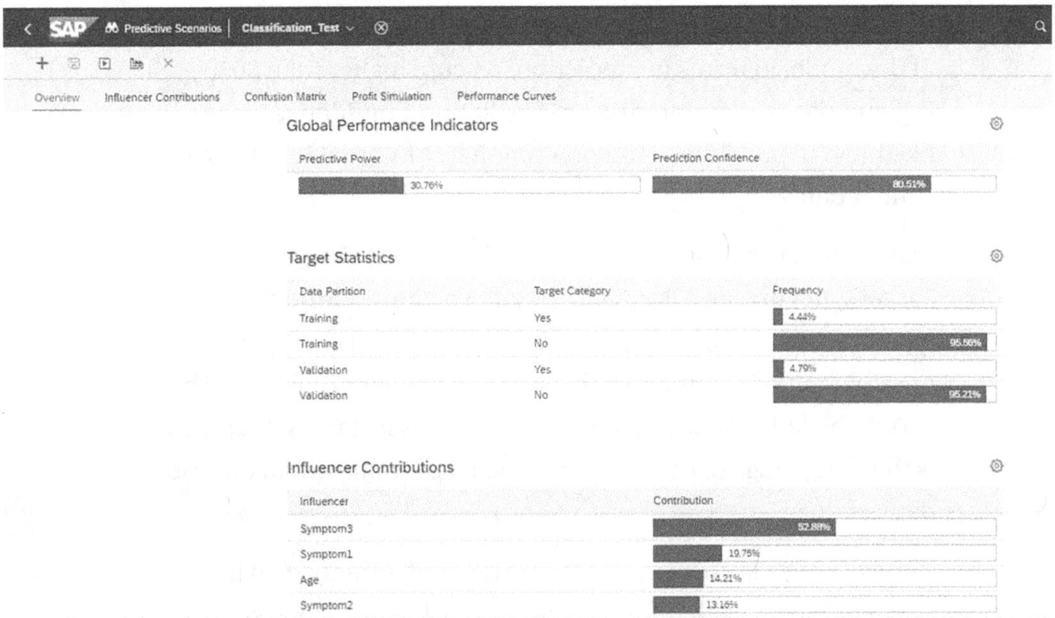


***Figure 6-3.** Overview of classification result*

As shown, the following information is generated:

- Overview
- Influencer contribution
- Confusion matrix
- Profit simulation
- Performance curves

**Overview**

This page will give an overview of the data the model is trained on and the important KPIs. The following information is displayed:

> *Global Performance Indicator*: Two KPIs are shown: Predictive Power and Prediction Confidence. Predictive power is the strength of the model in terms of prediction. A score higher than 80% is generally good for prediction. Prediction Confidence is the likeliness of providing good prediction if the model is applied on similar data.

> *Target Statistics*: This shows the following KPIs: Data Partition, Target Category, and Frequency. Data Partition shows the data type that was involved in training. Target Categories are the possible values of the result that will be used for prediction. There should be only two categories for binary classification. Frequency is the percentage of occurrence of the result value out of the entire dataset.

> *Influencer Contribution*: Here the percent of influence on the result based on each influencer specified will be displayed. This data is also used for the ranking if the number of influencers is predefined.

**Influencer Contribution**

In this section the results shown in Figure 6-4 will be displayed.

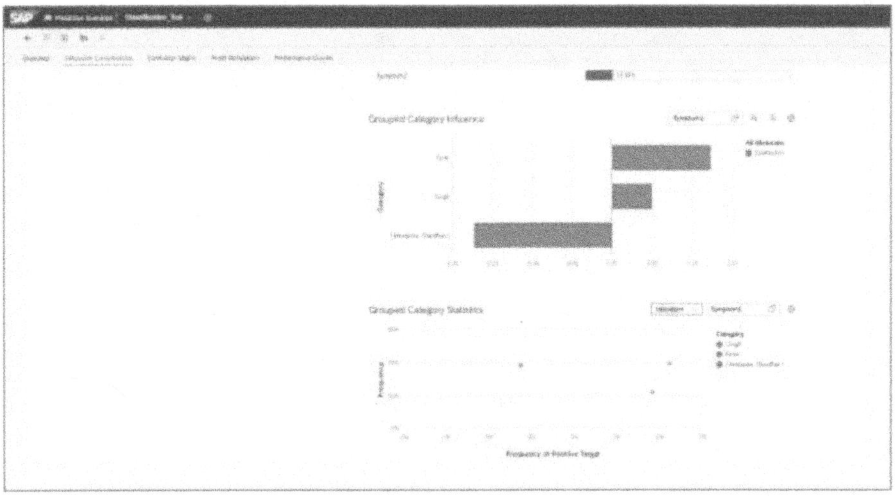

***Figure 6-4.*** *Influencer contribution in classification*

Two main KPIs are reported:

> *Grouped Category Influence*: This is displayed based on one of the influencers. In Figure 6-4, "Symptom 1" is used. It shows the Influence % value on the final prediction.
>
> *Grouped Category Statistics*: This can be shown on the training or the validation data and for a particular influencer. Each value or group of values for any influencer will show the percentage occurrence of positive result of the prediction.

**Confusion Matrix**

Figure 6-5 is a confusion matrix that shows the positive and negative outcomes for both true and false.

It shows the following:

- Contacted population
- Detected target
- Confusion matrix
- Metrics

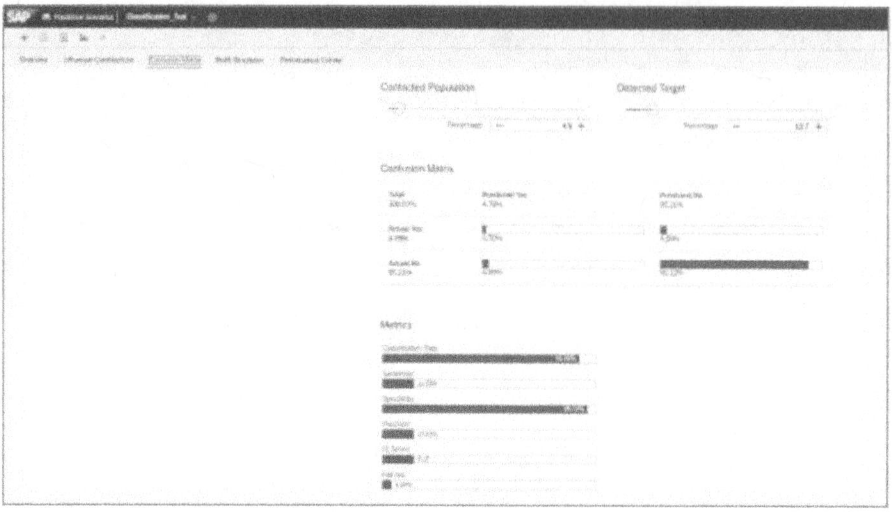

***Figure 6-5.*** *Confusion matrix in classification*

A contacted population is a KPI that can be used to predict the percentage of a positive outcome based on the total population of the data. This can be changed to see the effect on the prediction.

The confusion matrix is based on the following scenarios:

> *True Positive*: Both Actual and Predicted are True (0.7% here).
>
> *False Positive*: Actual is False and predicted is True (4.09% here).
>
> *True Negative*: Actual is true and Predicted is False (4.09% here).
>
> *False Negative:* Both Actual and Predicted are False (91.12%).

The metric also shows the following KPIs:

> *Classification Rate*: Percent of the total data classified in the predictive model (91.82% in the current model)
>
> *Sensitivity*: Percent of data that will leave the current classification (14.63% in the current model)
>
> *Specificity*: Percent of data that will stay as the current classification (95.71% in the current model)
>
> *Precision*: The strength of the model (14.63% in the current model)

*F1 Score*: Mean of Precision % and Recall % (0.15% in the current model)

*Fall-Out:* Percent of negative target that is incorrectly specified as positive (4.29% in the current model)

**Profit Simulation**

Profit simulation is used when the wrong or correct prediction is associated with a cost; see Figure 6-6.

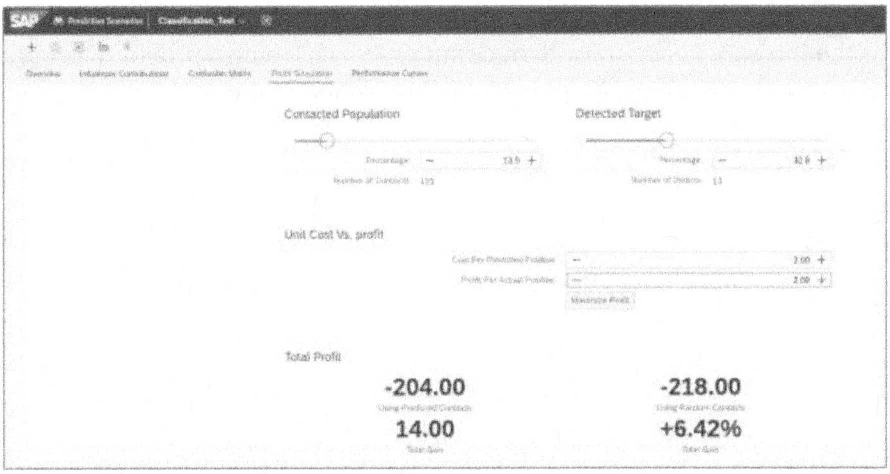


***Figure 6-6.*** *Profit simulation in classification*

The following KPIs are used:

*Cost per predicted positive*: This the cost associated with a True Positive and False Positive scenario.

*Profit per Actual Positive*: This is the profit for a True Positive scenario.

The cost and profit can be seen based on the actual prediction values. There is also an option to make a maximum profit. If you click this, then the threshold that can give the maximum profit will be displayed.

**Performance Curves**

Several performance curves are generated after the model is trained.

% Detected Target compares the model with a perfect and random model. A perfect model will always give you 100% precision in the predicted values. See Figure 6-7.

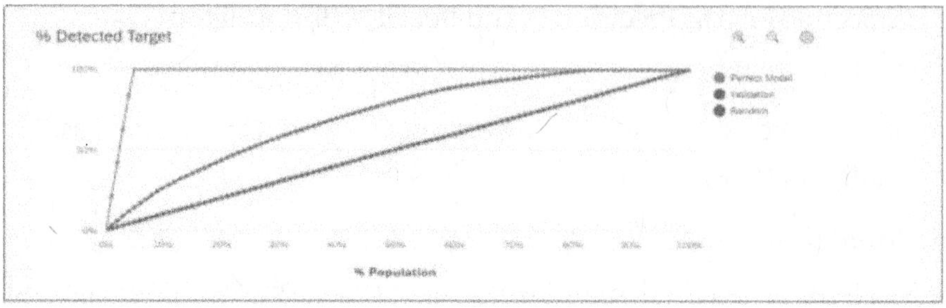


***Figure 6-7.** % Detected Target value in classification*

Lift is the increase in accuracy than a random model. It also provides an opportunity to see the comparison against a perfect model. See Figure 6-8.

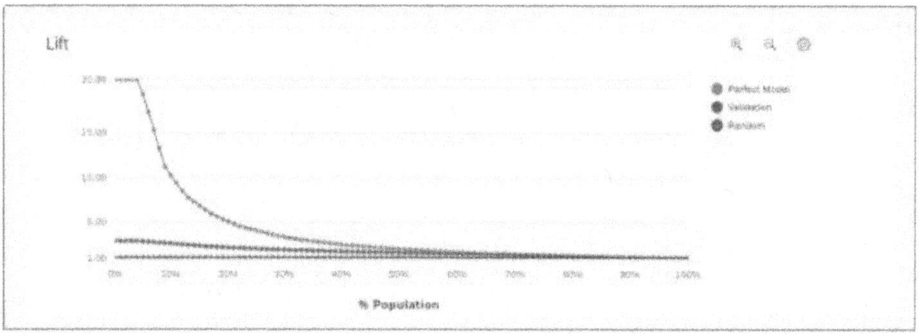


***Figure 6-8.** Lift in Classification*

Sensitivity versus specificity is displayed in the Figure 6-9 plot and shows the difference between right and wrong predictions.

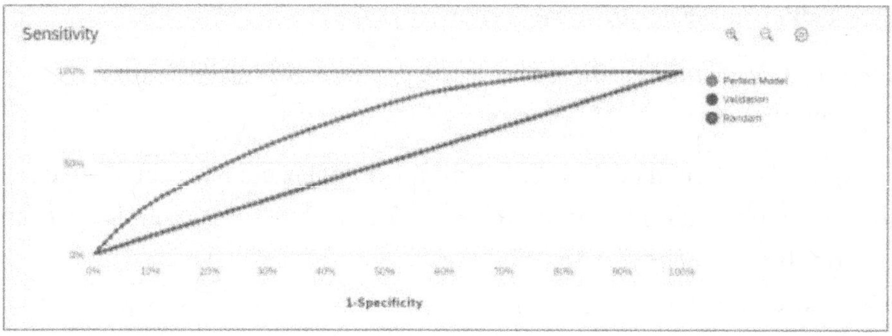


***Figure 6-9.** Sensitivity in classification*

A Lorenz plot can be shown for either Sensitivity (True Positive) or Specificity (False Negative). See Figure 6-10.

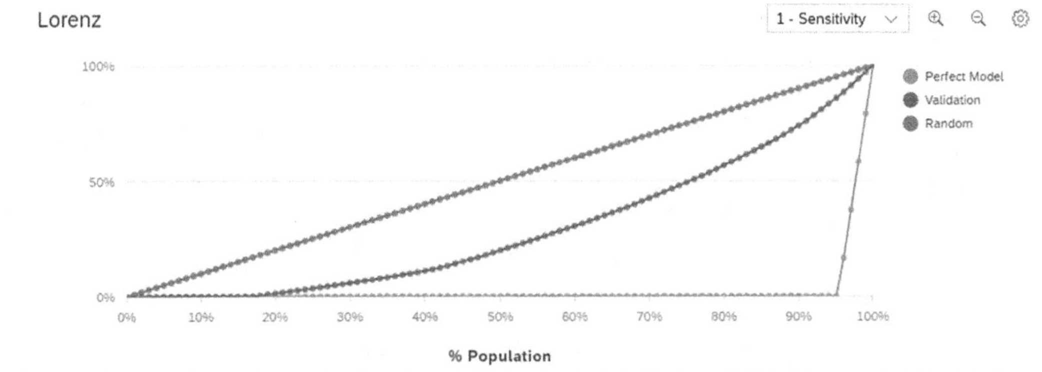


***Figure 6-10.** Lorenz in classification*

A density plot shows the density of the positive and negative outcomes in the overall prediction. A good predictive model always displays the peak value of positive and negative values in different areas of the plot. Therefore, based on the previous plot, the prediction model does not give a good prediction. See Figure 6-11.

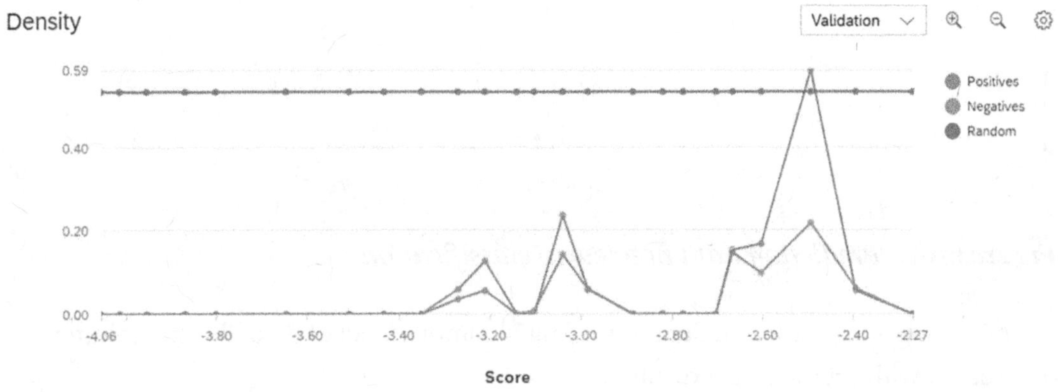


***Figure 6-11.** Density in classification*

<u>Generate Prediction</u>

The final step in creating the model is to generate the prediction for a new dataset. In this new dataset, the predicted column should not be present as it will be generated during the prediction. The data shown in Figure 6-12 is uploaded.

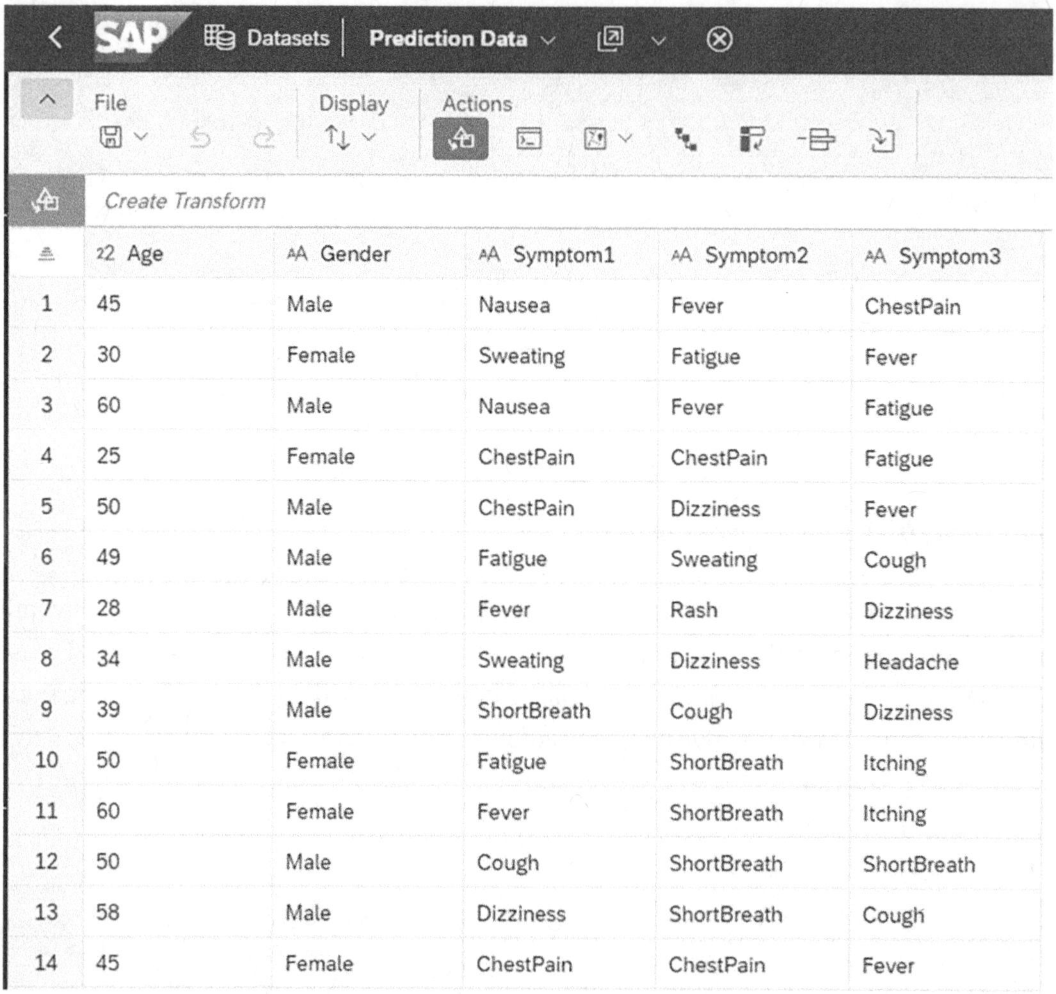


| | Age | Gender | Symptom1 | Symptom2 | Symptom3 |
|---|---|---|---|---|---|
| 1 | 45 | Male | Nausea | Fever | ChestPain |
| 2 | 30 | Female | Sweating | Fatigue | Fever |
| 3 | 60 | Male | Nausea | Fever | Fatigue |
| 4 | 25 | Female | ChestPain | ChestPain | Fatigue |
| 5 | 50 | Male | ChestPain | Dizziness | Fever |
| 6 | 49 | Male | Fatigue | Sweating | Cough |
| 7 | 28 | Male | Fever | Rash | Dizziness |
| 8 | 34 | Male | Sweating | Dizziness | Headache |
| 9 | 39 | Male | ShortBreath | Cough | Dizziness |
| 10 | 50 | Female | Fatigue | ShortBreath | Itching |
| 11 | 60 | Female | Fever | ShortBreath | Itching |
| 12 | 50 | Male | Cough | ShortBreath | ShortBreath |
| 13 | 58 | Male | Dizziness | ShortBreath | Cough |
| 14 | 45 | Female | ChestPain | ChestPain | Fever |

***Figure 6-12.*** *Prediction data preview in classification*

As shown, the prediction data is nothing but another set of data like the training dataset but without the target result field.

Now, go to your prediction model and apply the prediction model. See Figure 6-13.

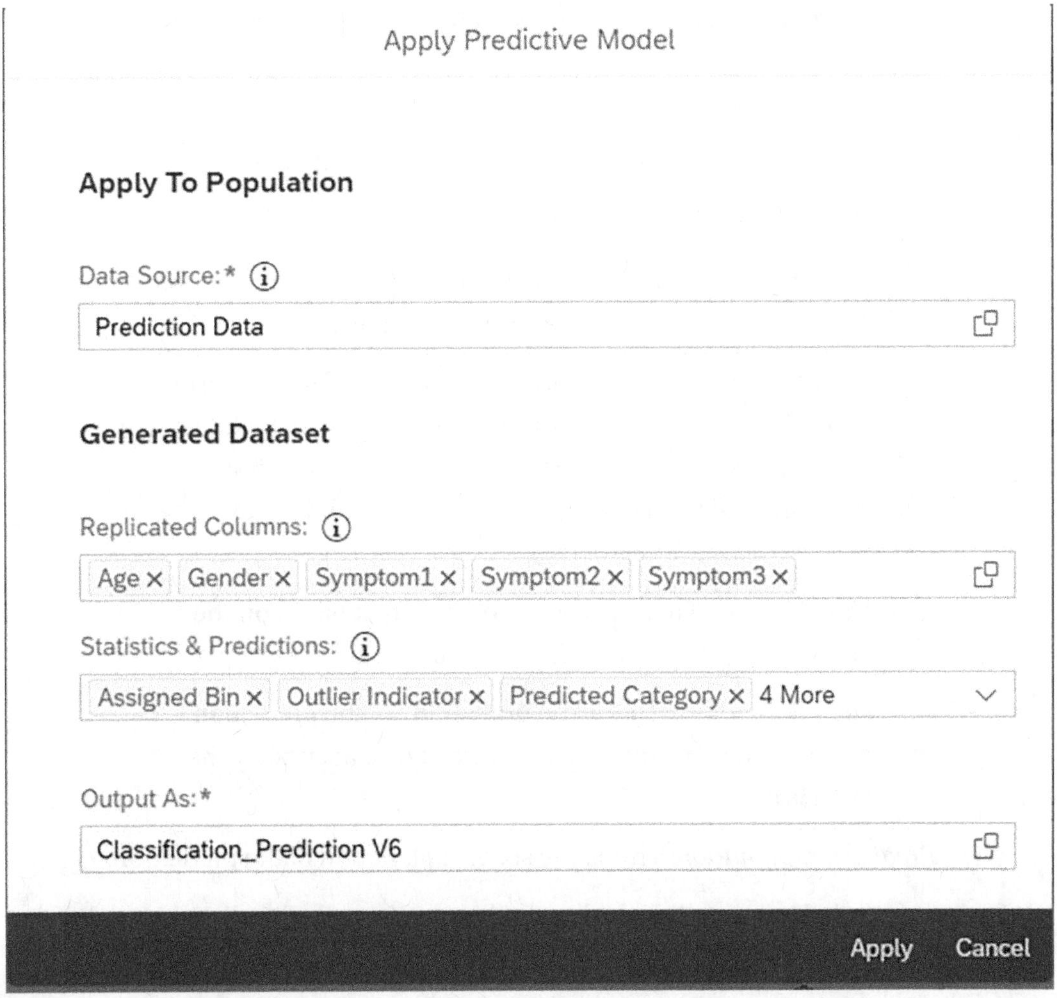


***Figure 6-13.** Applying a predictive model*

The Data Source value is the name of the dataset that contains the data required for the prediction. In our case, it is Prediction Data.

Replicated Columns are the fields from the dataset that will be available along with the predicted value. If you leave this as blank, then no fields will be transferred in the predicted dataset.

Statistics and Predictions are the KPIs generated during the prediction. During the prediction, these values will be available as separate fields in the predicted dataset. The following fields are possible:

- *Apply Date*: Date on which the prediction is applied on the model.
- *Train Date*: Date on which the model is trained.
- *Assigned Bin*: The observations are stored in 10 different bins, and each bin will have a 10% probability of occurrence.
- *Outlier Indicator*: For each row in the application dataset, the outlier indictor is 1 when the row is an outlier with respect to the target, else 0. The outlier observation is the prediction error, which is greater than three times of the average prediction error for the similar dataset.
- *Predicted Category*: This is the value of the target based on the prediction outcome. It can be Yes or No for the given example.
- *Prediction Probability*: This is the probability of the prediction category as the target value i.e., measure of how accurately the prediction is done.
- *Predicted explanation*: This is the set of explanation of the prediction.

Once the prediction is applied, the log can be seen from the Predicted Model drop-down. See Figure 6-14.

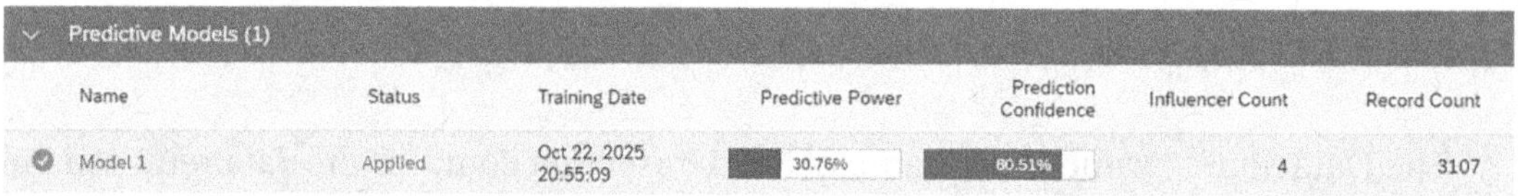


***Figure 6-14.*** *Log of model prediction*

Now, the values of the prediction and all statistics can be seen from the result set. See Figure 6-15.

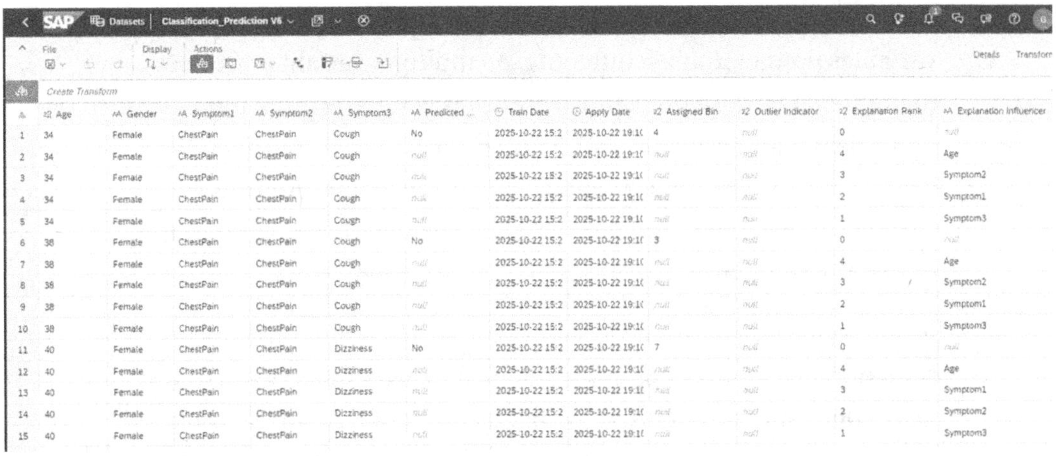


| | Age | Gender | Symptom1 | Symptom2 | Symptom3 | Predicted ... | Train Date | Apply Date | Assigned Bin | Outlier Indicator | Explanation Rank | Explanation Influencer |
|---|---|---|---|---|---|---|---|---|---|---|---|---|
| 1 | 34 | Female | ChestPain | ChestPain | Cough | No | 2025-10-22 15:2 | 2025-10-22 19:1( | 4 | null | 0 | null |
| 2 | 34 | Female | ChestPain | ChestPain | Cough | null | 2025-10-22 15:2 | 2025-10-22 19:1( | null | null | 4 | Age |
| 3 | 34 | Female | ChestPain | ChestPain | Cough | null | 2025-10-22 15:2 | 2025-10-22 19:1( | null | null | 3 | Symptom2 |
| 4 | 34 | Female | ChestPain | ChestPain | Cough | null | 2025-10-22 15:2 | 2025-10-22 19:1( | null | null | 2 | Symptom1 |
| 5 | 34 | Female | ChestPain | ChestPain | Cough | null | 2025-10-22 15:2 | 2025-10-22 19:1( | null | null | 1 | Symptom3 |
| 6 | 38 | Female | ChestPain | ChestPain | Cough | No | 2025-10-22 15:2 | 2025-10-22 19:1( | 3 | null | 0 | null |
| 7 | 38 | Female | ChestPain | ChestPain | Cough | null | 2025-10-22 15:2 | 2025-10-22 19:1( | null | null | 4 | Age |
| 8 | 38 | Female | ChestPain | ChestPain | Cough | null | 2025-10-22 15:2 | 2025-10-22 19:1( | null | null | 3 | Symptom2 |
| 9 | 38 | Female | ChestPain | ChestPain | Cough | null | 2025-10-22 15:2 | 2025-10-22 19:1( | null | null | 2 | Symptom1 |
| 10 | 38 | Female | ChestPain | ChestPain | Cough | null | 2025-10-22 15:2 | 2025-10-22 19:1( | null | null | 1 | Symptom3 |
| 11 | 40 | Female | ChestPain | ChestPain | Dizziness | No | 2025-10-22 15:2 | 2025-10-22 19:1( | 7 | null | 0 | null |
| 12 | 40 | Female | ChestPain | ChestPain | Dizziness | null | 2025-10-22 15:2 | 2025-10-22 19:1( | null | null | 4 | Age |
| 13 | 40 | Female | ChestPain | ChestPain | Dizziness | null | 2025-10-22 15:2 | 2025-10-22 19:1( | null | null | 3 | Symptom1 |
| 14 | 40 | Female | ChestPain | ChestPain | Dizziness | null | 2025-10-22 15:2 | 2025-10-22 19:1( | null | null | 2 | Symptom2 |
| 15 | 40 | Female | ChestPain | ChestPain | Dizziness | null | 2025-10-22 15:2 | 2025-10-22 19:1( | null | null | 1 | Symptom3 |

***Figure 6-15.*** *Reviewing the classification results*

As shown, the predicted values are displayed for the new dataset. In some cases, the value is not available, which means that the training data was not enough to generate predictions for this dataset. It can be possible that the data used for training does not talk about the value of the influencer that is there for this dataset.

You have now learned how to perform binary prediction using the classification model in SAC Smart Predict.

**Regression**

Regression is another type of prediction model that predicts the outcome as continuous numeric values. This is based on several variables that are responsible for making good predictions. In contrast with binary classification, regression models can provide several different outcomes.

Two types of variables are generally defined in the regression theory:

- Dependent variables (the value changes based on changes in other variables)
- Independent variables (other variables do not influence the change)

Many regression models are available, such as:

> *Simple linear regression:* A linear co-relation between the dependent and independent variables in the dataset exists. A line will be drawn that can predict the missing values. The line will be the best fitted line in a plot of dependent and independent variables. this is also called *least square regression line.*

*Multiple linear regressions:* This is when multiple independent variables predict a single outcome. As multiple variables are used to influence the outcome, the accuracy is generally more than a simple linear regression. If the Categorical value is received like healthy and ill, then it will be converted using a dummy variable with a binary outcome. The process is used to support the regression modeling.

*Polynomial regression:* If your data does not fall under the linear category (i.e., it is not possible to draw a straight line between your dependent and independent variables), then the model suitable for regression would be polynomial regression. The best drawn regression line can be of nonlinear shape.

*Ridge regression:* This is used when linear regression becomes unstable due to highly correlated values. This model solves this by applying a penalty factor to streamline the output. The penalty is also known as *L2 penalty*.

*Lasso regression:* This model is like the ridge process and is suitable for the scenario when a correlation exists between the variable influencers. This applies a Shrinkage method to regularize the output. It shrinks the outcome toward the central point by introducing a penalty factor. This is also known as *L1 regularization.*

*Support vector regression (SVR):* This is based on SVM and can be applied both for classification and regression.

*Decision tree regression:* This regression is based on different decision trees to find the outcome. Each decision tree will represent an outcome. This model is also valid for classification.

*Random forest regression:* This method uses multiple decision trees to generate a number of outcomes. The final prediction is based on the average of the outcomes from all the trees. These trees will made from a smaller set of data from the entire dataset.

The process of drawing the best fitted line in case of regression can follow many alternatives:

*Least square method:* This method is generally used to get the equation of best fitted line using a sum of squared errors. This is determined by the square of the difference between the actual and predicted outcomes. The sum of square should be made as minimum as possible to find the best fitted line.

The following are the disadvantages of this method:

- Only two variables are considered. Other relationships are not considered.
- Evenly distributed data is required. For uneven dataset, this method will not be suitable.
- This method is sensitive to outliers.

*Gradient descent*: This process in regression uses an iterative model to reduce the slope of the regression line until the difference between actual and prediction becomes small. This allows a step-by-step process to follow and improve the accuracy in every step. The difference between the actual and predicted value is also called the *cost function.*

Table 6-1 compares the classification and regression models.

***Table 6-1.*** *Classification vs. Regression*

| Features | Classification | Regression |
|---|---|---|
| Objective | Categorize the data systematically using the current available dataset | Outcome is based on numeric values |
| Decision boundary | Boundary is clearly defined | Based on the best fit line |
| Tree algorithm | Multiple outcomes from trees are voted to find the best result | Subset of the data is used to predict the outcome and then average of the outcome is used (since numeric) |
| Target values | Usually, discrete | Usually, continuous |
| Metrics | F1 Score, ROC, etc. | R Squared, mean absolute error etc. |
| Learning process | Patterns in the training data | Relation between variables |

**How It Works in SAP Analytics Cloud**

Regression follows the similar process as classification during training and prediction. It starts by creating a new dataset that should be providing the data based on historical observations. The only difference is that the goal can have numeric outcomes.

In Figure 6-16, the dataset contains the insurance cost based on several parameters (like age, sex, smoking, and BMI). These variables contribute toward the insurance cost.

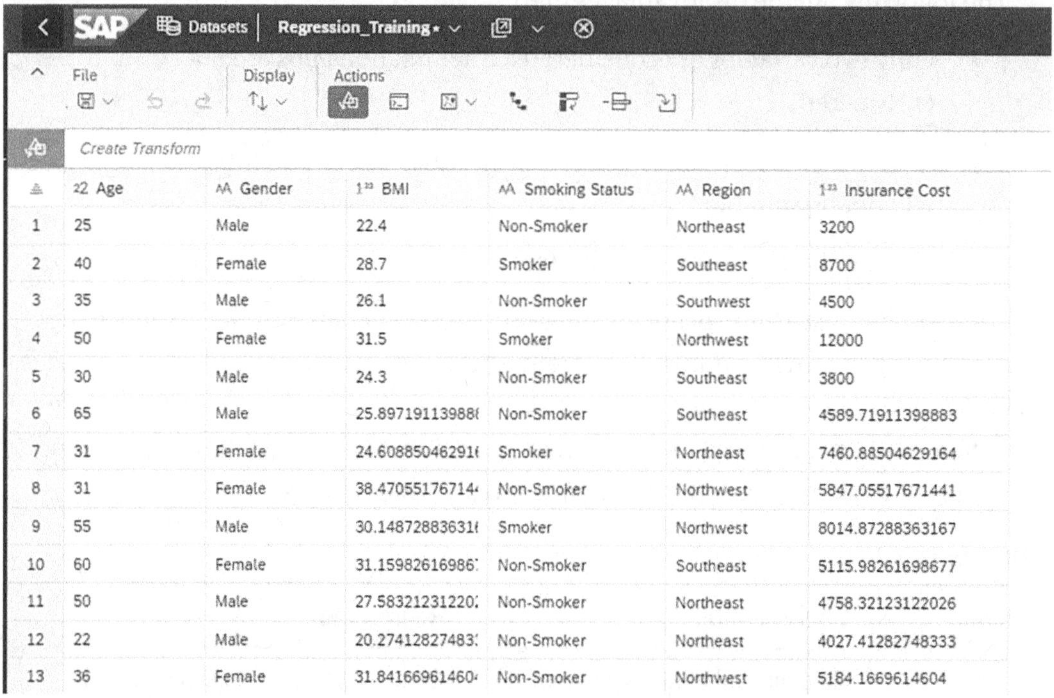


| | Age | Gender | BMI | Smoking Status | Region | Insurance Cost |
|---|---|---|---|---|---|---|
| 1 | 25 | Male | 22.4 | Non-Smoker | Northeast | 3200 |
| 2 | 40 | Female | 28.7 | Smoker | Southeast | 8700 |
| 3 | 35 | Male | 26.1 | Non-Smoker | Southwest | 4500 |
| 4 | 50 | Female | 31.5 | Smoker | Northwest | 12000 |
| 5 | 30 | Male | 24.3 | Non-Smoker | Southeast | 3800 |
| 6 | 65 | Male | 25.89719113988 | Non-Smoker | Southeast | 4589.71911398883 |
| 7 | 31 | Female | 24.60885046291 | Smoker | Northeast | 7460.88504629164 |
| 8 | 31 | Female | 38.47055176714 | Non-Smoker | Northwest | 5847.05517671441 |
| 9 | 55 | Male | 30.14872883631 | Smoker | Northwest | 8014.87288363167 |
| 10 | 60 | Female | 31.15982616986 | Non-Smoker | Southeast | 5115.98261698677 |
| 11 | 50 | Male | 27.58321231220 | Non-Smoker | Northeast | 4758.32123122026 |
| 12 | 22 | Male | 20.27412827483 | Non-Smoker | Northeast | 4027.41282748333 |
| 13 | 36 | Female | 31.84166961460 | Non-Smoker | Northwest | 5184.1669614604 |

***Figure 6-16.** Dataset for regression*

As shown, the insurance cost is the outcome that depends on other fields in this dataset.

Once the dataset is created, a regression type prediction model needs to be created. Before the actual training, we can define the type of data in each column. See Figure 6-17.

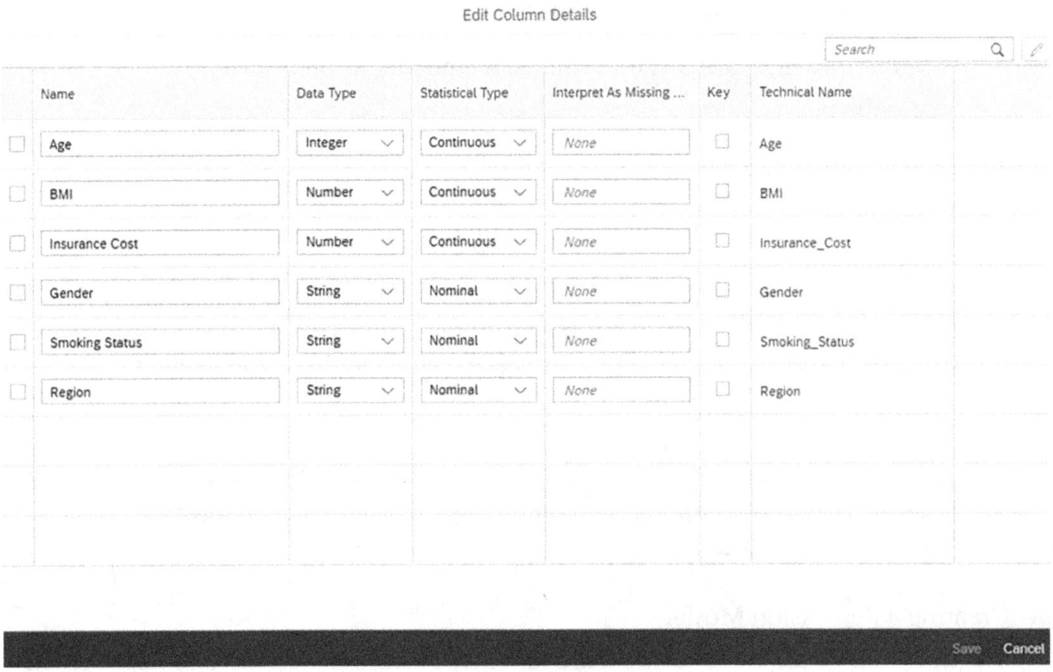


***Figure 6-17.** Defining column properties for regression*

The statistical type shown in Figure 6-18 is available.

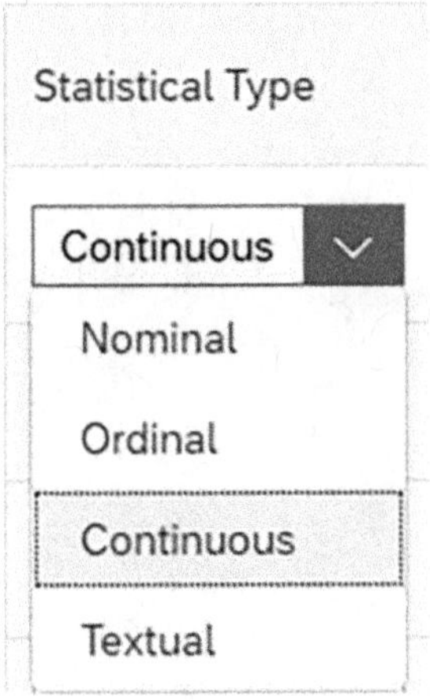


***Figure 6-18.** Statistical type for regression*

Details of each statistical type are given here:

*Nominal:* These are discrete values. A categorization is also possible.

Nominal variables can show only two values.

*Ordinal*: Values are discrete. There could be numerical values or text values.

*Continuous*: Values are generally numeric. They are also continuous in nature. During the training process, the variables are grouped into several bins.

*Textual:* They are used for the text analysis. This can be a single word, phrase, or sentence. Currently the SAC predictive feature does not allow this type of variable.

Creating a Regression Model

The next step would be to create a model of type Regression in SAC Smart Predict. See Figure 6-19.

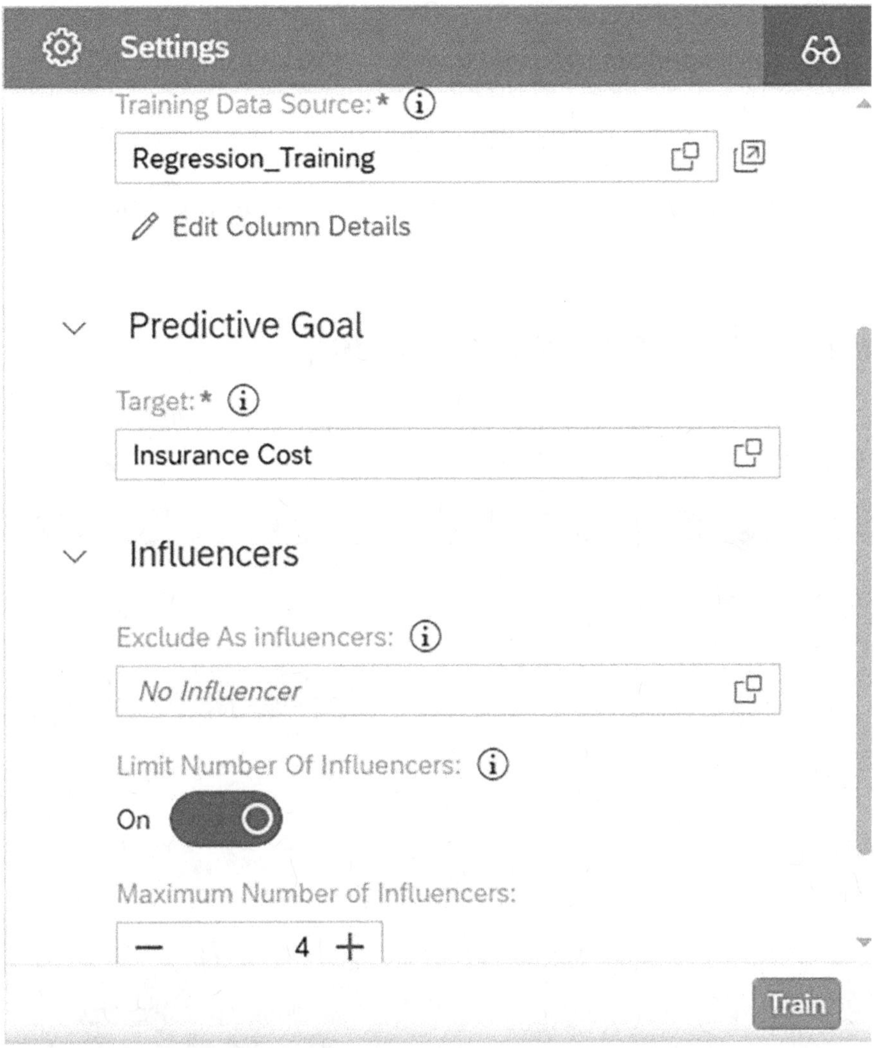


***Figure 6-19.*** *Create Regression model*

The following details are entered:

*Training Data Source:* This is the dataset that was uploaded. In our example, it is Regression Training Dataset.

*Target:* Target is the outcome of the prediction. From the training, the model will study the behavior of this field based on the other variables available in the model. The variation of the data is used to understand the impact on the target variable. The target variable is a dependent variable in the dataset. In our case, this is the field Insurance Cost. After successful prediction, Insurance Cost will be determined based on new values for other variables in the data.

*Limit of Influencer:* In this case, we have marked it as 4; therefore, the four variables that had maximum impact on the prediction will be used in this model.

## Understanding the result of training

After the training of the model, several KPIs will be displayed for further analysis and to find the strength of the model developed. See Figure 6-20.

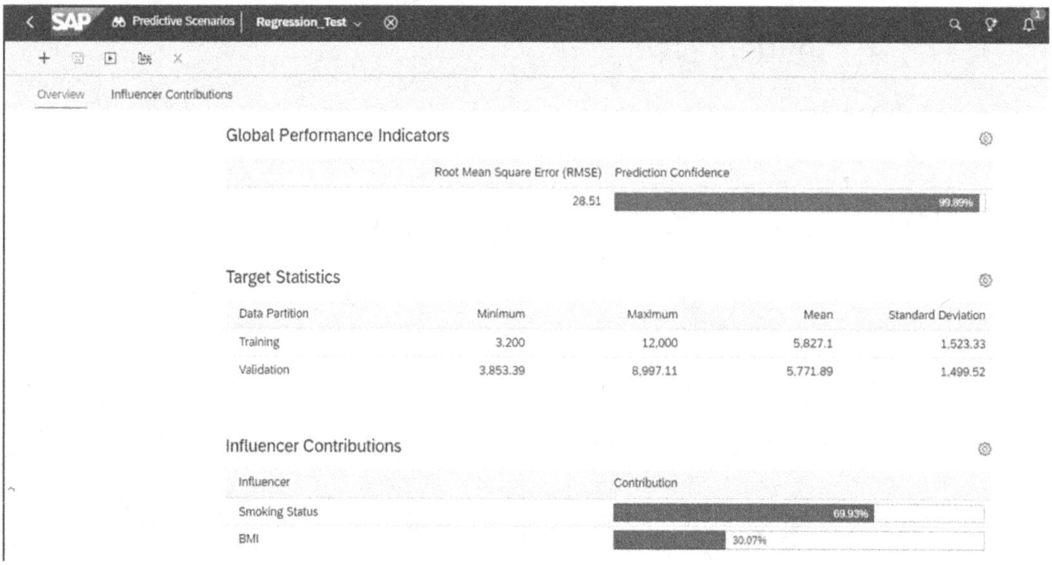


***Figure 6-20.*** *Overview of the regression model*

On the Overview page, the following details will be displayed:

- *Root Mean Square Error (RMSE):* This is a measure to determine the accuracy of the model. It is the distance between the predicted value and the actual value. The formula can be applied by first calculating the distance between the predicted and actual value for each data point, then finding the mean of them, and finally applying a square root on that mean. The aim is to get a smaller value for this KPI.

A zero value represents that no error exists, and the predicted value equals the actual value. It has the following advantages:

- Measures the error in the prediction
- Outlier sensitivity
- Makes the model easy to interpret
- Acts as an optimization criterion for the model
- Can be used to compare the effectiveness with other models

- *Target Statistics:* The following data is shown:
    - Minimum
    - Maximum
    - Mean
    - Standard deviation

  Based on the mean and standard deviation, you can predict the quality of our model.

- *Influencer Contribution*: You can see that the Smoking status has the maximum influence on the result followed by the BMI. These are the main variable used for performing the prediction. See Figure 6-21.

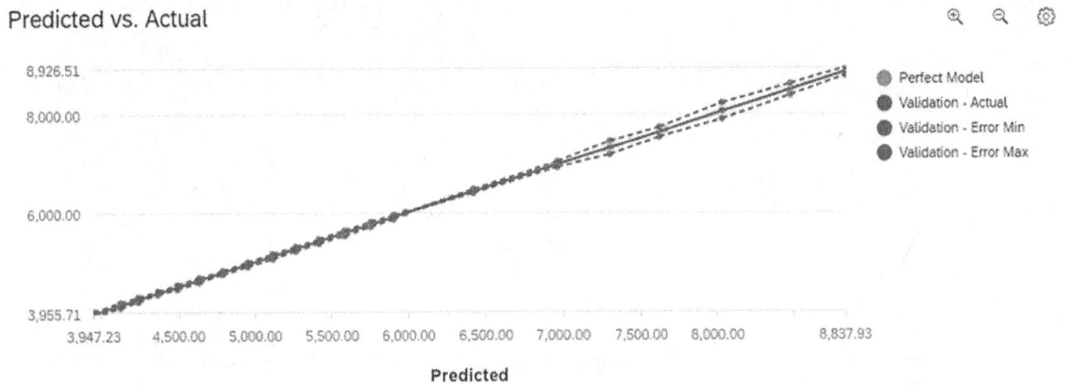


***Figure 6-21.** Predicted versus actual in regression*

A perfect model is shown in the plot as a green line. Now, the validation data shows how accurate the prediction will be in comparison with the actual data.

A more detailed influencer contribution analysis will be available on the Influencer Contribution tab. Here the following will be displayed:

> *Grouped Category Influence*: This will show the contribution of any of the influencer variable on the result. See Figure 6-22.

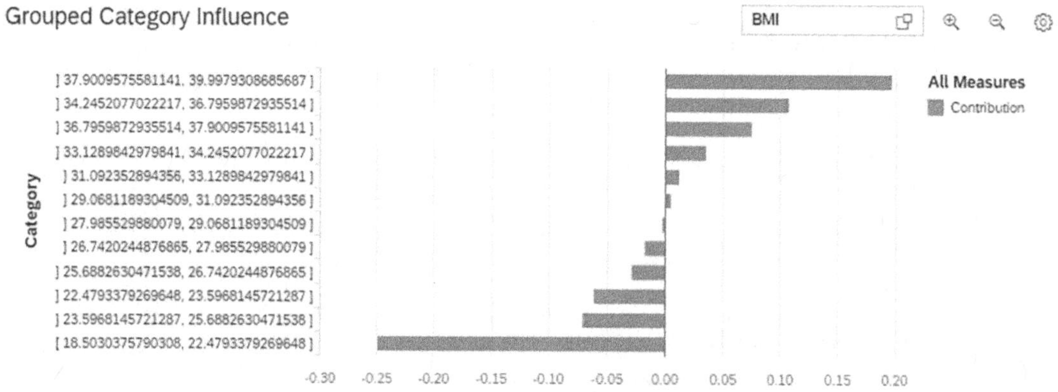


***Figure 6-22.*** *Grouped category influence in regression*

> *Grouped Category Statistics*: This is the frequency of a particular value against the target mean. See Figure 6-23.

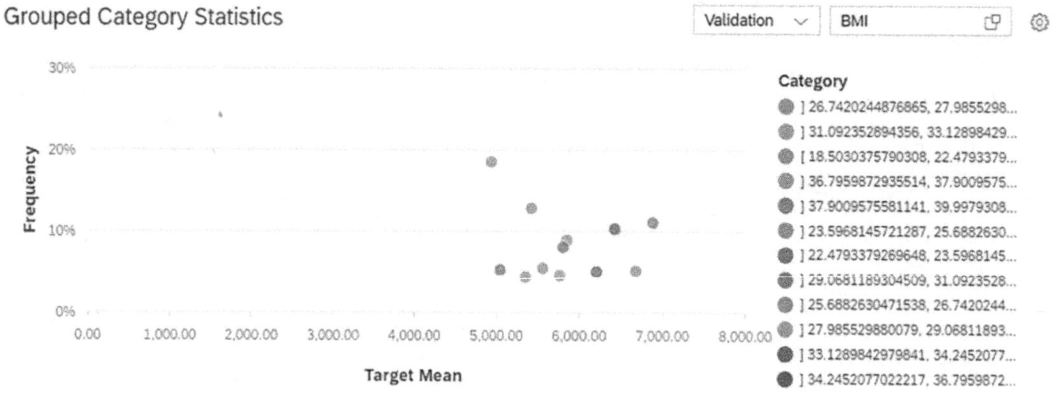


***Figure 6-23.*** *Grouped category statistics*

Upload Prediction Sample Data

The next step is to upload a dataset that is similar in nature but without the target Predicted column, as it will be updated at runtime. See Figure 6-24.

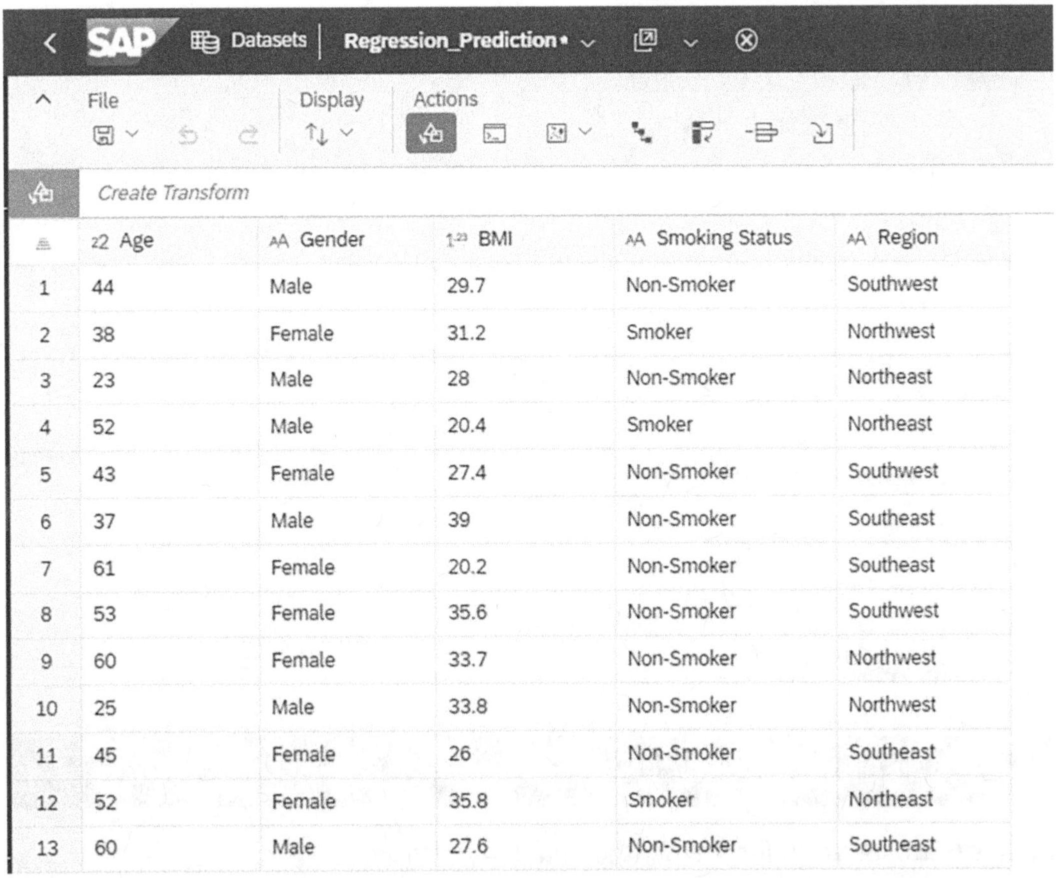


| | Age | Gender | BMI | Smoking Status | Region |
|---|---|---|---|---|---|
| 1 | 44 | Male | 29.7 | Non-Smoker | Southwest |
| 2 | 38 | Female | 31.2 | Smoker | Northwest |
| 3 | 23 | Male | 28 | Non-Smoker | Northeast |
| 4 | 52 | Male | 20.4 | Smoker | Northeast |
| 5 | 43 | Female | 27.4 | Non-Smoker | Southwest |
| 6 | 37 | Male | 39 | Non-Smoker | Southeast |
| 7 | 61 | Female | 20.2 | Non-Smoker | Southeast |
| 8 | 53 | Female | 35.6 | Non-Smoker | Southwest |
| 9 | 60 | Female | 33.7 | Non-Smoker | Northwest |
| 10 | 25 | Male | 33.8 | Non-Smoker | Northwest |
| 11 | 45 | Female | 26 | Non-Smoker | Southeast |
| 12 | 52 | Female | 35.8 | Smoker | Northeast |
| 13 | 60 | Male | 27.6 | Non-Smoker | Southeast |

***Figure 6-24.** Dataset for storing result: regression*

The previous data is uploaded without the target field and will be used for prediction.

Creating the Prediction

In this section, you will create the prediction (Insurance Cost) based on the experience and the training model algorithm. See Figure 6-25.

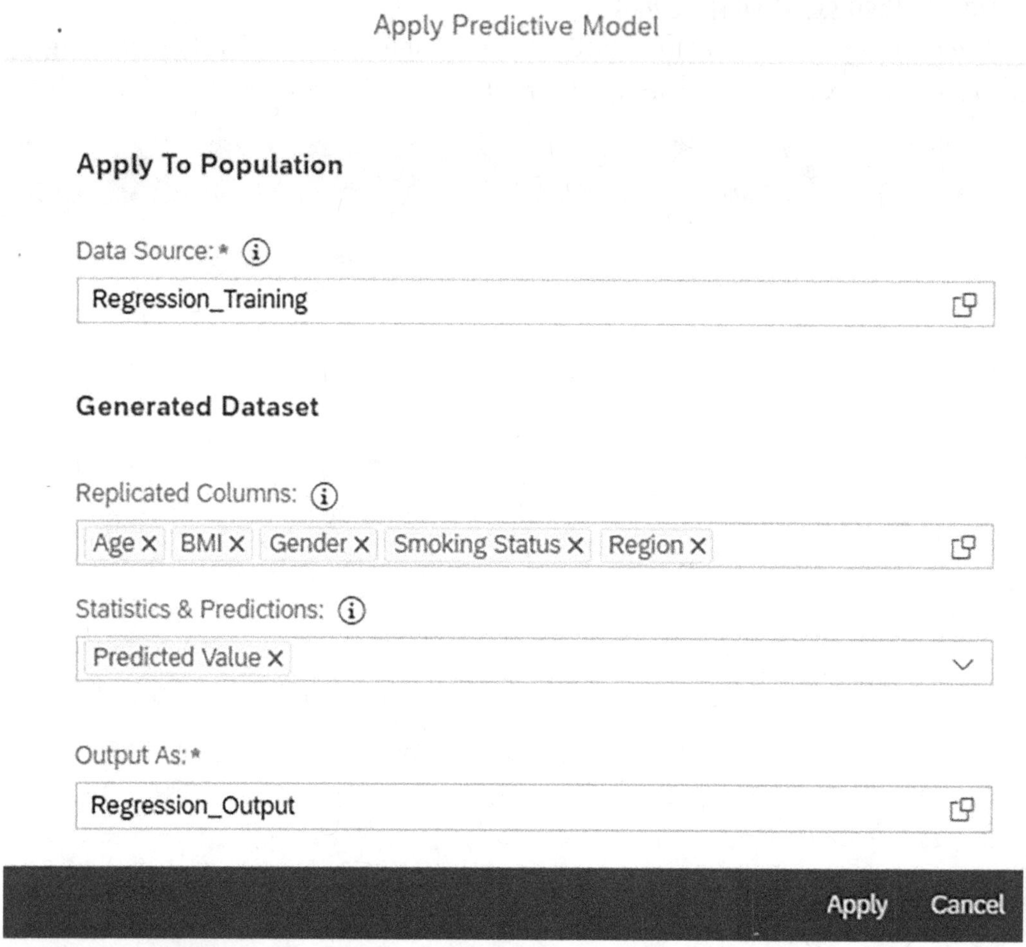


***Figure 6-25.** Settings for predictive model: regression*

**Datasource** is the dataset that will supply the independent variable values for making a prediction. In our case, it is the Regression_Prediction dataset.

Replicated Columns are the fields available in the data source that need to be replicated in the final prediction dataset. No fields will be replicated unless specified.

Out of many parameters defined, **Predicted Value** will show the value of the target field after making a prediction.

**Output as** is the name of the dataset which will be created to store the predicted values.

Once the details are added, click Apply. See Figure 6-26 shows the process status at the bottom of the screen.

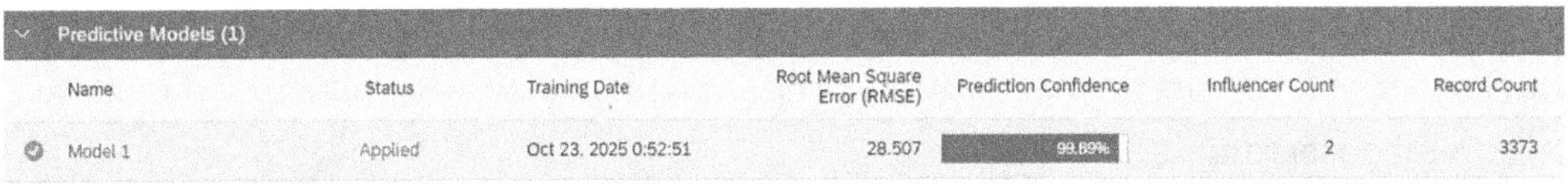
Predictive Models (1)

| Name | Status | Training Date | Root Mean Square Error (RMSE) | Prediction Confidence | Influencer Count | Record Count |
|---|---|---|---|---|---|---|
| Model 1 | Applied | Oct 23, 2025 0:52:51 | 28.507 | 99.89% | 2 | 3373 |

***Figure 6-26.** Log of predictive model: regression*

As shown, the prediction is now successfully calculated for 3,373 records, and two major influencers are used in this model.

The data records are shown in the dataset in Figure 6-27.

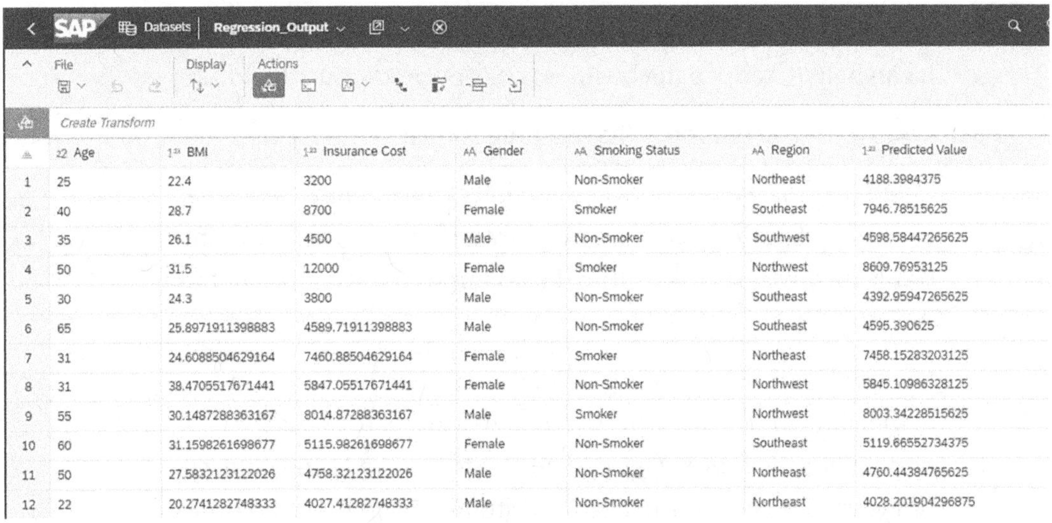


| | Age | BMI | Insurance Cost | Gender | Smoking Status | Region | Predicted Value |
|---|---|---|---|---|---|---|---|
| 1 | 25 | 22.4 | 3200 | Male | Non-Smoker | Northeast | 4188.3984375 |
| 2 | 40 | 28.7 | 8700 | Female | Smoker | Southeast | 7946.78515625 |
| 3 | 35 | 26.1 | 4500 | Male | Non-Smoker | Southwest | 4598.58447265625 |
| 4 | 50 | 31.5 | 12000 | Female | Smoker | Northwest | 8609.76953125 |
| 5 | 30 | 24.3 | 3800 | Male | Non-Smoker | Southeast | 4392.95947265625 |
| 6 | 65 | 25.8971911398883 | 4589.71911398883 | Male | Non-Smoker | Southeast | 4595.390625 |
| 7 | 31 | 24.6088504629164 | 7460.88504629164 | Female | Smoker | Northeast | 7458.15283203125 |
| 8 | 31 | 38.4705517671441 | 5847.05517671441 | Female | Non-Smoker | Northwest | 5845.10986328125 |
| 9 | 55 | 30.1487288363167 | 8014.87288363167 | Male | Smoker | Northwest | 8003.34228515625 |
| 10 | 60 | 31.1598261698677 | 5115.98261698677 | Female | Non-Smoker | Southeast | 5119.66552734375 |
| 11 | 50 | 27.5832123122026 | 4758.32123122026 | Male | Non-Smoker | Northeast | 4760.44384765625 |
| 12 | 22 | 20.2741282748333 | 4027.41282748333 | Male | Non-Smoker | Northeast | 4028.201904296875 |

***Figure 6-27.** Output of the regression model*

Predicted values appear in the last column. The details can be combined with the actual data to present this in terms of a story where actual versus prediction can be displayed for a more meaningful analysis.

You have now learned how the prediction model works for the regression type model. Here all the values that are predicted are different and of type number. On the other hand, the outcome of the SAC Classification model does not have variety and follows the binary rule.

**Time Series**

Time series is the third category in SAC Smart Predict. As the name suggest, this model works only when the variables change over a period and should be continuous and evenly spaced. For example, it can be based on dates, months, quarters, or years.

A time series is usually defined by a plot with time-related characters on the x-axis and the variable of interest on the y-Axis. Thus, it will produce a trend of the data based on several observations.

The main advantages of a time series are the following:

- It can be used to predict the trend of the variable in the future. It can consider the spikes in the data during a specific time (for example, a holiday period in that region).
- It can detect the pattern in the dataset; the longer the plot, the better the detection possible.
- It can help to reduce the business risks by predicting the future.

The following are the components of a time series:

*Trend:* Trends are patterns in data that can be helpful to understand. A trend can be gradually descent or ascent or remain stable. In any case, a trend can be an important measure to train the model.

*Seasonality:* Seasonality is generally identified by a portion of the plot behaving differently than the rest of the area for a particular time range. This can be due to a spike in the dataset (for example sales) during the Christmas period or a lead time of delivery delays during weekends or the holiday season. All these observations can help the model understand what it means to the predicted dataset for future forecasting.

*Cyclicality:* This includes long-term fluctuations in the series, which is not due to seasonality.

*Irregularity:* This is also known as noise in the plot. These are the patterns that do not have any explanation. They could be due to some scenario that can happen only one time. For example, a sudden cyclone for the first time in four years can result in a delay in transportation, or the outbreak of COVID-19 can slow down the sales of a restaurant for a specific time. These events create randomness in the data that can't be used for the prediction of future events because they are one-time events.

**How It Will Work in SAP Analytics Cloud**

The first step to implement the cloud-based prediction model is to create a dataset that can be used to train the model. Please note the presence of a time character is mandatory.

Creating a Dataset

The example used in this process is the total cost of transportation from a warehouse to retailers for laptops. The data will contain the distance, mode of transport, weather, liters of fuel required, source, destination, and overall cost of transfer.

To train the model correctly, we must ensure the following:

- The training data must have sufficient information in order to get insight.
- The data needs to have continuous dates in ascending order.
- For large number of influencers, data with continuous date range in ascending order needs to be applied for each combination of influencer.
- If dates are broken or sufficient data is not available for training, then the system would throw an error to stop the process.
- For a large volume of data, it may require a lot of time in the training process.
- Unlike other prediction methods in SAC, the training and forecasted data sources need to be available as a single dataset. The predicted values will be added based on the period specified during the training process. See Figure 6-28.

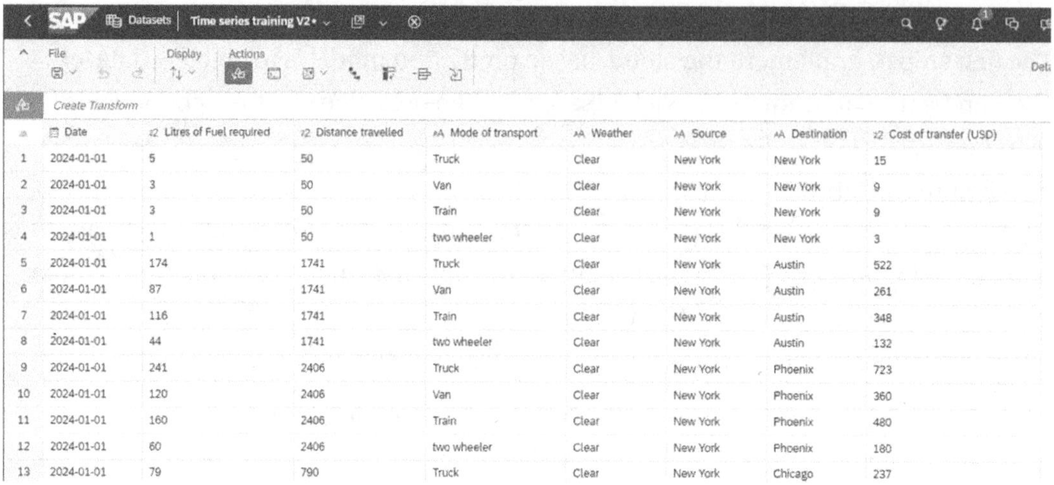


| | Date | Litres of Fuel required | Distance travelled | Mode of transport | Weather | Source | Destination | Cost of transfer (USD) |
|---|---|---|---|---|---|---|---|---|
| 1 | 2024-01-01 | 5 | 50 | Truck | Clear | New York | New York | 15 |
| 2 | 2024-01-01 | 3 | 50 | Van | Clear | New York | New York | 9 |
| 3 | 2024-01-01 | 3 | 50 | Train | Clear | New York | New York | 9 |
| 4 | 2024-01-01 | 1 | 50 | two wheeler | Clear | New York | New York | 3 |
| 5 | 2024-01-01 | 174 | 1741 | Truck | Clear | New York | Austin | 522 |
| 6 | 2024-01-01 | 87 | 1741 | Van | Clear | New York | Austin | 261 |
| 7 | 2024-01-01 | 116 | 1741 | Train | Clear | New York | Austin | 348 |
| 8 | 2024-01-01 | 44 | 1741 | two wheeler | Clear | New York | Austin | 132 |
| 9 | 2024-01-01 | 241 | 2406 | Truck | Clear | New York | Phoenix | 723 |
| 10 | 2024-01-01 | 120 | 2406 | Van | Clear | New York | Phoenix | 360 |
| 11 | 2024-01-01 | 160 | 2406 | Train | Clear | New York | Phoenix | 480 |
| 12 | 2024-01-01 | 60 | 2406 | two wheeler | Clear | New York | Phoenix | 180 |
| 13 | 2024-01-01 | 79 | 790 | Truck | Clear | New York | Chicago | 237 |

***Figure 6-28.*** *Training data preparation for time series*

As shown, for each combination of source, target, and mode of transport, the dates are repeated, which makes the combination available for each date in the window.

The main influencers here are the source, target, and mode of transport. The cost in USD is the target field for the prediction.

Training Your Model

See Figure 6-29.

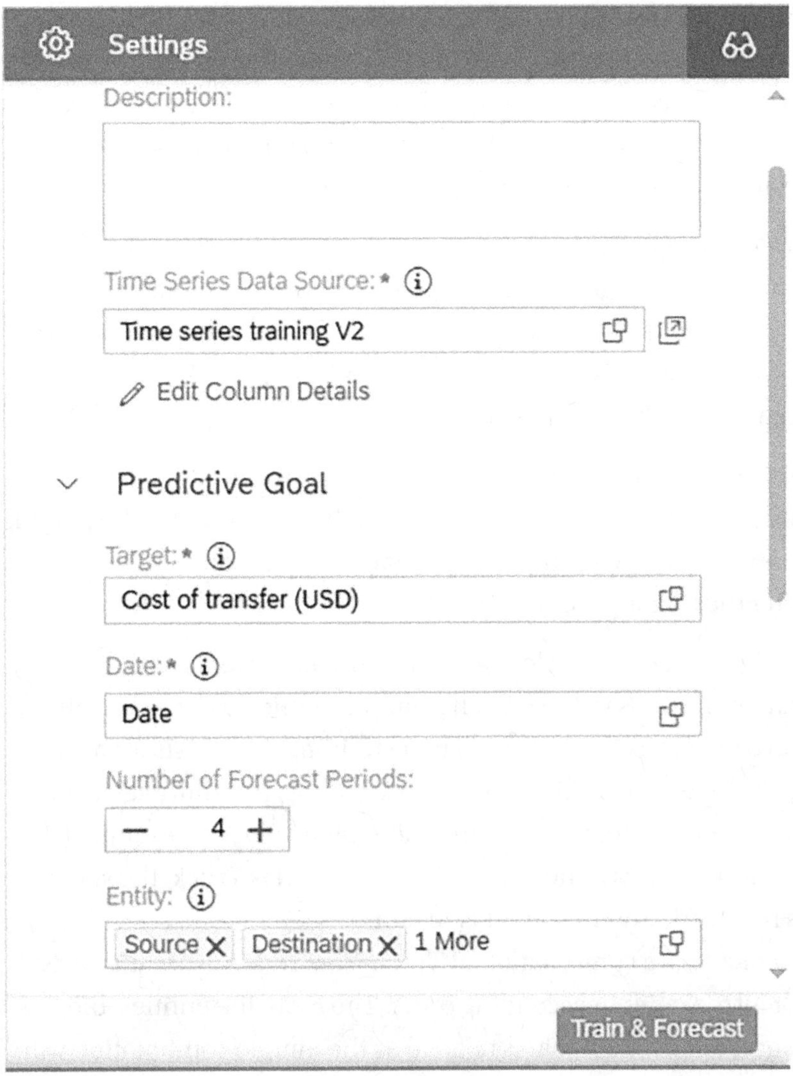


***Figure 6-29.*** *Settings for time series model*

The following settings are displayed in Figure 6-29:

> *Data source*: In this section, please enter the source of the training data. As explained earlier, it must have a date field and at least one numeric field to understand the aim of this prediction. In our example, it is Time Series Training V2, the dataset that was uploaded earlier.

*Target:* This is the goal of the prediction; i.e., it is the field on which the prediction will be made after the training for the future dataset. This has to be a numeric field and should be filled for all the past observations that are required for the training. In our example, it is Cost of transfer (USD).

*Date:* Date is a field that is used for the time selection for the training. Although the name suggests it is date, we can use a month or quarter as well. In such cases, the base dataset should have this format specified before introducing it as a training data. In our case, the field is Date.

*Number of forecast period:* This will define the limit up to which the prediction needs to be made. As I defined here, 4 is the period; therefore, the prediction will be made for four consecutive days after the training window ends.

*Entity:* Entity is the field that acts as influencer to find the patterns/trends in the data. If multiple entities are selected, the developer must make sure that the training data exists for all the dates for each combination. In my example, the entity selected is the mode of transport, source, and target. For one example scenario, let's assume the mode of transport is Truck, the source is New York, and the target is Austin. To generate successful predictions, a combination of Truck-New York-Austin must exist for all the dates in ascending order. The more the entities, the more training data that is needed as the unique combination will increase. See Figure 6-30.

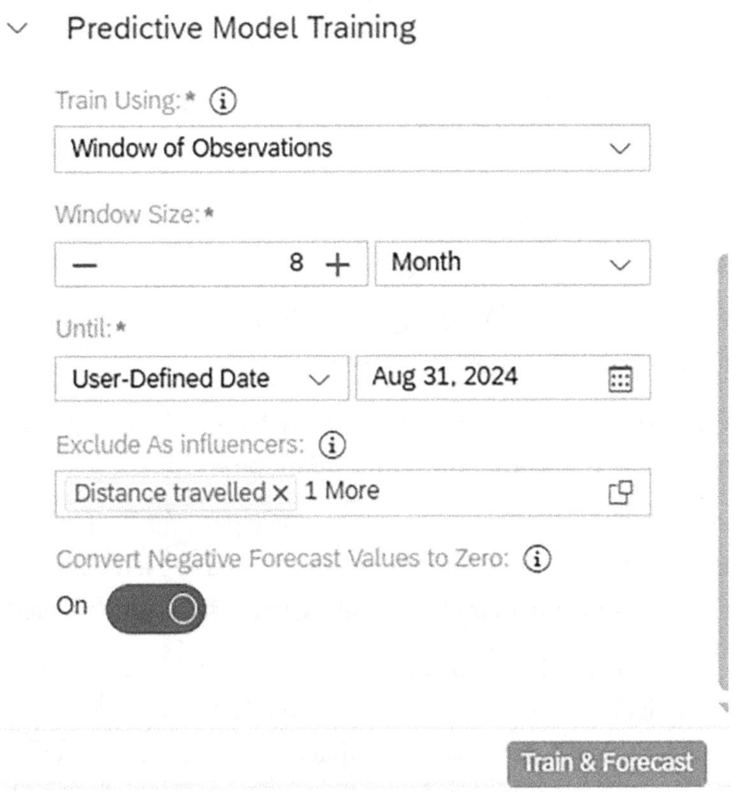


***Figure 6-30.*** *Training properties: time series*

Further settings include the following:

*Train Using:* This will specify how much data will be used for the training of the dataset. The rest of the data is for validation purposes. We have two options here:

- Window of Observation: Here you need to specify the subset of data that will be used for training. If this option is selected, then the window size needs to be mentioned.
- All Observations: This option will be selected when all of the base dataset is required for the training. In this case, no window needs to be mentioned.

*Window Size:* In this option, you need to add the size of the time window in case the training was requested for a window of observation. The possible units are as follows:

- Day
- Week
- Month
- Year

In this example, we used a window of observation of 8 months.

*Until:* In this field, you can select a date up to which the training data will be considered. There are two options:

- Last Observation: This option is selected when the training set of data needs to be considered until the end of the window.
- User-defined date: Here you can specify a particular date up to which the data for training will be considered. Anything left within the window is not considered for training if a custom date is selected.

*Exclude as influencer*: Here you can exclude any variable that does not have any impact on the result. I have excluded Distance Travelled and Liters of fuel as they do not have any impact on the variation of the result. For example, the distance between New York to Austin remains the same for all the observations and for a specific transport type. So, they are not influencers. On the other hand, the mode of transport can be an influencer as it can have different costs associated for different modes; i.e., the cost of fuel is higher for a truck than a van for the same distance traveled and therefore influences the cost.

*Convert Negative Forecast value to zero*: An observation value can become negative during the forecasting process due to several reasons or an error in the training process. As this will have no business relevance, you can make it zero with this option.

Deep Dive into the Result of the Training and Forecasting

Once the training process is complete, several details of the model and the accuracy will be displayed on the screen for further analysis. Please note that at this stage the model is ready with the prediction data and requires only a dataset to be created to store the outcome.

### Overview

In the Overview section, the following details will be displayed (see Figure 6-31):

- Top & Bottom Entities
- Global Performance Indicators
- Training Issue by Entity
- All Entities

***Figure 6-31.** Overview of time-series model*

As shown, the entities (a combination of mode of transport, source, and destination) are sorted based on MAPE. MAPE stands for Mean Absolute Percentage Error and is used to perform an accuracy check of the model.

The metric determines absolute error, which is the difference between the predicted and actual values in positive values. MAPE is always shown as a percentage. The average error is zero in case the predicted value always matches with the actual value. In general, the aim is to decrease the value of MAPE because the lower the value, the more accurate the model is.

In the previous example, the top and bottom entities are shown differently as SAC creates separate models for each combination. See Figure 6-32.

***Figure 6-32.*** *Global performance indicators for time series*

In the Global Performance Indicators section, the following values are shown for analysis of the model:

> *Expected MAPE (%):* Mean Absolute Percentage Error (MAPE) is the percentage of difference between the predicted and actual results in terms of absolute values. This shows how the model is behaving in terms of producing the predicted values.
>
> *Expected MAE:* Mean Absolute Error (MAE) is the measure to determine the average error of the absolute differences between the predicted and actual results. By making an average, it gives equal weight to big and small errors at the end while displaying the MAE.
>
> *Expected MASE:* Mean Absolute Scaled Error (MASE) is a measure to find the accuracy of the model by comparing the predicted values with that of the naïve forecasting approach. Naïve forecasting does not consider any seasonality effect as it always considers the last period's value; i.e., the forecast is equal to the actual data for the last season of the window. The value of MASE is therefore determined by the MAE of the model divided by the MAE of the naïve forecasting process. This is a comparison ratio; i.e., if the ratio is < 1, it means that the model is more effective than the naïve forecasting method.
>
> *Expected RMSE:* Root Mean Square Error (RMSE) is a measure that calculates first the Mean Square Error by squaring the differences between predicted and actual (negative errors and positives errors cancel each other during the average). Then the root of the value will be calculated to convert the error into the actual unit (as

previously squared). This determines how the errors are spread from the best fit line.

*Expected $R^2$:* This is a measure of how accurately the time series model fits the training data. This is very helpful in prefiltering operations. This provides accuracy in terms of how the past values of the dependent variables impact the forecasting. This is determined by finding the ratio of the squared residual of the predicted outcomes and the squared deviation of the dependent variables from the sample mean. The ratio is then subtracted from 1. If the prediction does not have a constant term in the model, then it is not very significant to measure $R^2$.

For all these metrics, the following values are displayed:

- Median: This is the mid value of the outcome range.
- Third Quartile: When the outcome is divided equally in four groups, the third group is called the third quartile.

In our example, the values in Table 6-2 are observed.

***Table 6-2.*** *Metric, Median, and Third Quartile*

| Metric | Median | Third Quartile |
|---|---|---|
| Expected MAPE% | 3.35 | 3.36 |
| Expected MAE | 4.64 | 8.77 |
| Expected MASE | 0.13 | 0.13 |
| Expected RMSE | 16.38 | 30.95 |
| Expected $R^2$ | 0.78 | 0.78 |

Figure 6-33 shows the entity details.

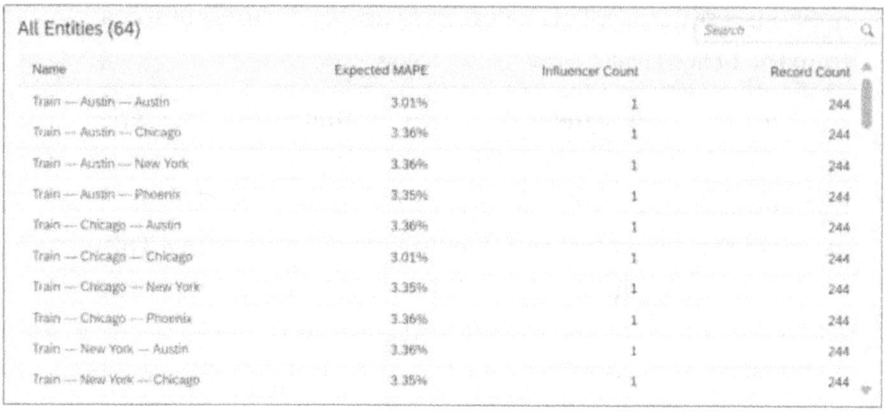

All Entities (64)

Search

| Name | Expected MAPE | Influencer Count | Record Count |
|---|---|---|---|
| Train — Austin — Austin | 3.01% | 1 | 244 |
| Train — Austin — Chicago | 3.36% | 1 | 244 |
| Train — Austin — New York | 3.36% | 1 | 244 |
| Train — Austin — Phoenix | 3.35% | 1 | 244 |
| Train — Chicago — Austin | 3.36% | 1 | 244 |
| Train — Chicago — Chicago | 3.01% | 1 | 244 |
| Train — Chicago — New York | 3.35% | 1 | 244 |
| Train — Chicago — Phoenix | 3.36% | 1 | 244 |
| Train — New York — Austin | 3.36% | 1 | 244 |
| Train — New York — Chicago | 3.35% | 1 | 244 |

***Figure 6-33.*** *All entities in time series*

For each entity, the following information is shown:

> *Name*: This is the combination of the values that creates the entity, i.e., mode of transport, source, and destination.
>
> *Expected MAPE*: The MAPE value of the said combination.
>
> *Influencer Count*: This is the count of the influencer.
>
> *Record Count*: This is the number of records that exist for each combination in the training dataset.

### Forecast

The forecast data is displayed in different variations. The following data is available:

- Global performance indicators
- Forecast vs. actual
- Forecast breakdown
- Forecasts
- Outlier (past)
- Outlier (future)

*Global Performance Indicator*

See Figure 6-34.

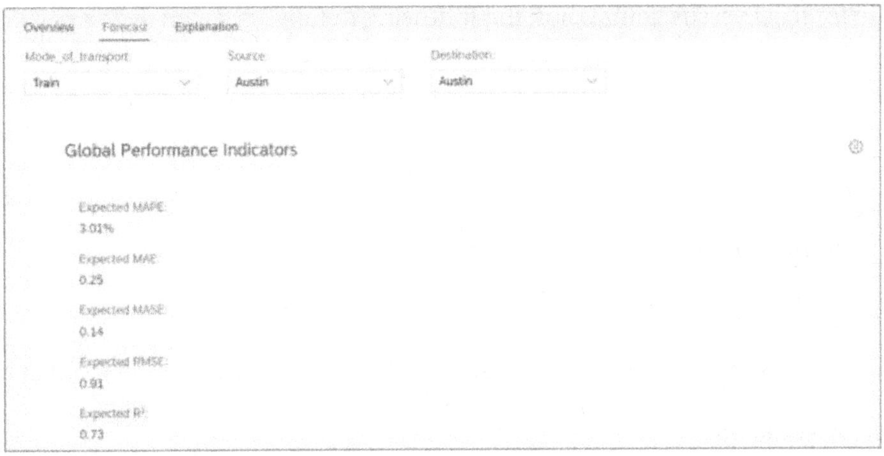


***Figure 6-34.** Forecast dashboard: time series*

All the performance matrices are displayed with the variation of the fields that construct an entity. This gives an opportunity to see all the results for a combination at once plus the navigation of the statistical result of the model becomes easy. The following matrices are displayed:

- Expected MAPE%
- Expected MAE
- Expected MASE
- Expected RMSE
- Expected $R^2$

**Forecast vs. Actual**

See Figure 6-35.

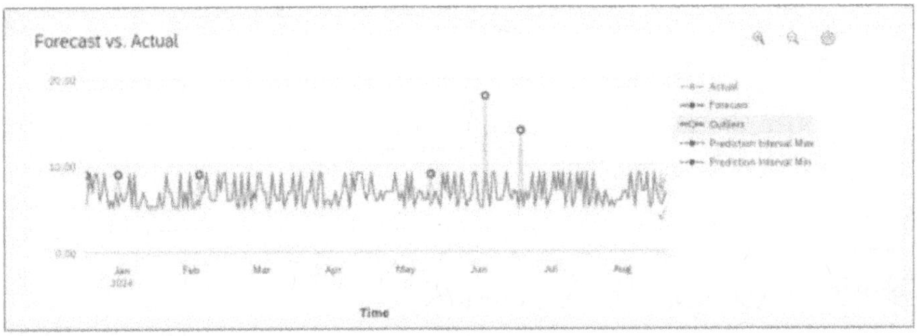


***Figure 6-35.** Forecast versus actual in time series*

In the forecast versus actual plot, the following details are given over a period:

- Actual data
- Forecast data
- Outliers
- Prediction interval max
- Prediction interval min

The data is plotted in a single graph so that the variation can be seen and analyzed.

**Forecast Breakdown**

The components that have an impact on the values predicted are shown for each period (date) in Figure 6-36.

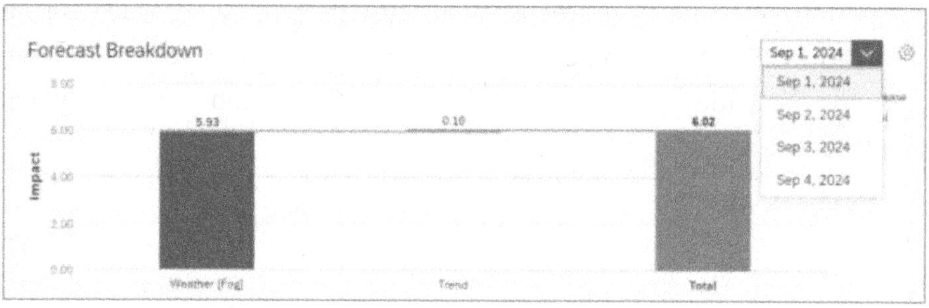


***Figure 6-36.** Forecast breakdown for time series*

As the prediction was done for only four periods (dates) after the training date, it is now possible to verify the impact of the variables on the predicted result for each case.

**Forecasts**

See Figure 6-37.

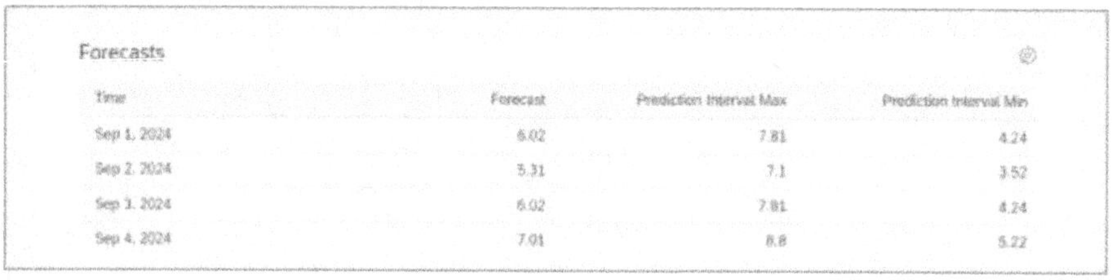

Forecasts

| Time | Forecast | Prediction Interval Max | Prediction Interval Min |
|---|---|---|---|
| Sep 1, 2024 | 6.02 | 7.81 | 4.24 |
| Sep 2, 2024 | 5.31 | 7.1 | 3.52 |
| Sep 3, 2024 | 6.02 | 7.81 | 4.24 |
| Sep 4, 2024 | 7.01 | 8.8 | 5.22 |

***Figure 6-37.** Forecasts in time series results*

The real forecast values for all the given period of prediction are shown in Figure 6-37. This also includes the maximum and minimum of the Prediction interval.

**Outlier (Past)**

See Figure 6-38.

Outliers (Past)

| Time | Actual | Forecast |
|---|---|---|
| Jan 1, 2024 | 9 | 5.31 |
| Jan 15, 2024 | 9 | 5.31 |
| Feb 19, 2024 | 9 | 5.31 |
| May 27, 2024 | 9 | 5.31 |
| Jun 19, 2024 | 18 | 9.19 |
| Jul 4, 2024 | 14 | 7.01 |

***Figure 6-38.*** *Past outliers for time series*

An outlier is a measure of the data point that does not follow the patten of the series. In this case, some of them are due to the holiday period when the cost of transport significantly differs from the rest of the data in the series.

**Outlier (Future)**

See Figure 6-39.

Outliers (Future)

| Time | Actual | Forecast |
|---|---|---|
| Sep 2, 2024 | 9 | 5.31 |

***Figure 6-39.*** *Future outliers for time series*

Future outliers are a deviation of the data for the future. In this example, one outlier exists.

**Explanation**

In the explanation section, the following details are shown:

- Time Series Breakdown
- Time Series Component Impact
- Trend

- Impact of Cycles
- Impact of Categorical Influencers
- Impact of Numerical Influencers
- Fluctuations
- Target Statistics

*Time Series Breakdown*

See Figure 6-40.

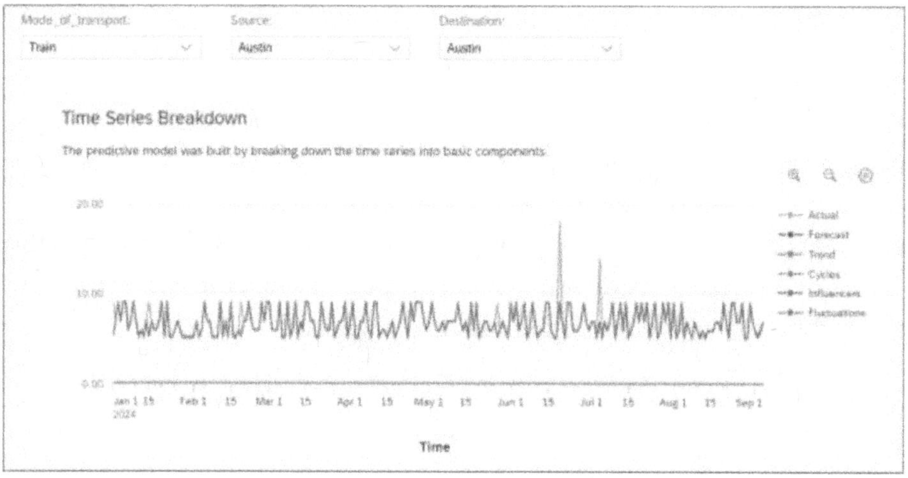


***Figure 6-40.*** *Time series breakdown*

In the previous plot, the following details are shown:

- Actual Data
- Forecast
- Trend
- Cycles
- Influencers
- Fluctuations

All this data will be shown with a variation of time and is overlapping in nature, i.e., plotted in the same graph. The data can be checked against the combination of mode of transport, source, and destination as they construct one single entity. This is also because the model is subdivided into many smaller models each for one entity.

*Time Series Component Impact*

See Figure 6-41.

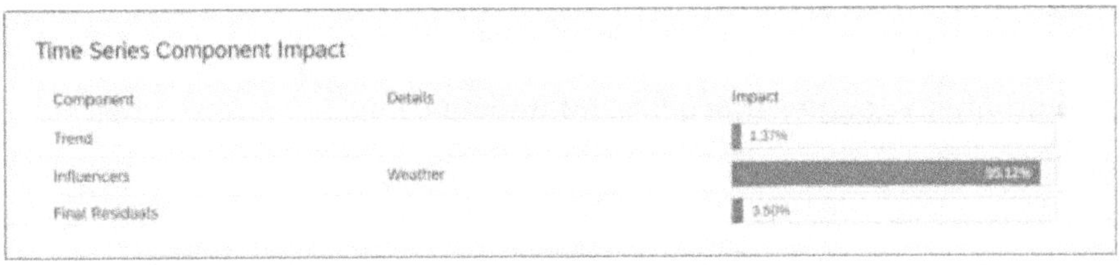


***Figure 6-41.*** *Component impact: time series*

In the previous plot, it is defined how the prediction is made. As shown, most of the impact is due to the presence of influencers in the data.

*Trend*

A trend usually specifies the pattern in the past result that can be translated into the future predictions. In our case, there is no trend found.

*Impact of Cycles*

Cycles are long-term fluctuations in the series that are not caused by the seasonality of the data. In our example, there are no cycles found.

*Impact of Categorical Influencers*

See Figure 6-42.

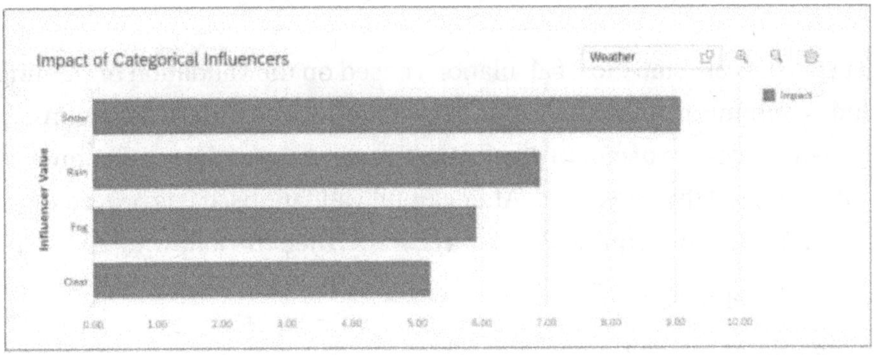


***Figure 6-42.*** *Categorical influencers in time series*

Categorical influencers are the variables that influence the result and are of type categories; i.e., they are text values that can create a group. In Figure 6-42, Weather is one of the influencers with the possible values Snow, Rain, Fog, and Clear. Each category will have an impact on the predicted values.

*Impact of Numerical Influencers*

Numerical Influencers are numbers that can impact the prediction. In this case, there are no number variables that act as influencers.

*Fluctuations*

Fluctuations are randomness in the series that can't be explained. This can be a sudden spike of the data due to COVID-19, for example. In this example, there are no such fluctuations noticed.

*Target Statistics*

See Figure 6-43.

***Figure 6-43.*** *Target statistics in time series*

Target statistics are statistical calculations based on the validation or training dataset. This includes minimum, maximum, mean (average), and standard deviations.

All these matrices are useful to determine the accuracy of the prediction and strength of the model thus prepared. After careful validations, if it is proved that the model does not show the required level of accuracy, then the following can be possible:

- Change entity design
- Change/exclude the influencers
- Add more data to re-train the model

<u>Save the Prediction</u>

When you are satisfied with the quality of the model, the next step is to save the forecast data for further reporting. See Figure 6-44.

***Figure 6-44.*** *Save forecast for time series*

Once the forecast is saved, the new dataset will display the outcome of the prediction. See Figure 6-45.

***Figure 6-45.*** *Log for time-series model*

The results show the target dataset (Figure 6-46).

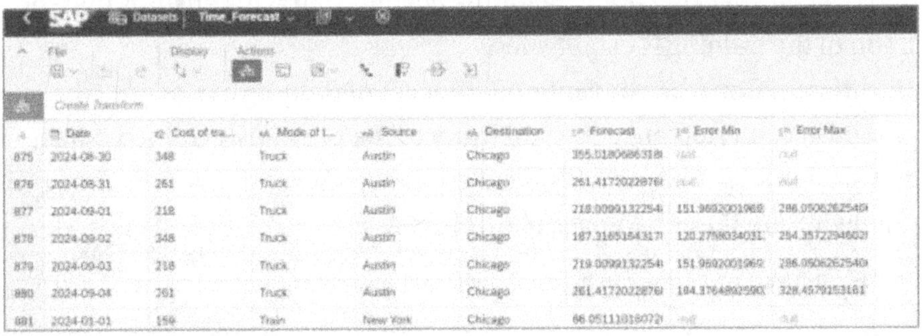


***Figure 6-46.*** *Time-series prediction data*

As you can see, some of the predicted values for (Sept 1. to Sept. 4) are extremely accurate when compared with the actual values.

In this section, you learned about the machine learning processes in the SAP Analytics Cloud Smart Predict application.

If your predictive model needs to define a group (for example, based on certain descriptions and characteristics, you want to define whether it is a book, a journal, or a research paper), then you can use a classification model. To find a sales trend of a product and to predict how much sales the product is likely to have in the future, you can use a time-series model. If you need to get the expected sales of a product based in a region based on similar products in some other region with driving factors such as product mix, discounts, subscriptions, marketing feedback, supply chain methods, etc., then you can use a regression model for prediction.

## 6.2 Deep Learning

Deep learning is a subset of machine learning and uses an artificial neural network to perform a more sophisticated prediction. A neural network functions like a human brain where multiple neurons are responsible for making decisions. Ideally the learning process is much more detailed than the normal machine learning process. Here the patterns, grouping, features, etc., are considered while performing the training.

There are many deep learning algorithms available.

**Recurrent Neural Network**

A recurrent neural network (RNN) is useful for time-series prediction as it uses patterns in the sequence of data during the training process. A memory of the past observation is considered when checking the data for the current step. This ensures that the continuation of the training is established.

This is different from the conventional process of training as not only the current dataset is used at each step but a past memory of the previously trained data is also considered at each step. This process is called *back propagation through time* (BPTT).

The following are the advantages of this process:

- Check how past data influences the present data.
- The dependency of the variables/influencers over a period can be identified.
- This can adapt the calculation due to gradients easily.
- This is very useful for sequential data where a connection from the present data to the past is inevitable.

The following are the disadvantages of this process:

- The gradient can grow very high at times; therefore, the values are normalized to avoid explosion.
- When the dataset is very large, due to the continuous back propagation, the gradients tend to decrease and ultimately lead to the disappearance of the observations that are dated long back.

**Convolutional Neural Network**

A convolutional neural network (CNN) is a useful algorithm to train data for images. The process involves creating a feature map that produces useful details like edges, patterns, and textures. This process continues multiple times until a more recognizable object is classified.

The following are the advantages of this process:

- Accurate image and video classification.
- When the data consists of noise, this model is a very efficient way to remove that data while training.

The following are the disadvantages of this process:

- The training process is difficult due to the process complexity.
- It requires a high volume of data for training.
- The entire process consumes a high volume of memory during training and computation.

**Long Short-Term Memory Network**

Long Short-Term Memory Network (LSTMs) is a deep learning method that uses an RNN method and can learn long-term dependencies within the data. It introduces memory cells that are capable of holding the information for an extended period. This overcomes the difficulty of such a process in the RNN method.

The following are the advantages of this process :

- It can handle long-term sequential data.
- A memory cell can store and extract information about any training experience with past data.
- It prevents gradient vanishing.

The following are the disadvantages of this process:

- The process is very complex to execute.
- It does not work well with insufficient data.
- The results are often difficult to interpret as there are many iterations involved during the training and prediction processes.
- The training time is very long.

**Transformer Network**

A transformer network is often found similar to the NLP models. As it is useful for the text or speech learning/recognition process, it first compares one part of the data with another to find weightage of each part. This is useful when a complete sentence is read, which allows the model to see how the words are impactful within a sentence.

The following are the advantages of this process:

- The process is highly parallelizable, which speeds up the training process.
- It can capture long-term dependency with the data.
- The process is highly scalable.

The following are the disadvantages of this process:

- The process is very complex and requires a lot of memory during the training and computation.
- It does not work well with smaller datasets.
- It does not work well with biased datasets.

**Generative Adversarial Network**

A generative adversarial network (GAN) is widely used for the training of images, video, and audio data. It works by comparing two neural networks. It generates a fake dataset from the noise of the data and then compares the authentic and fake data.

The following are the advantages of this process:

- It can generate new authentic data to support the anomaly detection.
- The results are realistic.
- The learning process does not require any supervision.

The following are the disadvantages of this process:

- The complexity and costs are high.
- Sometimes the training leads to a vanishing gradient.
- Finding the configuration required for the training environment requires lots of experiments.

There are many other deep learning methods used in the industry. With the evolution of deep learning, a more sophisticated outcome is produced.

## 6.3 Test Your Knowledge

Q1: Which of the following model uses a neural network?

a) Long short-term memory network

b) IOT

c) Classification

d) Regression

Q2: Which of the following model overcomes some of the limitations of RNNs?

a) Long short-term memory network

b) GAN

c) All of the above

d) None of the above

Q3: Smart Predict can be used for which the following (choose all that apply)?

a) Transformer network

b) Classification

c) BPTT

d) Time series

Q4: An entity in the time series can't have multiple fields.

a) True

b) False

Q5: SAC only supports binary classification.

a) True

b) False

Q6: Fluctuations are patterns in a time series.

a) True

b) False

Q7: Which of the following metric compares the predicted value with that of the Naïve Bias Forecasting Method?

a) MAPE

b) MAE

c) MASE

d) RMSE

# 6.4 Summary

In this chapter, you learned about the types of AI applications including the machine learning and deep learning methods. You also learned about the use cases on SAC Smart Predict.

AI/ML use cases are often the differentiating factor to decide on which product to implement. This, however, can't be the only thing to decide whether to move to BDC or not. The modernization of the landscape requires strong business and technical reasons to allocate budget for this change.

In the next chapter, you will learn about the reasons organizations are now actively looking at modernizing their landscapes.

## CHAPTER 7

# Need for Modernization

Over time, the analytics landscape has grown older and requires the adoption of new tools and techniques. This is called the *modernization* of the ecosystem. Often, we find that the modernization of ERP goes hand in hand with the analytics modernization.

Most organizations that are on ECC are moving into S/4 HANA (on-premise or in the cloud) or have a roadmap to do so. At least this is the vision of most SAP customers. The question remains is that with this move to S/4 HANA, should the organization also think of upgrading the analytics landscape? The answer is yes. These are the reasons:

- Modern cloud-based SAP Analytics products offer more flexibility and smooth integration with S/4 HANA.
- The trusted data platform can retain the business semantics of the data.
- The federation of data becomes more and more popular over the persistence because of the following:
    - It saves money.
    - Governance of the data is easier especially for sensitive data.
    - Data becomes more trusted as the source remains the same.
    - Analytics does not require any wait time; i.e., all data from different platforms can be seen, immediately offering more flexibility to the users for data reconciliation.
    - There is a pass-through scenario to move data one place to other without any intermediate storage.



© Sourav Banerjee 2025
S. Banerjee, *Modernizing SAP Business Warehouse*, https://doi.org/10.1007/979-8-8688-2192-9_7

- There is reduced operational overhead on the server side (like patch implementation, downtime, and system upgrade). With a cloud-based infrastructure, the availability of the server becomes excellent without any unforeseen scenarios (like unplanned downtime).
- AI-related applications and machine learning can be done with ease. This also provides several built-in AI agents.

Now that the vision is clear, the next important point is what the landscape should look like. Each customer will have a different set of legacy and third-party applications that are required to the integrated in the new architecture.

It is therefore useful to first understand the current landscape, which includes source systems, type of data exchange with frequencies, data platform, reporting layer, data lake solutions, and outbound interfaces.

## 7.1 Issues with the Current Landscape

The term *issues* is not probably valid for all landscapes. There could be customers who are running their current operation efficiently with no pain areas. It would be difficult to convince those customers on the need to move to cloud. The main reasons are the following:

- Unable to produce a strong business case for the implementation as there are no blockers in the day-to-day operations.
- The cost of implementation and the cost to purchase the new products are not justified.
- The return on investment is unclear.
- There is risk in disrupting a smoothly running BAU operation.
- The customer is unclear on how the new product would fit into the overall ecosystem.
- Many customers are in favor of other products like Microsoft or Oracle.
- There is a lack of awareness on the SAP products within the customer architecture committee.

There are many other reasons apart from these items. The bottom line is that there are customers who do not know how the new SAP solutions can help them to simplify their business solutions.

We can divide the customers into three broad categories:

- Customers who have their ERP system on SAP, data platform on SAP, and planning and reporting also on SAP with outbound data lake on non-SAP products
- Customers who have their ERP system on SAP, data platform on SAP, and planning and reporting and data lake on non-SAP products
- Customers who have their ERP system on non-SAP products, data platform on non-SAP products, and planning and reporting also using non-SAP products

For the third category, there is no need of discussion as chances are they will never move to SAP for their analytics landscape. The driving factor to use an SAP solution in analytics is whether they are using SAP for their ERP solutions.

In the following sections, you will see some scenarios that many SAP customers have. The list is not exhaustive, but it will give you an idea of the target audiences.

### 7.1.1 Scenario 1

Figure 7-1 shows the architecture designed for the first scenario.

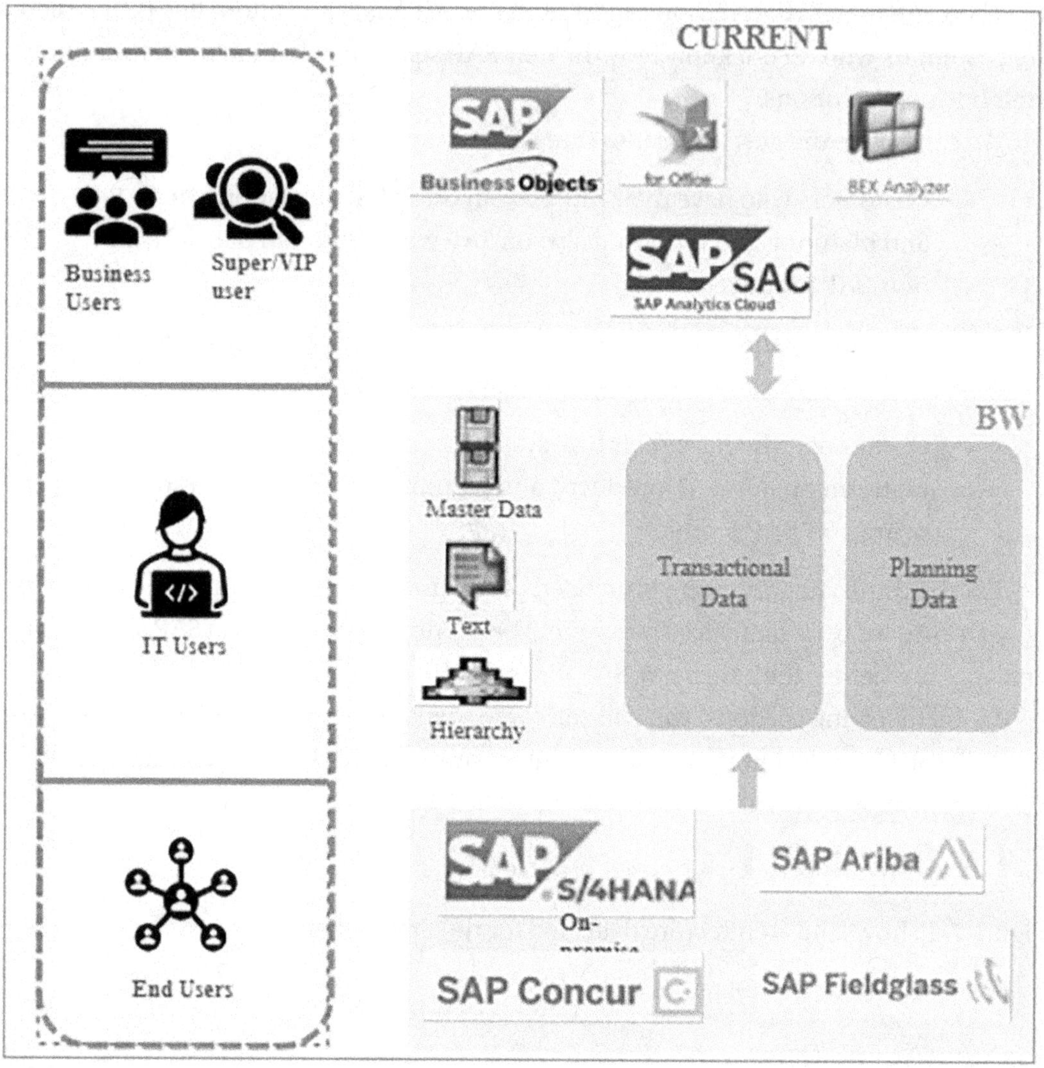


***Figure 7-1.*** *Scenario 1: SAP-driven landscape*

*Source systems*

The source systems in this example consist of S/4 HANA (or ECC), SAP Concur, SAP Ariba, and SAP Fieldglass.

Data Platform

The data platform or data warehouse is created using SAP Business Warehouse (or BW/4 HANA). The model takes data from different sources and combines it. Integrated planning or BPC (different box) can be used for the planning-related needs.

Reporting Layer

In this example, the reporting layer is mainly based on Bex query (or BW queries). Then it is viewed using Business Objects or Analysis for Office or SAP Analytics Cloud. In some cases, Lumira is also used.

In this scenario, the following issues exist:

- Business Warehouse is not capable of producing the integration scenario with other SAP applications. They could have been integrated in the long route, which creates operational difficulty, has poor performance, and has several limitations.
- There are no products that can be extensively utilized for the machine learning and AI-related applications.
- There is a delay in the data reporting as it is in most cases persisted (although there are techniques available to perform real-time reporting, but they are not very widely accepted).
- The cost of procuring and maintaining the BW server is high.
- The full capability of SAP Analytics Cloud is not utilized. Especially for planning purposes, IP/BPC does not have a good interface for end users in terms of custom functionalities or look and feel.
- The source of truth is duplicated within BW.
- One must constantly keep looking at the product versions and software installed to check if some version/product is approaching the end of maintenance or end of life.

It is useful to know that customers are often not even aware that such issues exist. There could be issues behind the curtain with no reason to worry on the front end.

Business Warehouse has ruled the SAP analytics space for quite a lot of time, and therefore it is also a preferred product for many customers in such way that they would sink with it rather than get rid of it. Therefore, it is important to create a future landscape in a way that suits the business needs. In return, there could be a small disruption of services during the implementation, which is the price to pay for the long-term benefits.

## 7.1.2 Scenario 2

Figure 7-2 shows the explains the second scenario.

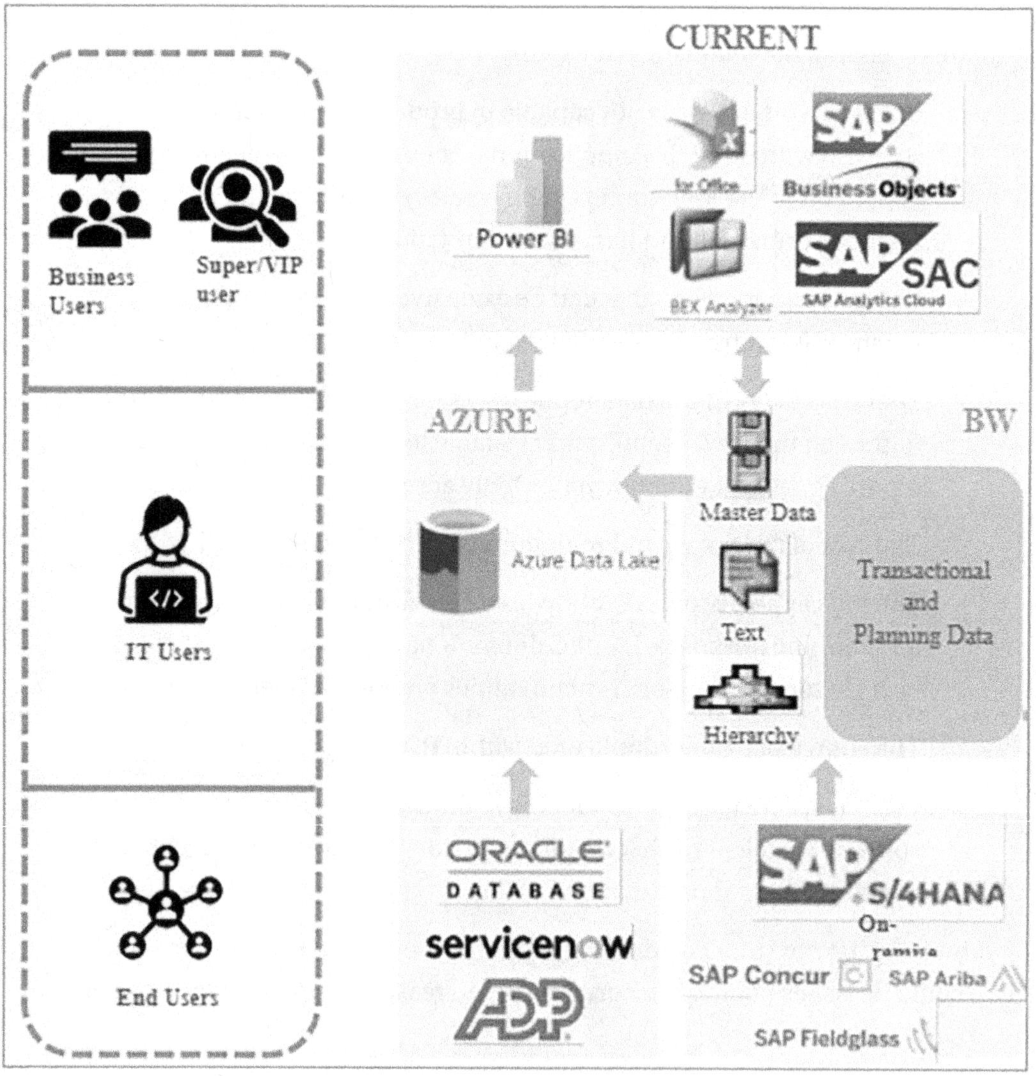


*Figure 7-2.* *Scenario 2: SAP and non-SAP*

*Source Systems*

The source systems are a combination of SAP and non-SAP products. SAP ERP would include S/4 HANA or ECC, and some of the SAP cloud applications are included. Some of the ERPs are on Oracle. The payroll system's data comes from ADP, and ticket-related details are from Service Now.

Data Platform

Traditional BW or BW/4 HANA does most of the data integration and transformation. It also sends the data to an MS Azure data lake to create a layer of semantics.

Reporting

The reporting layer consists of Power BI (reporting the data on ADLS) and Business Object/Analysis for Office/SAP Analytics Cloud for reporting the data on top of the BW layer.

In this scenario, the following issues exist:

- The outbound interface to Azure Data Lake is either using a file-based transfer mechanism from Business Warehouse or through other connectors provided by SAP within Azure. Owning the data transfer process will be an issue as SAP may not be able to support this integration scenario.
- The data transfer to Azure, if file-based, may have issues with the delta management. In many cases, customers use the full load every day with some filters to create a pseudo delta. This is not a robust delta management approach.
- SAP Analytics Cloud uses only planning data and a few simple reports. The majority of the reporting is done in Power BI. SAC is a preferred reporting tool for SAP dataset, which is not used here.
- ADLS extracts data from different non-SAP source systems, and therefore the data platform does not include this data.
- There is an issue with the integration methods for the SAP cloud apps. There are several issues related to performance and handling the business semantics of the data.

- Business Warehouse is on-premises, which mean that there is additional overhead of the server maintenance, patch upgrades, etc. Additionally, there are challenges due to unplanned outage of the server, i.e., availability.
- A single source of truth is not maintained for all data; therefore, there are issues related to the governance and security of the data.
- No known major innovations are planned in the BW/4 HANA area.
- SAP BW/4 HANA persists the data in the majority of the cases, which leads to additional costs to scale up the server.
- The architecture is very complex due to the many components that co-exist in the ecosystem.
- Most importantly, if the customer has plans to move to S/4 HANA (if on ECC currently), then the landscape requires lots of changes due to operational changes in the dataset.

## 7.2 Innovation in the Analytics Space

There are many innovations that are performed in SAP Analytics that are attractive in nature. The situation started evolving with the introduction of S/4 HANA on-premises and the public cloud edition. They mainly evolved because of the following reasons.

**A More Scalable Architecture**

Scalability is one of the important factors when discussing the robustness of any server. With static memory and the space requirements in the earlier scenario, it was not possible to effectively utilize the size of the servers, so in many cases, customers end up paying extra money for no reason. A scalable architecture is primarily the capability to utilize the memory based on the actual needs, which is sometime less and sometimes more. A dynamic design therefore ensures that the server can scale up or down based on the memory requirements.

**Real-Time Data Reporting**

In the era of AI, it is extremely useful to have an architecture that supports real-time data reporting at scale. This enables the true machine learning capabilities to be unleashed. For example, the Business Data Cloud Databricks component uses data products from the Datasphere to implement a data layer that combines different sources' data and available without delay or without any physical data movement. This overcomes the issue with governing and maintaining a large and sensitive dataset. It also allows the users to decide what data to share to the AI agents created to automate certain tasks.

**Gen-AI Applications**

In the earlier days, it was extremely difficult to create an AI agent that works with Generative AI models and include them within real-time dashboards. With the help of the new cloud-based analytics products, there were many Gen AI–capable models already embedded inside the product that can be used without the overhead to define the model or to have skilled partners to develop them.

**Self-Service Capability**

In most analytics products for data engineering and reporting, it is more and more useful to use the self-service reporting capabilities for slicing and dicing the data, creating useful and interactive dashboards, studying data insights, finding lineage, etc. It is no longer needed to create a predefined report/dashboard that merely works based on the training given by the developer. Users are more inclined to navigate the data themselves at their own pace by generating their own reports. This is why the concept of a data lake becomes more and more useful nowadays.

**Creating a Data Fabric**

Traditionally, it was difficult to combine the data from different parts of the organizations. Therefore, the reporting capabilities were very complex. With the help of the new cloud-based analytics products, it is now simple to ingest and combine the data in one place to create a data fabric. With the concept of Business Data Fabric, it became even more useful to retain the business definition of the fields even at the top layer for reporting. Earlier, due to the complexity of the ingestion, the true definition of the data fields was lost during the entire process. The Business Data Fabric concept overcomes this difficulty with ease.

**Integration Capabilities**

One of the main reasons to move to the cloud-based SAP analytics products is to provide the capability to integrate with other SAP applications like ARIBA, CONCUR, etc. This also helps to overcome some of the challenges that previously exist on the on-premise products like BW/4 HANA.

### 7.2.1 Types of Data Architecture

Data architecture is different from data modeling. A data architecture provides a strategic vision toward a future-proof ecosystem for customers. The following are the types of Data Architecture that exist today.

**Data Lake Architecture**

A data lake generally consists of three layers (see Figure 7-3).

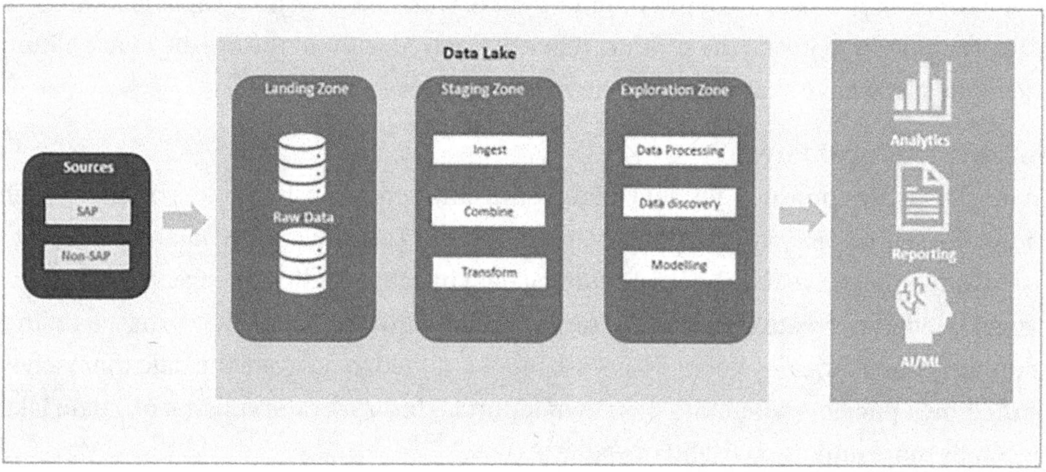


***Figure 7-3.*** *Data lake architecture*

> *Landing Zone*
>
> This is the area where the data first appears within the data lake. Data is generally stored in an unorganized manner without applying any logic; i.e. it is a replica of the sources that are feeding to the data lake.
>
> *Staging Zone*
>
> In this zone, the raw data from the landing zone is used for further processing. It is first ingested in the layer and then processed to create more meaningful information from the dataset.
>
> *Data Exploration zone*
>
> In this zone, the processed data is fed into the analytics engine where the main modeling is done. In other words, the data is now ready to be ingested into a visualization platform.

A data lake usually stores data in raw format. It can store structured, semistructured, and unstructured data. The idea is to remove the singularity from the dataset; it will no longer exist in a silo. All the dependencies are considered and then combined in a way that provides answers to all the business problems.

A data lake can be one of four types.

- On-premises data lake
- Cloud data lake
- Hybrid data lake
- Multicloud data lake

A cloud-based data lake is the preferred solution because of the following advantages:

- Because of the variety of cost models available, cost effectiveness is achieved.
- The security of the data is more robust due to its Shared Responsibility Model. This is a model where the responsibilities for different security aspects are divided between the cloud service provider and the customers. If we take an example of AWS as a provider, customers are generally responsible for controlling the OS-level security, patching, and firewall configuration, while AWS is responsible for the security of the software, applications, and hardware. This allows the security model to be free from vulnerabilities and security breaches.
- Based on the user needs and memory requirements, the server can scale up and scale down to arrive at an optimum number.
- Cloud-based models provide a built-in mechanism to dive deep into the data, which is useful for IOT and machine learning models.

### Data Warehouse Architecture

A data warehouse generally consists of three different layers. See Figure 7-4.

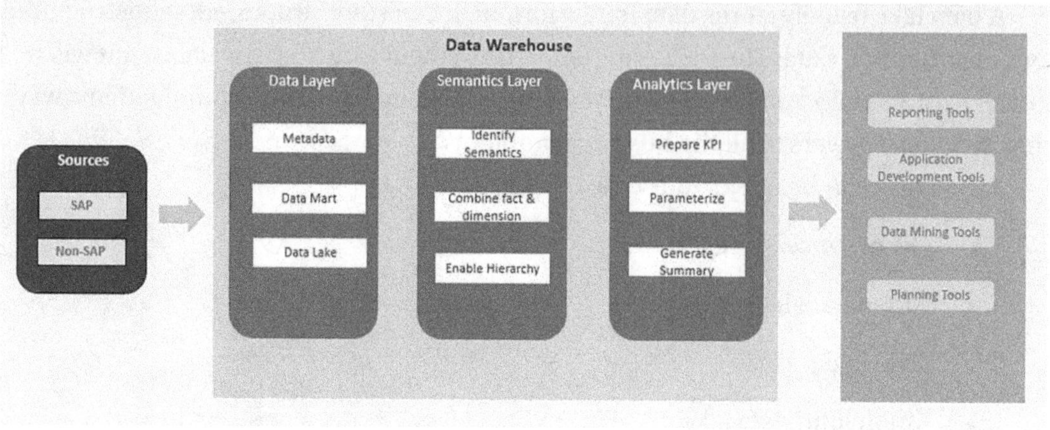


***Figure 7-4.*** *Data warehouse architecture*

**Data Layer**

In this layer, the outcome of the ETL process is stored. Here the following operations are done:

- *Metadata creation*: Define the fields, identifying the type of the field, possible value help, descriptions, master data, etc.
- *Data mart*: Define the model based on the type of functional areas such as finance or sales.
- *Data lake*: This provides the comprehensive storage of data from different places in a single container.
- *Central database server*: This is responsible for storing the data at scale and applying the necessary security and governance.

**Semantics Layer**

In this layer, the semantic definition is stored. This means the context of the data is retained at this layer. This requires data construction from the data in the previous layer. Additionally, the preparation of the data for a more sophisticated analytical model is done here. It also includes the definition of hierarchies, combining facts and attributes.

**Analytics Layer**

In this layer, the tools for the analytics are available. This includes tools used for visualization purposes such as SAP Analytics Cloud and tools used for data mining purposes such as SAP Signavio.

The following are the advantages of cloud-based data warehousing:

- The desired scalability is achieved for a high volume of data.
- Long-term cost forecasting is not needed as the majority of the costing model just needs a prediction of one year.
- It has a strong backup strategy that makes sure the data and models are available to be restored for disaster recovery purposes.
- Data processing is extremely fast compared to on-premise data warehouses.
- The integration with other applications is seamless and does not necessarily need intervention from the IT side. The self-service capability is so robust that even end users can connect the data with other applications and combine it.

As covered, other data architectures include the data mesh architecture, business data fabric architecture, and data mart architecture.

A data lake is generally used to create all the KPI definitions in a single place for more of a glossary. A data warehouse, on the other hand, performs semantic modelling on the data to make them report-ready.

## 7.2.2 Just Ask

Just Ask is functionality in SAP Analytics Cloud stories that can perform tasks based on the questions asked. Basically, this is a Generative AI application built within SAC. This generally works only with the acquired models or the models defined within Datasphere.

Assume you are running a finance dashboard using an SAC story and you identified a number of abrupt changes in the incoming invoice details for a region. You would then need to display the result in tabular format and add multiple filters and navigations to find out details about the reason of these sudden changes of trend. This is very time-consuming, especially when you are figuring this out during at year-end. In this case, you can use the Just Ask functionality to train the model to prepare the result of your analysis in terms of a table/chart. Then in the Just Ask input field, you can ask your question to provide a detailed breakdown of the data based on certain conditions. This helps you get to the root of the problem quickly.

Prepare Your Models

In this demo, I will use one of the acquired models to perform the setup.
I have previously set up the data for the following:

- Regression
- Classification
- Time series

I will create three models using these data and then implement Just Ask for demonstration purposes.

*Model 1: Regression*

See Figure 7-5.

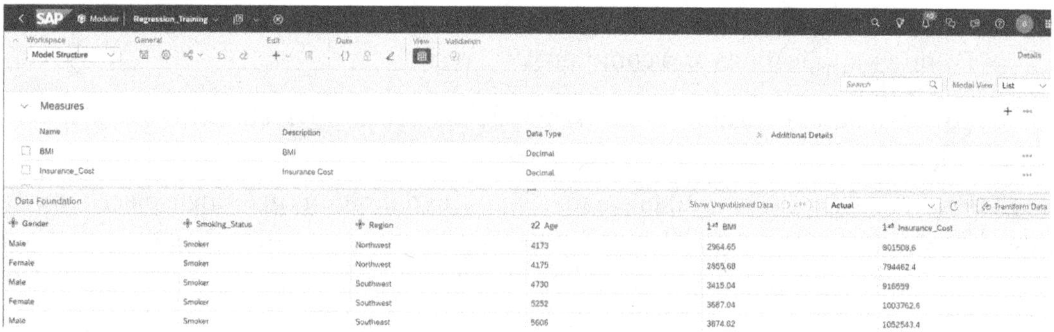

***Figure 7-5.** Regression model*

*Model 2: Classification*

See Figure 7-6.

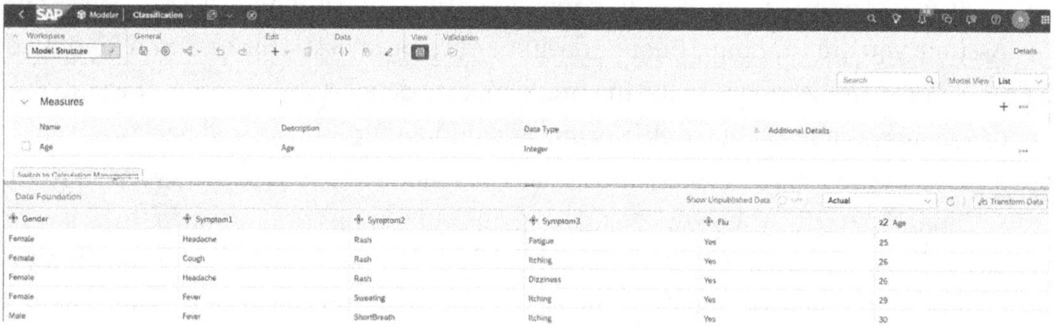

***Figure 7-6.** Classification model*

*Model 3: Time Series*

See Figure 7-7.

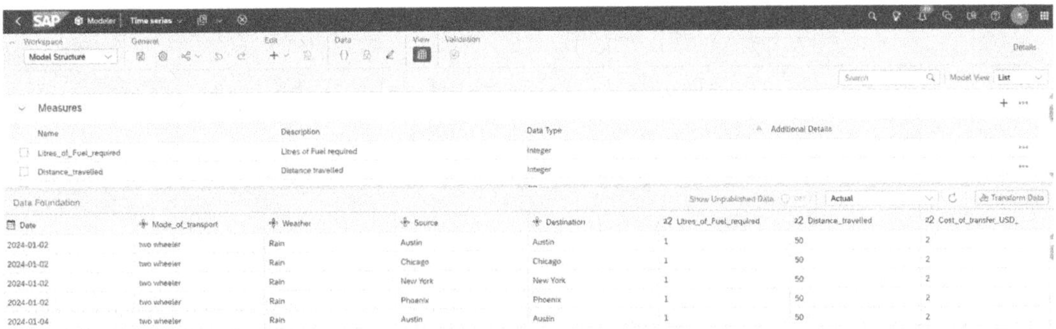

***Figure 7-7.*** *Time-series model*

Add Models to Just Ask

Before adding any model to Just Ask, you need to set the default appearance in the administration. Go to System ➤ Administration ➤ Default Appearance and turn on Conversational Analysis. If this is not marked, then Just Ask won't appear on the home page. See Figure 7-8.

***Figure 7-8.*** *Enable Just Ask*

After the Just Ask functionality is added, the next step is to add models to the Just Ask functionality. Open Just Ask and select Manage Model. In this section, select add model. The model once added will be indexed automatically. This process helps the AI engine to communicate with the model's data in natural language. See Figure 7-9.

Indexed models have the following advantages:

- Make the data readable by the AI engine
- Synonyms can be added to the dimensions and measures

- Rules to train the model for interpreting similar future scenarios
- Sample questions can be added to the model

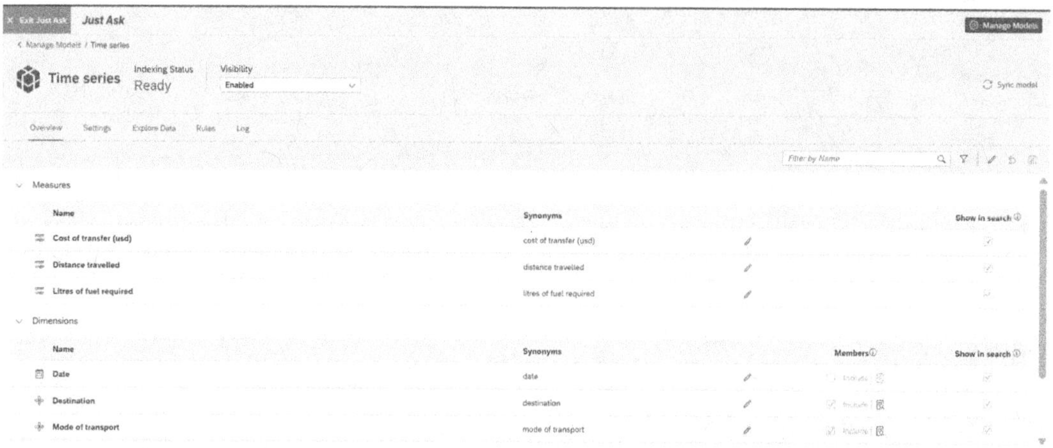


***Figure 7-9.*** *Indexed model*

In the Add Model section are five tabs. See Figure 7-10.

In the Overview section, you can update the following:

- List of measures and dimensions. Here you can include/exclude them from the search results.
- You can create synonyms for faster searching.
- You can search for help for all dimensions. For each of the values against any dimension, you can add a synonym.

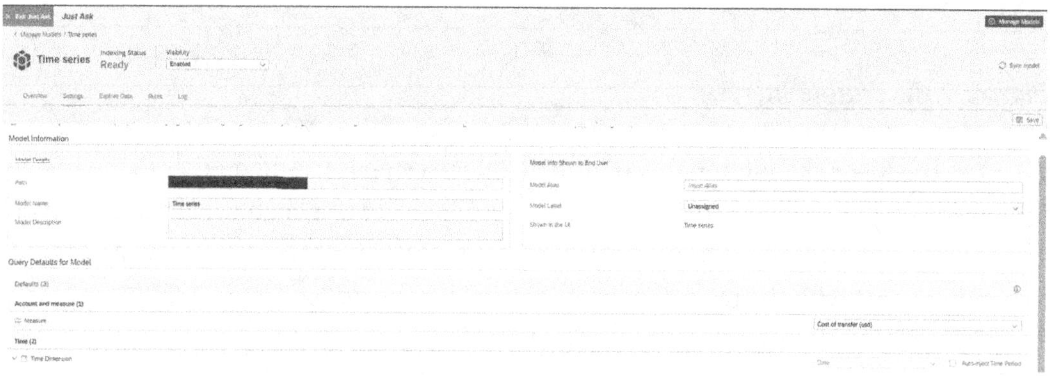


***Figure 7-10.*** *Settings: Just Ask*

In the Settings section, you can view the model information and pass default values to the model. You can make one measure default, and you can set a default time dimension. See Figure 7-11.

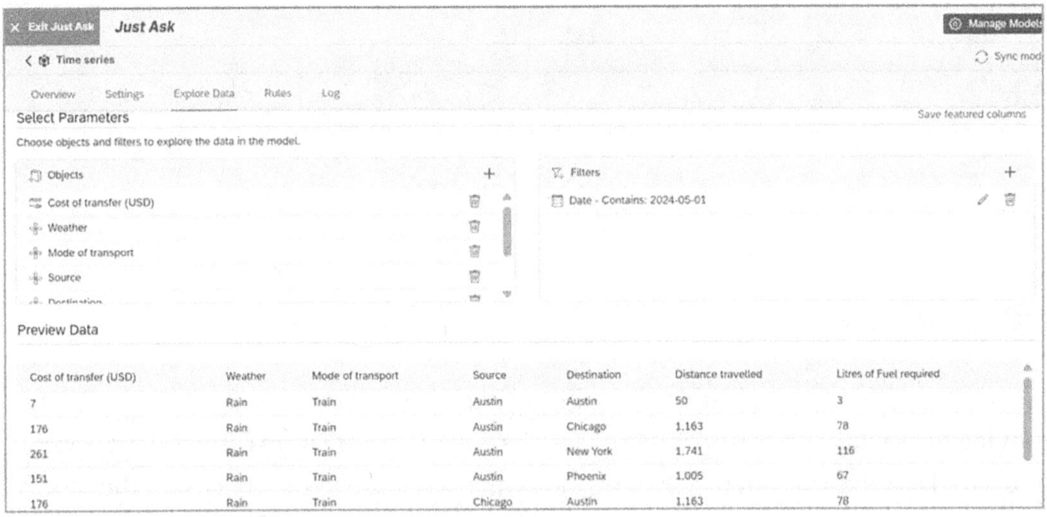


**Figure 7-11.** *Exploring data: Just Ask*

In the Explore Data section, you can perform the following tasks (see Figure 7-12):

- You can add any parameters that are essentially the list of fields to be displayed for the preview of the data. This will allow you to study the data in depth.
- In Filters, you can add filters based on any dimensions to slice the dataset for preview. You can either use a single value or use a range with inclusion or exclusion options.
- In the preview data, you can see the subset of the data for which the parameter was passed.

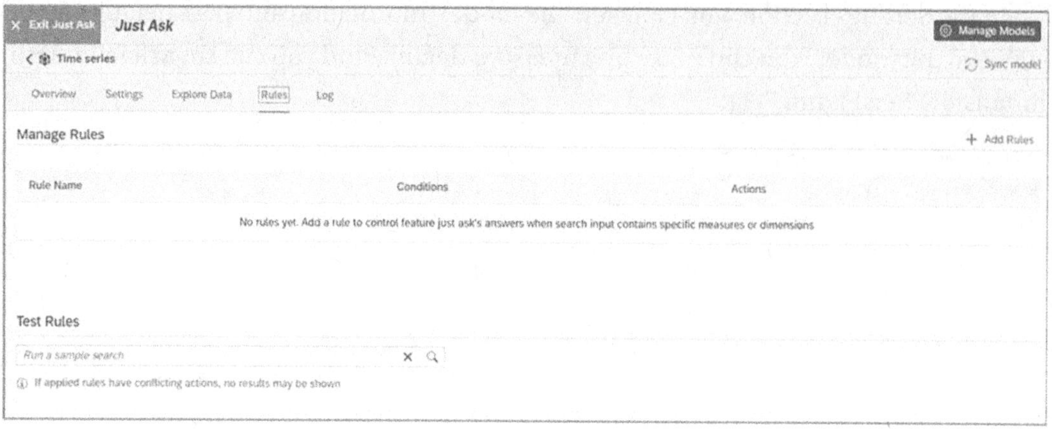


***Figure 7-12.*** *Rules in Just Ask*

In this section, you can add rules for our GenAI agent (see Figure 7-13). This is like training the model to perform certain tasks based on the questions asked. This is very important as the variety of the training data will contribute to the success of the model. Let's create some rules.

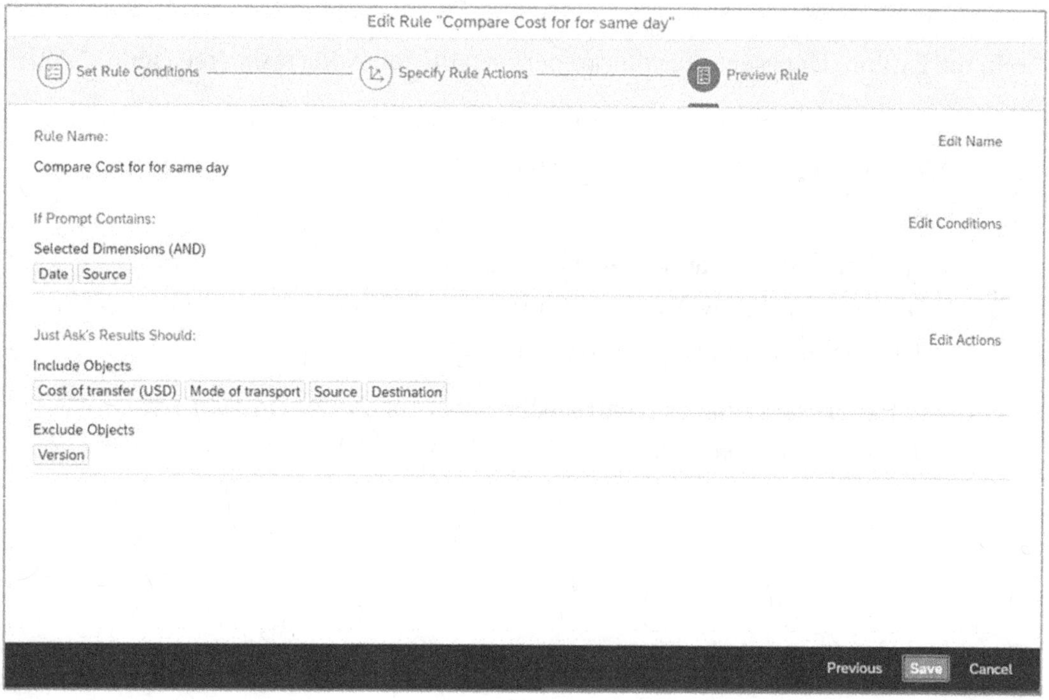


***Figure 7-13.*** *Creating rules*

In this rule, I defined the search condition that consists of the date and source. Here Just Ask will include cost of transfer (USD), mode of transport, source, and destination.

Now let's test the question. See Figure 7-14.

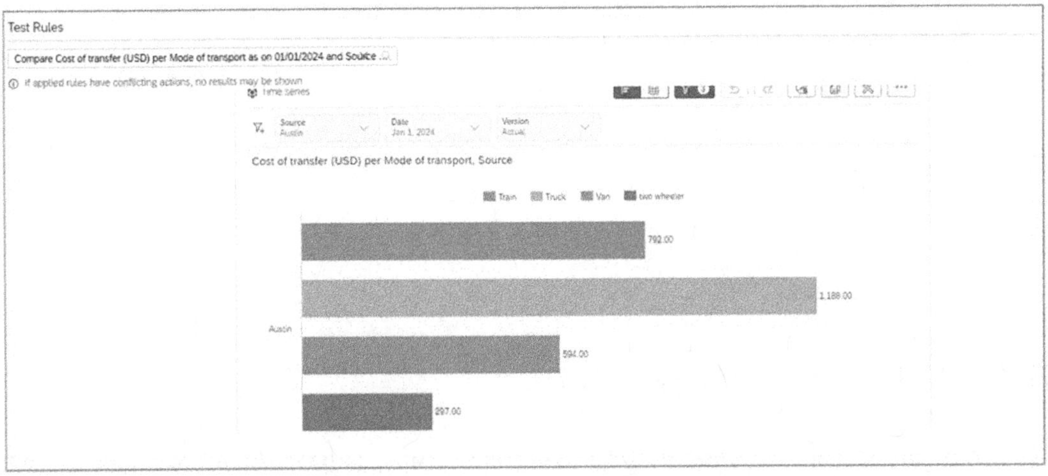


***Figure 7-14.*** *Test rules: Just Ask*

*Trend*

See Figure 7-15.

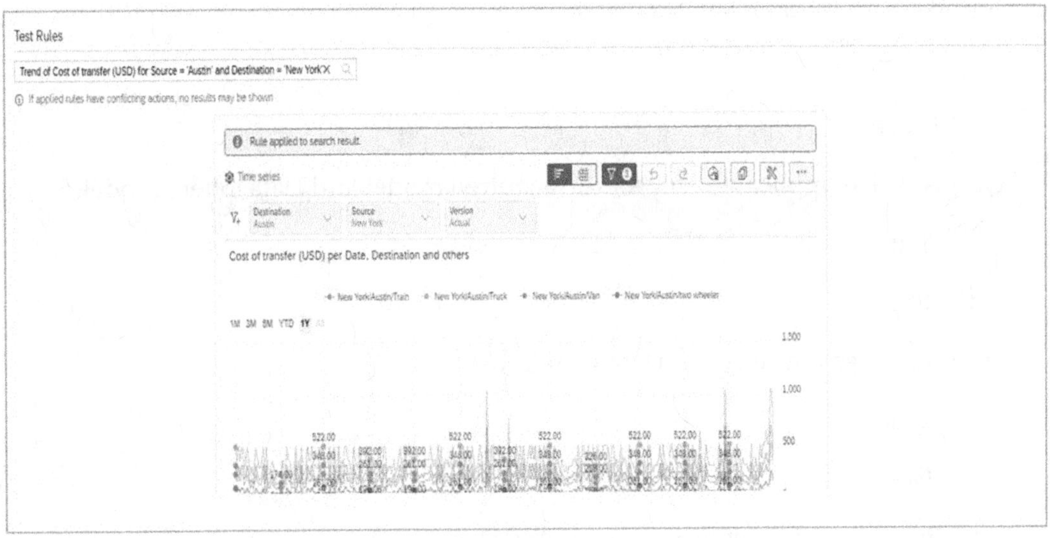


***Figure 7-15.*** *Applying a rule*

Now the model is fully added to Just Ask. See Figure 7-16.

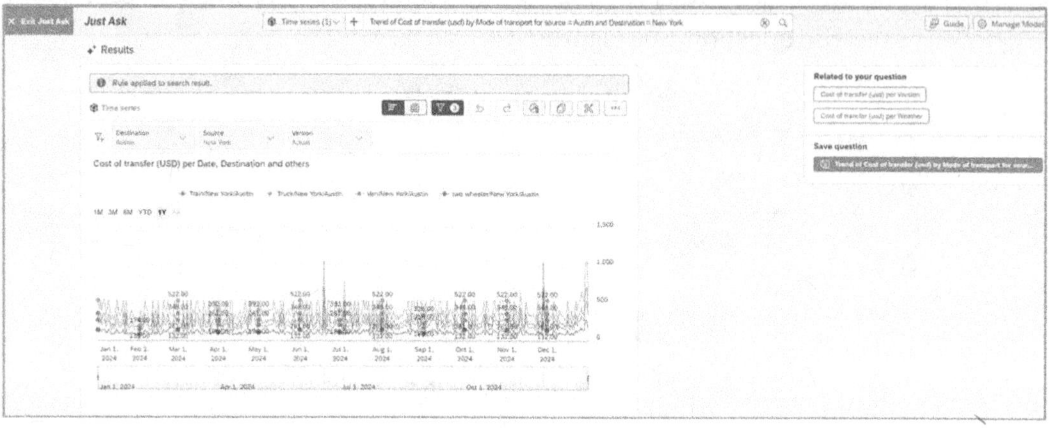


***Figure 7-16.*** *Adding the model to Just Ask*

As shown, the plot is prepared based on the example you tried earlier, and the question is also saved here.

## 7.3 Test Your Knowledge

Q1: Just Ask is relevant for a particular story.

a) True

b) False

Q2: Just Ask is applicable only for the acquired model and Datasphere model.

a) True

b) False

Q3: Data mesh is a subset of Data Warehouse.

a) True

b) False

Q4: Which of the following is a data mining tool?

a) SAP Analytics Cloud

b) SAP Ariba

c) SAP Concur

d) None of the above

Q5: Indexed SAC models are useful for creating a semantics layer.

a) True

b) False

Q6: Which one of the following is not a layer in a data lake architecture?

a) Landing Zone

b) Staging Zone

c) Data Exploration Zone

d) Analytics Zone

Q7: Which one is not a type of data lake?

a) Hybrid

b) On-premises

c) Multicloud

d) Multilayered

## 7.4 Summary

In this chapter, you explored examples based on an different customer's landscape, different data architectures, and Just Ask functionality.

Until this stage, you learned about knowing the problem better. Once the problem statement is clear, the next important question is how the short- and long-term path is defined.

In the next chapter, you will learn more about the adoption path and how to migrate the current landscape to Business Data Cloud.

## CHAPTER 8

# Path of Adoption

Now that we have discussed the features and new functionalities of the Cloud Analytics applications of SAP, the next question is how the adoption is done. This is not an easy journey where you can adopt the new products overnight; the process requires careful investigation, scoping, cost assessment, and roadmap preparation.

We can categorize the situation in three possible scenarios:

- **Customers have already moved their ERP system to S/4 HANA on-premises or in the public cloud:** This is a perfect modernization scenario for analytics. Customers who are heavily relying on SAP as their ERP system were mostly in the ECC version. Based on SAP's strategic move toward a cloud-based product, many customers are preferring to use S/4 HANA.
- **Customers are on ECC for their ERP and have plans to move to S/4 HANA in future:** These are customers who are relying on SAP data for their ERP system but still can use ECC without any major disruption. Normally, such organizations have plans for the S/4 HANA migration, but they are not urgent.
- **Customers are on ECC for their ERP and no plans for S/4 HANA in future:** These are customers who are going to continue with ECC or have future plans to use non-SAP ERPs. Only a handful of such customers exist as it is a tedious task for them to move everything to a non-SAP environment, study and convert the historical data according to the new product's definition, and educate business users on how to use a completely new interface for their day-to-day activities.

The third scenario is not very common as it is preferred to follow SAP's guidelines and stay up-to-date. But it could be applicable for small organizations.



© Sourav Banerjee 2025
S. Banerjee, *Modernizing SAP Business Warehouse*, https://doi.org/10.1007/979-8-8688-2192-9_8

From an analytics point of view, usually organizations adopt a mix of SAP and non-SAP products. In general, the applicability of a data lake is common in Microsoft products like Azure. SAP Analytics products in such scenarios were merely used to connect the SAP ERP with the data lake hosted in Azure, and reporting was done in Power BI.

For a more SAP-driven landscape where the reporting is also done in SAP, the full capabilities of the SAP Analytics products can be used.

One other important aspect is integration with various systems. Prior to the cloud era, it was not possible to seamlessly integrate all non-SAP products and SAP data into a single place. Many organizations therefore adopted a file-based transfer (through middleware like SAP PI).

Thanks to the integration suite on BTP, you can now connect to most of the SAP cloud apps to Datasphere through a push mechanism.

Another bottleneck is the preference of Business Objects over SAP Analytics Cloud. Most users are not in the agreement about changing reporting approaches that have been running smoothly for years. Even with the evolution of AI- and ML-related applications in SAP Analytics, it is in general difficult to convince users to start using the new SAP Analytics products. From an end-user perspective, including Datasphere or Business Data Cloud does not make much of a difference; what matters most are the following:

- Look and feel
- Ease of use
- Performance
- Resolve some of the pain areas
- A product without much of complexity to run
- Self-service capability
- Real-time data display
- Simpler design of the reports
- Ability to perform master data management
- Simplicity of the report functionalities

- Ability to report most of the key elements of the business in one place
- Slice and dice of the data efficiently
- Report downloads and automated broadcasting functionalities
- Alert mechanism
- Possibility of automatic validation of data
- Ability to perform financial planning with ease
- Automate tasks that are part of the planning process
- Self-data load possibilities
- Ability to investigate differences from summary level to detail level

It is therefore a good start to find a scenario that is most useful for the business and demonstrate some of these capabilities in terms of a proof of concept. Engaging in communication with superusers may also help them understand the "nice-to-have" features.

There are many analytics tools on the market. It is easier to get users on board who are already using products like SAP Business Warehouse. Those who are more inclined toward the non-SAP Analytics product often choose to stay with it, with the exception of the financial planning process for which SAP Analytics Cloud can be introduced.

The following are some of the products:

**Integration:** For integration with SAP cloud applications, SAP Datasphere can be adopted along with SAP Integration Suite in BTP.

**Data Warehousing:** Data Warehousing can be used within SAP Datasphere to combine data from different sources and prepare a business semantics layer for consumption.

**Pass-Through Solutions:** SAP Datasphere can be used for connecting SAP data and sending it to a data lake without any storage requirements. This will enable organizations to make use of the delta loading functionalities.

**Reporting:** SAP Analytics Cloud can be used for visualization purposes and to combine multiple reports together in a single place. It can also be used to push back data to the ERP system, which is sometimes required for data synchronization purposes.

**Planning:** SAP Analytics Cloud planning operations can be used for typical planning needs like versioning, data copy, reclassification, revaluation, currency conversions, and more.

## 8.1 Getting Started with the Modernization Journey

The main requirement is to create a path that can be followed for both short-term and long-term perspectives. Starting the modernization is not an easy task as there are many dependencies for other key decisions in the organization.

Some of the important dependencies are as follows.

**Decision on the ERP Side**

You will often see that the modernization of the analytics ecosystem is largely dependent on the roadmap for SAP ERP. For example, when organizations move toward S/4 HANA from ECC, it happens in most cases in phases. This can be done by:

- **Creating an S/4 HANA template** via a pilot for a small set of data in most cases based on geography. For example, you can perform an S/4 HANA migration for a particular country or for a specific plant or division. This will ensure that the impact of the implementation on day-to-day operations, user acceptability, and investment made can be achieved. Once this is stabilized, then the same template can be used for rolling out the implementation for other divisions. This process will have a severe impact on the analytics landscape and co-existence of products. Let's assume that the division where the implementation was done also implemented Datasphere and SAP Analytics Cloud for a data and reporting solution. Now, the rest of the division continues to use SAP Business Warehouse and Business Objects for the reporting. In such a case, the operational overhead, cost, and support effort increase exponentially as each area requires manpower of different skills and can't be merged. A long-term approach could be to roll out the template everywhere and eventually merge the support team and decommission all the old components. The shift is time-consuming and requires a considerable amount of development and testing. Therefore, the return on investment can be realized only after the decommissioning happens.

- **A full-blown implementation of S/4 HANA** can ensure that the additional costs to keep the old analytics product alive are no longer necessary. Often, you see that an ERP migration and an analytics migration go hand in hand to ensure that the reporting solution is available at the same time that the ERP is live.

### Licensing Cost

With the new products, the question of what type of license is necessary also comes into mind. In many cases, you can see that organizations end up procuring higher licenses than required. This would also include the server capacity cost, which is very difficult to assess. The cost is an important factor to allocate budget for the project and to realize the return on investment to make a more strategic decision.

### Considering Sunset of Products

One of the driving factors for the modernization could be to identify the components in the architecture that are approaching end of support or end of life. For example, organizations that are using SAP Data Intelligence for ETL and pass-through solutions need a replacement product to avoid approaching end of life. In some cases, the support for some of the integration APIs also approaches end of support, which is a significant risk to the "business as usual" processes. In such cases, a new product must be identified that can replace the old product with similar functionalities.

### Overlapping Projects

There could be overlapping projects like version upgrades, other implementations, etc., that are planned to be executed during the modernization journey. This will have severe impact on the project scoping and delivery as these changes can slow down the migration process, and dual maintenance would be required in the case of a parallel configuration.

### Data Migration

If there is some data that is transformed and stored within Business Warehouse, it is difficult to get the same data from ERP. As an example, we can imagine some time-dependent master data that is not time dependent in ERP. Therefore, the data migration/access from ERP directly will lose the history of the changes. In such cases, a migration from existing BW is required. In solutions like Business Data Cloud, the existing BW can be used within BDC and combined inside Datasphere as a SAP-managed data product.

To perform a successful migration to new product, the following questions need to be answered:

- What are the reports and objects in scope?
- How do I handle the outbound interfaces?
- Can all my SAP applications be combined in a single place?
- How can I create a uniform data layer where all my data can be stored and accessed easily without losing its context?
- Which data can be federated, and which data must be persisted?
- How do I ensure that a robust authorization of the dataset is maintained?
- Can the sizing be done prior to implementation?
- What will happen to the existing Business Warehouse Server?
- What type of user training would be required?
- How does the administration and governance of the server take place?
- What is a typical timeline for the implementation?
- How the planning will be performed?

### 8.1.1 Step 1: Introduce a New Component

At this stage, typically a small set of the data models is identified to start the migration process. Assume that we have Business Warehouse as a reporting solution and S/4 HANA as the source (see Figure 8-1).

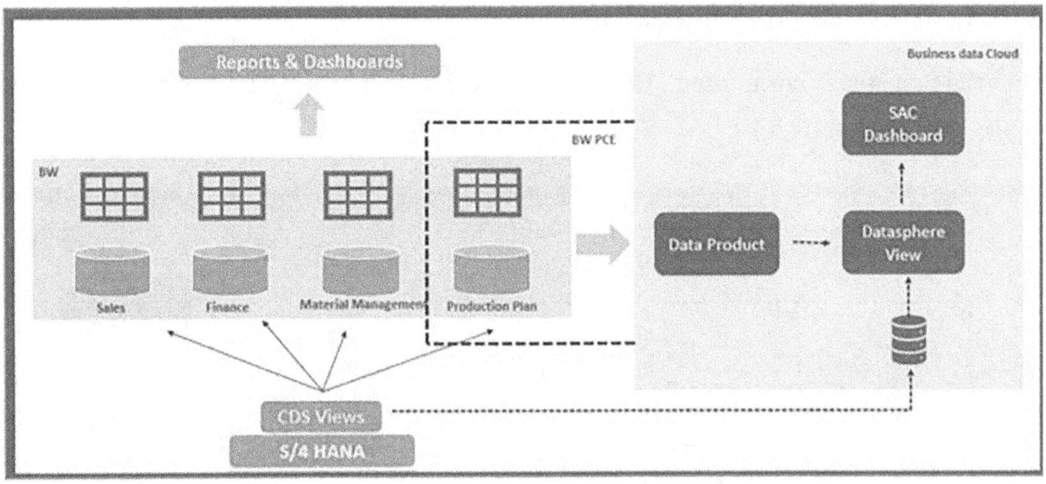


***Figure 8-1.** Step 1 for Business Data Cloud*

The following will happen:

1. Identify a dataflow that can be used to initiate the implementation.
2. Procure Business Data Cloud with Datasphere and SAP Analytics Cloud as two components.
3. Use Data Product Generator to convert the BW flow into an SAP-managed data product. Here the flow must first be moved to the BW Public Cloud Edition server.
4. Consume the data product within Datasphere.
5. Create a Datasphere view to combine the data product's data with the other datasets available.
6. The same CDS views that are connected with BW data sources are also connected to Datasphere in terms of a remote table. This is for a future-ready architecture.
7. Datasphere view is exposed to SAP Analytics Cloud via Analytical view and then visualized through dashboards.
8. Decommission BW or continue to use BW within Business Data Cloud. In this example, we will concentrate on BW existence after the migration.

## 8.1.2 Step 2: Full Migration

After the first step is completed, the next step is to perform the migration for the entire landscape (see Figure 8-2).

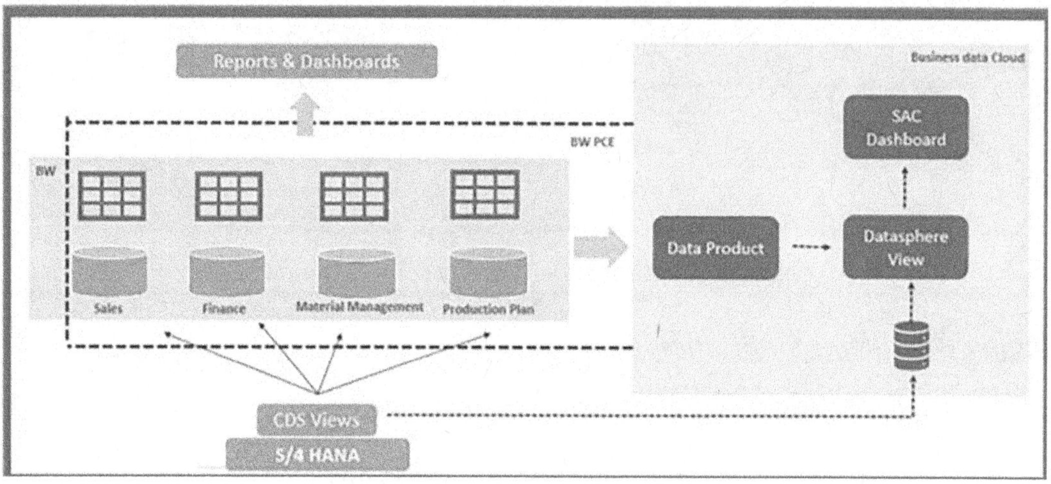


***Figure 8-2.*** *Step 2 for Business Data Cloud*

The following steps will be executed here:

**Step 1:** Migrate the rest of the data flows into the BW Private Cloud Edition server. At this stage, the BW PCE will also be connected with the S/4 HANA server so that the consistency will be maintained. The delta from CDS views will now be consumed within PCE.

**Step 2:** Generate the data product for all the new flows.

**Step 3:** All new data products will be consumed within Datasphere views.

## 8.1.3 Step 3: BW Decommissioning

Once the data flows moved into Datasphere, the next step is to plan for a decommissioning of the BW server (see Figure 8-3).

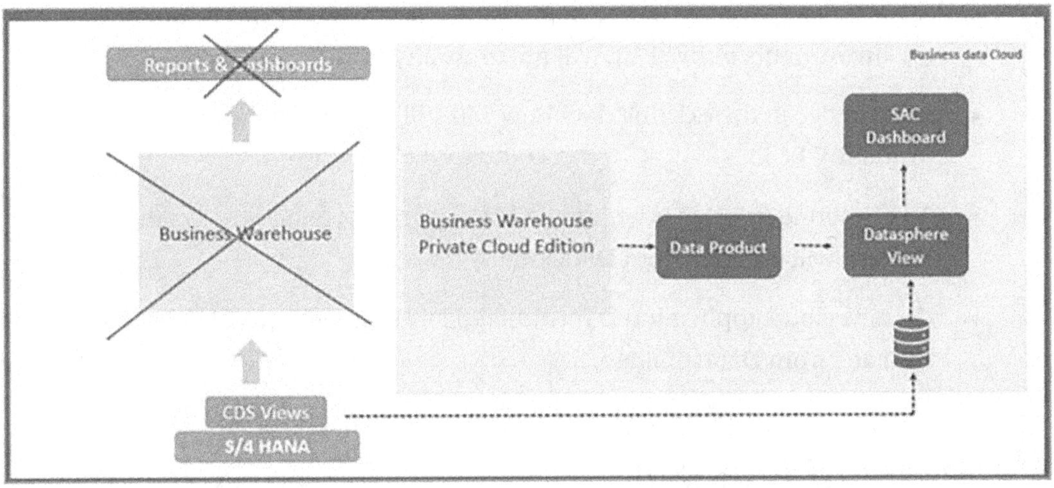


***Figure 8-3.*** *Step 3 for Business Data Cloud*

In this step, the following tasks will be executed:

1. Identify any dependencies with the existing BW server.
2. Re-verify if all the required data flow and reports are moved within Business Data Cloud.
3. Stop loading into the existing BW server.
4. Revoke access of all reports for the end users.
5. Clean up data.
6. Stop all the batch jobs running in the BW server.
7. Decommission the server completely.

After all the steps are executed, then the flows are up and running within Business Data Cloud. The next step is to decide whether the BW objects can be natively redesigned. In such cases, the BW PCE objects also need to be mirrored within Datasphere, and then the BW PCE can also be planned to be decommissioned. If the BW investment is very high, the customer will be inclined to keep the BW objects alive. In that case, the following can be done:

- All BW objects will continue to exist within BW PCE. This will need an assurance that the data loads are continuing to run on the BW PCE from S/4 HANA. Datasphere will be fed continuously through data products.

- All new developments are to be performed within Datasphere so that the investments in BW PCE will not grow anymore.
- Any change to the existing data flow will still need to be done inside BW PCE.
- All outbound interfaces where the BW data needs to be sent to other systems will be done from Datasphere.
- If a new cloud application is introduced, the connection will have to be made from Datasphere.

## 8.2 Proof of Concept

Customers who are looking to find a clear path for migration and have doubts about the feasibility of certain solutions need to perform a proof of concept (POC) based on predefined criteria.

The advantages of performing a pilot project are as follows:

- Typically it comes with a small scope, and therefore the cost is low. The number of licenses is also less compared with a live system.
- The server capacity needed is small. In some cases, SAP products come with a pay-as-you-go model, which can be utilized to pay a small amount to support the POC. Datasphere, for example, provides a small license at the beginning of purchase, which can then be converted into a standard plan.
- As the project runs with a small set of data flow, the implementation cost is also very less, and a focused approach can be taken just to prove certain points.
- A POC is useful to showcase the capabilities to the decision-makers in the organization to clear up ambiguity with the product.
- There is no impact on the BAU process as the box is completely different and has no connection to the current landscape. However, one need to monitor the source (S/4 server) system loads periodically to ensure that the system is not overloaded due to querying the data.

## 8.2.1 Scope and Deliverables

The first step to define a POC is to understand and agree on the scope of deliveries. One point to note is that a POC is typically not a complete project, so there will be lots of loose ends.

The following are generally *excluded* from the scope:

**Housekeeping**

Typically, POCs are conducted only for a specific topic and mostly for a feasibility study. Therefore, there is no need to have any housekeeping activities. Once the purpose is fulfilled, then the objects and the data within it are no longer required. It can be cleaned up, and data doesn't have to stream into it any longer.

**Batch Jobs**

Batch jobs are generally not considered. In most cases, one-time data loading would be sufficient to perform the required tasks, or if it happens periodically, then it would be required for only a specific time frame. There is no need to schedule any job to continuously update the data (even if is required, then the jobs must be cancelled after the demonstration).

**Data Migration**

In general, for POC purposes, the following should be done:

**Master Data**

All master data needs to be loaded, but no update is needed after the first load because small changes in the master data attributes won't impact the outcome of the POC to a great extent.

**Text**

There is a one-time full load of all master data. Master data objects can also be considered for real-time data access without any data movement. No update needs to be scheduled.

**Transactional Data**

Based on performance, some datasets will be federated without any need for data migration. For others where replication is required due to performance implications, perform loading only for a certain time range, for example, two years and delta after that. This depends on the KPIs in the report. If there are KPIs in the report that calculate the data for last year, then last year's data is required to be migrated to the POC.

**Slicing**

If the volume of the data even for one complete year is too high, then one can pick an example scenario, e.g., a couple of profit centers or company codes that can be used for demonstration purposes. In such cases, it is no longer necessary to load a complete year's data; rather, only a subset of data can be loaded.

- **All functionalities:** If the report in scope contains much functionality including performing some updates, running a job, etc., then you can choose to decide which one could be part of the scope. In general, POCs are not meant to show everything.
- **Authorizations:** Generally, the authorization framework implementation is not part of POCs. If there is a specific requirement to demonstrate how authorizations can be applied to the dataset, then it can be set up with a minimum scope only to support the POC. All roles and user access will not be set up.
- **Integration:** POCs usually do not include connecting all the apps in the environment unless this is one of the acceptance criteria and for identified systems only. In all other cases, picking one SAP and one non-SAP application would be good enough to perform the POC.
- **Outbound interfaces:** Any data moving out of SAP is generally considered out of scope for the POC. The exception is the case where the POC is executed to check the feasibility to send certain data into non-SAP applications (for example, Azure Data Lake).
- **Connectivity with live systems:** In many cases, customers can access the live source system (S/4 HANA) to get a feel of the visualized data. In this case, a test environment contains sufficient data to perform the demonstration, which should be the first choice.

<u>How to Define the Scope of the POC</u>

Defining the scope of the POC is not an easy task as this is the foundation of the full-fledged implementation. Therefore, the scoping can be an important factor toward the success of the main project.

The following are some of the desired outcomes of the POC:

- Demonstrating some of the key features of the new product
- Demonstrating how the pain points of the customer can be addressed using the new approach.
- Demonstrating how the new product fits into the overall analytics ecosystem
- Deciding on the feasibility of some of the functionalities (existing and nice to have)
- Demonstrating how long the new product will co-exist with the old product
- Demonstrating the end user acceptance based on the demonstration
- Analyzing feedback from the users who were not part of the scoping of the POC
- Deciding to move ahead with the product or not
- Deciding on the short-term and long-term implementation roadmaps

## Scope

In an ideal situation, a best practice is to have a small set of dataflows along with the administrative tasks move to the new environment. It is also useful to work with real-time data for demonstration purposes or refresh the sandbox/text environment with production data before the start of the POC.

The typical scope of the POC (although it differs from customer to customer) on a high level is as follows:

**Sizing**

Sizing analysis is one of the first exercises that needs to be done before the POC execution. This analysis will make sure you have good knowledge to procure servers with the desired capacity. This should also be added to the overall cost planned for this POC. Ideally, from a Business Data Cloud point of view, the following analysis is required:

- Number of capacity units needed
- Number of tenants required

- Space configuration, i.e., how much memory will be allocated to each space created
- If planning is in scope, then whether SAC planning would be required
- If the BW server will be consumed within Datasphere, then how much capacity unit needed for BW in Business Data Cloud
- If BW PCE is used, then what is the procurement cost of the BW PCE environment
- If there is a plan to demonstrate some of the AI capabilities, then the Databricks Capacity unit and services need to be assessed.

**Licenses**

Once the server is ready, the users need to be set up. At this stage, the requirement is limited as only the developers will have access to the tool. The demonstration typically does not give an opportunity to the end users to navigate on their own; rather, it is more of "read and watch" from a user's point of view. The following information is required:

- Number of users required for BW
- Number of users required for Datasphere
- Number of users required for SAP Analytics Cloud
- Number of users required for SAP Analytics Cloud Planning
- Nature of access required for each user

**Integration**

Here, you define how many connections need to be built. This also talks about any non-SAP or SAP cloud applications that are in scope. It is useful to define all this at the beginning of the project to avoid delays and conflicts at a later stage. Ideally the following could be scope of the integrations:

- SAP ERP (ECC or S/4 HANA) to Datasphere
- SAP BW to Datasphere (if PCE is used, then the connection with BW PCE and Datasphere need to be built)
- One non-SAP server (can start with the simpler server) to Datasphere

- One cloud application on SAP to Datasphere
- Datasphere to SAC (bidirectional)
- Datasphere to Databricks
- Outbound to data lake (only if the success of the entire project depends on this criteria)

## Deliverables

The deliverables for the POC are outlined in this section.

**Feasibility**

One of the main reasons why a POC is useful is to check the feasibility of the new product in terms of the activities that are critical to the success of the organization. It can also help in further decision-making. The following feasibility checks are performed:

- Whether SAP ERP connects to Datasphere without any problems. It is also to conclude that the data exchange is seamless, be it replication or federation. The incremental loading approach needs to be checked and concluded.
- Whether the cloud application identified can connect with Datasphere and the data is consumed within the other layers of Business Data Cloud.
- Whether the connection can handle the high volume of data during loading and reporting.
- How the outbound interface works with the Datasphere.
- How a data product can be used within Datasphere.
- How SAP and non-SAP data can be combined and used within the other components of Business Data Cloud.
- How Databricks can be used to create an AI-related use case leveraging the data products from Datasphere.
- How the planning processes can work in SAP Analytics Cloud.

- How the Datasphere models are consumed within the SAP Analytics Cloud and how SAP Analytics Cloud can push data into Datasphere.
- How the Native HANA models can be consumed within Datasphere.

**Documentation**

Documentation becomes an important deliverable in the POC stage as this will help the design of the main implementation. The documents should outline the following:

- Connectivity parameter and processes
- Guidelines on the overall architecture including data exchange process
- Details on the models need to be prepared
- Prerequisites
- Server setup guidelines including user setup
- Naming conventions
- Data loading and migration strategy
- Objects in scope (name, functionalities, and metadata)
- Deliverables in each sprint
- Test scripts
- Test results
- Detailed technical specification that should include model names, pseudo logic, field list, filters, etc.
- Acceptance criteria

**Authorizations**

Authorizations need to be set up only to support the POC. For example, a business scenario can be picked up like company codes, and the roles can be set up based on different values of company code. A positive and one negative result on the access can be a good start to demonstrate the authorization process.

**Demonstration**

A product demonstration is typically planned at the end of the POC where some of the key users, decision-makers, and project sponsors will be present. A demonstration should be divided into two parts: a document (often a set of slides) explaining the new features of the products and a document performing a simulation on the product page with a well-defined scenario. During the demonstration process, users won't get access to the system themselves, but they can review the results through screen share.

**Environment Preparation**

Environment preparation is typically done during the final stages of the POC, but it is useful to agree on the criteria for the preparation in advance (during the early stages of the project). This includes the following:

- Number of years of data to be extracted from the ERP system. This can be identified based on discussing with the users or by assessing the reports that exist today
- If there is a particular filter that can be imposed on the dataset for demonstration purpose. This can be a set of company codes or profit centers, etc.
- Master data update frequency.
- If there is a dependency on other dataflow, whether they can be made out of scope, and if a one-time data load to those objects will be sufficient for the POC.
- If batch jobs need to be scheduled during the last few weeks (how many and in what frequencies).
- Set up a one-time data upload for the planning process (how many years and for what versions).
- Data loading from other servers that are not connected and out of scope of the POC. In such cases, if this is important, then perform you can perform a one-time load by Excel file upload from the source just to support the scenario.
- If the outbound interface is in scope, then delete the content of the target object in the data lake (in development system) and load using Datasphere to avoid duplicates. An agreement on how much data needs to be pushed must be made before.

**Design**

The design of the new artifacts should be based on the scenario planned, i.e., the existing data flow. There may not be a one-to-one relation with the existing objects, but at the end all the required reports must be re-created.

**Financial Planning**

If there is a financial planning use case that is to be included in the scope, then the following must be performed:

- Ability to perform the end-to-end planning scenario
- Ability to be able to input data for different planning versions through the new tool
- Any manual tasks that are in scope completed using the new tool, for example, copy or delete or customer calculations, etc.
- Ability to save and retrieve the data using SAP Analytics Cloud and Datasphere

## 8.2.2 Timeline

Proof of concepts for the area of analytics are generally executed within three to four months. As the scope is defined very accurately, the execution is focused on delivering the scope. Any new requirement occurring during the projects are documented but not acted upon. This ensures that the project does not go over budget.

The timeline of the POC also ensures that the main project plan can be made based on the percent work delivered during the POC and what is left. This can automatically give a rough estimate of the actual delivery. About 20–30% scope for the POC is a good start for the modernization. A large amount of scope loses its purpose and is therefore difficult to complete within short time. A quick execution is always preferred for the following reasons:

- To keep the user community motivated for the actual implementation
- To spend less money during the POC
- To avoid stakeholder oversight especially when the project runs for a longer period

- To avoid losing interest on the product
- To avoid doing a complete rework due to eventual delay and knowledge is lost in the muted period

Please consider the timeline in Figure 8-4 for performing a proof of concept.

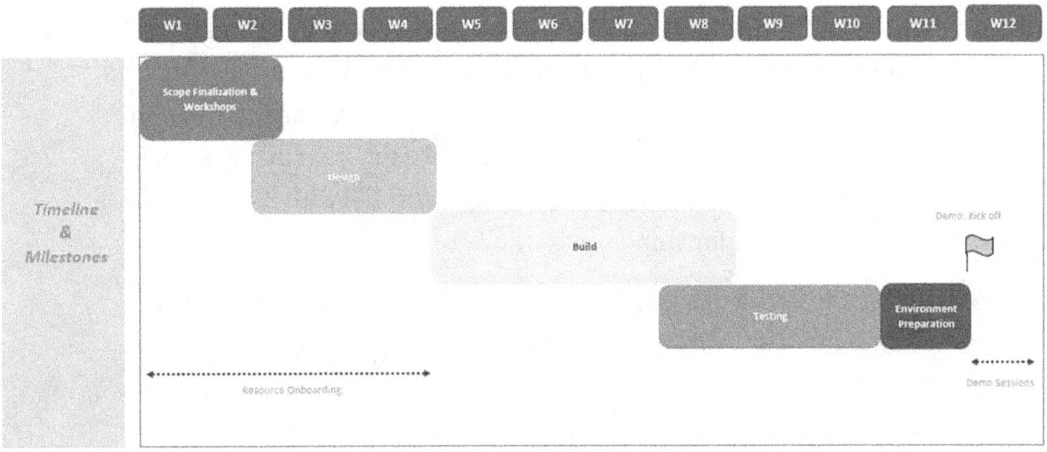


***Figure 8-4.*** *Timeline for POC*

## Scope Finalization and Workshops

This phase lasts about two weeks where the following activities will be done:

- Prepare the workshop agenda, concentrating on the delivery planned.
- Execute the interactive workshop, keeping everyone informed on the context of this workshop. Workshops need to be very precise and should not deviate from the agreed area of interests.
- Finalize the scope of objects; this can include the data flow or process or both.
- Document the outcome.

## Design

This phase lasts about two to three weeks and can overlap with the scope phase. The following activities are done at this stage:

- Prepare the business blueprinting document.
- Document the models that need to be created under different components of Business Data Cloud, their relevance to the POC, and the logic to implement them. The logic is not necessarily written in a specific technical language, but it can be explained using a block diagram, a decision chain, or simply an Excel file with the source and target field's relationship.
- At the end of the design phase, all the technical documents need to be signed off on by the customer architect or IT owner or project sponsor.

## Build

This phase generally lasts about four weeks, and during this period, the following tasks will be executed:

- All major developments are done.
- Unit testing of the artifacts is executed.
- Data loading to perform further testing.

## Testing

This phase lasts about three weeks, and during this period the following tasks are performed:

- Test the new product with production-like data.
- Compare the result from the new reports with existing reports for a specific criterion.
- Performance test to make sure that the report/dashboard and all the functionalities are running within an acceptable limit. A complex report execution with a large volume of data can be considered

within the acceptable limit if they take no more than one minute. Smaller reports, planning tasks, and jump reports should be executed within 5 to 10 seconds.

- Stress test to make sure that the source database is not overstressed during multiple parallel jobs or remote query runs.

## Environment Preparation

This phase lasts about one week, and during this time the following activities are performed:

- Do a one-time data migration for the replicated flows. This can be based on a time period and/or values of certain fields (for example, profit center or country, etc.).
- Clean up any test data that exists during the unit testing.
- Reload master data, text, and hierarchies to make it up to date.
- Make any data corrections.
- Set up users for the demonstration activities.

## Demonstration

This is performed for about one week (one to two hours a day), and during this phase the following activities are performed:

- Conduct a kick-off session that clearly highlights the agenda for the next five days when the demo will be conducted.
- The first three days are typically reserved for the demo, and the next two days are for acquiring the feedback and finalizing the next step.
- Document all the outcomes and feedback in a clear and actionable format.
- Prepare a change request list that can be used as an input for the next phase of the project.

### 8.2.3 Next Steps

As there are many stakeholders involved in such project and everyone will have their own point of view and interest, it is difficult to come to a common conclusion in only one meeting. Therefore, it should not be attempted. However, the following points should be discussed and agreed on before all stakeholders confirm that the POC project can be formally closed.

#### Documentation

Ensure that all documents are correctly placed and all modifications/updates are done in the documents that might have changed during the project. In other words, the documents written during the design phase must capture all the changes made to the objects based on the testing outcome.

#### Feedback Analysis

All feedback gathered during the demonstration should be documented in an actionable format, and the complexity/time needed to perform such change must be categorized in a high-medium-low scale.

#### Efforts

Get a go-ahead to start the full system assessment and prepare a study on the manpower needed to complete such changes.

#### Pros and Cons

All the limitations, product bugs, dependencies, etc., should be captured. These are lessons learned during the POC.

## 8.3 Outcome of the POC

Now when the POC is officially closed, let's see what can be done next. POCs are generally executed to prove certain pre-agreed points. These are some of the blockers in the path of the execution based on the anticipation of the sponsor or IT head. A successful POC means that all these blockers either removed or a viable alternative is found during the execution. All these points help to steer the discussion on the next step.

The next step of the project generally requires the following information for analysis:

- Overall sizing requirements
- One-time server procurement cost, recurring maintenance cost and licensing cost
- Implementation cost from the service providers
- Run cost after implementation
- User training requirements
- Any other alternative program for which the ongoing decisions can contradict the existence of this product
- Number of users required to be set up
- How the current and new components will co-exist for some time
- What the risks are to the BAU processes
- Any uncertainty due to S/4 HANA implementation on the ERP side
- Any component that is approaching end of service or end of life that has a direct or indirect impact on this implementation
- The disaster recovery process
- What will happen during the implementation phase where there is a new change request that has to be immediately worked upon from the BAU process
- How soon the next phase can be started, assuming all the financial approvals are in place, and how long it will take for the entire project to complete followed by the decommissioning of the old servers and/or products

## 8.4 Test Your Knowledge

Q1: What activity is not done during the Environment Preparation Phase?

a) Clean up old data

b) Perform a one-time load

c) Configure the tenant

d) Set up the users

Q2: Why is proof of concept useful in analytics modernization?

a) It can help to perform a feasibility check on an approach.

b) It can find out product limitations.

c) It can help to assess the estimation of the entire implementation.

d) All of the above.

Q3: All system (SAP and non-SAP) connectivity is generally a scope of POC.

a) True

b) False

Q4: Datasphere can be used as a pass-through solution without any replication.

a) True

b) False

Q5: Which one of the following should not be part of the demo kick-off session?

a) Planned agenda discussion for the entire demo period

b) Solution overview

c) Detailed design overview including the pseudo logic, metadata, loading methodology, naming conventions, etc.

d) None of the above

Q6: A batch job schedule for updating data is generally considered out of scope from the POC.

a) True

b) False

Q7: It is usually beneficial to keep the POC execution period short because of the following reasons.

a) To keep the cost controlled

b) To generate quick results

c) To onboard resources quickly

d) Both a and b

## 8.5 Summary

In this chapter, you learned about planning the POC, scope, and deliverables. You also learned how to plan for the next steps.

Once the pilot project is successful, it provides an enormous number of data points on the feasibility of a larger implementation, blockers, and pros and cons. It is often too hard to run a full implementation on a complex product; therefore, a robust project management plan and technique will be required to avoid delivery slippage.

In the next chapter, you will learn about the project management aspects while handling the full implementation.

## CHAPTER 9

# Project Planning

Planning for the end-to-end implementation including decommissioning the old server/product is not an easy task. It requires a careful assessment of the cost and the scoping before you can proceed. The project sponsor is generally looking for the costs incurred and the benefits obtained by the process so that a fair idea about the return on investment can be obtained.

Usually, an assessment is performed first on the landscape. The aim is to understand the different aspects that will help to decide the implementation path. Some of these parameters are as follows:

**Objects in scope:** This includes data flow, master data, and connectivity/data exchange with all components and outbound services.

**User requirements:** This is the role-specific categorization of the users and the activities performed by each one of them. Products like SAC planning comes with a very expensive license; therefore, an optimum level of agreement is required between the business users and IT users to make sure that the costs are controlled.

**Reports in scope:** A full implementation gives an excellent opportunity to get rid of unnecessary reports, merge reports, and create new versions of the reports for the cleanup.

**New functionalities:** Some of the pain areas, flaws in the calculations, etc., can be reviewed and made in scope for the new implementation. New functionalities like automating certain manual tasks, automatic reconciliation, etc., can also be assessed against the current system landscape.

**Data migration:** An agreement with the users to limit the data to be transferred during the setup of the system can be obtained by discussing this with the end users and IT stakeholders.

**User training:** User training is needed after the implementation of the new tool to make the user community aware of how to perform certain tasks, become familiar with the navigation processes, etc.



© Sourav Banerjee 2025
S. Banerjee, *Modernizing SAP Business Warehouse*, https://doi.org/10.1007/979-8-8688-2192-9_9

**Outbound interfaces:** Assess the current outbound services to help plan the next phase, where the push mechanism can be established from Datasphere.

**AI/ML-related applications:** On top of the existing functionalities, it is good to identify a few cases where a machine learning capability or AI agent can be created to perform tasks that are manual in nature or to create a predictive scenario. One important implementation would be with SAP Joule, which can be used to automate planning-related tasks.

**Timeline and estimation:** Based on the previous points, you can estimate the number of days of effort required to complete the project along with the feasible timeline.

**Decommissioning strategy:** A clear path of decommissioning is prepared so you can provide important details like the phased approach, dependency check, where used list, etc. This need to be listed clearly along with the action that can be taken to decommission the server successfully.

**Resource investments:** It is very important to make sure that the key resources that worked in the POC are retained during the actual implementation. This is not always possible, especially when the implementation decision is significantly delayed after the completion of the POC.

**Change request from the POC:** There are several change requests based on the feedback received in sessions. They are nice-to-have features as mentioned by different users. They should be assessed in detail during this phase, and the efforts required should be added to the overall effort.

**Risk identification:** Before the start of the project, all risks that are open from the POC and the new risk identified during the assessment should be documented and categorized. A well-defined action plan for them is useful to add the contingency to the overall estimation and project planning process.

**User availability:** Users must be available during the initial phase (requirement gathering) and during the user acceptance testing. It is generally seen that there are many dependencies because it would be difficult to get most of the key users in a single platform even with adequate advanced notice. The following are the main reasons:

- Holiday period (like Christmas, bank holidays, Easter, etc.)
- During the month-end where most finance users are busy
- During the quarter-end
- During year-end

- Due to planned leaves
- Due to irregular availability every week (for example, some users do not work on Fridays)
- Choice of office working day in hybrid model (some users come only one day in the week to office and the rest of the days work from home)
- Business travel plans for some of the superusers
- Plans to visit events like SAP Sapphire, etc.

Although this is not a full list of activities performed before the start of the project, it will at least help to create a high-level plan of execution and the factors that drive it.

# 9.1 Prerequisites

There are several pre-requisites before the project can be started. They are items that must be met before the project execution starts. They can be technical or process related in nature.

## 9.1.1 SAP Analytics Cloud Licenses

SAP Analytics Cloud gives several licensing options, but it is useful to know which license is for what purpose. There are three different types of licenses available: SAP Analytics Cloud for Business Intelligence Predictive Edition, SAP Analytics Cloud for Planning Predictive Standard Edition, and SAP Analytics Cloud for Planning, Predictive Professional Edition.

**Subscription-Based Model**

A subscription-based model will have the following features:

- Any of the three license types can be used.
- A digital boardroom is an add-on to the existing license types.
- Only one tenant can be procured.
- There is no limitation on the contract duration.

### Consumption-Based Model

A consumption-based model will have the following features:

- The free plan has a fixed limit of six SAP Analytics Cloud for Business Intelligence Predictive Editions, one SAP Analytics Cloud for Planning Predictive Professional Edition, and two SAP Analytics Cloud for Planning, Predictive Standard Editions.
- The test plan has a minimum requirement of 20 test licenses.
- The production plan has a minimum requirement of 25 Analytics Cloud for business intelligence, Predictive Editions.

  or

  One *SAP Analytics Cloud* for Planning Predictive Professional Edition and 10 *SAP Analytics Cloud* for Planning Predictive Standard Edition
- The free plan will have a 90-day period, whereas the test and production systems will not have any limitations.

Table 9-1 shows the detailed comparison of the licenses along with the activities that are permitted.

We will use the following synonyms:

- SAP Analytics Cloud for business intelligence, Predictive Edition as "A"
- SAP Analytics Cloud for planning, Predictive Professional Edition as "C"
- SAP Analytics Cloud for planning, Predictive Standard Edition as "B"

***Table 9-1.*** *Different SAC Licenses*

| Features | "A" | "B" | "C" |
|---|---|---|---|
| Maintain Analytical model | X | X | X |
| Hierarchies | X | X | X |
| Data Export API | X | X | X |
| Data Import API | | X | X |
| User, role and team administration | X | | X |
| Read change log | X | | X |
| Create Story | X | X | X |
| Create and view value driver tree | X | X | X |
| Linked analysis | X | X | X |
| Calculate Dimension | X | X | X |
| Currency field | X | X | X |
| Maintain analytic application | X | X | X |
| Smart Predict | X | X | X |
| Smart Insight | X | X | X |
| Smart Discovery | X | X | X |
| R-Visualization | X | X | X |
| Maintain Planning model | | | X |
| View planning model | X | X | X |
| Create versions | X | X | X |
| Data Entry | X (only private version) | X | X |
| Data Entry on unbooked value | | X | X |
| Create Dimension member from table | | X | X |
| Maintain Data locks | | X | X |
| Maintain Data Actions and allocations | | | X |
| Run Data Actions | | X | X |

(*continued*)

***Table 9-1.*** *(continued)*

| Features | "A" | "B" | "C" |
|---|---|---|---|
| Run Multiactions | | X | X |
| Run Allocation | | X | X |
| Enter information on input tasks | | X | X |
| Distribute values with the planning panel | | X | X |
| Currency conversion | X (only view) | X | X |
| Run value driver simulation | X (Private versions) | X | X |
| Publish Simulation | | X | X |
| Add comments to table data cell | X | X | X |
| Create connection SAC to BPC | | | X |

## 9.1.2 Datasphere Capacity Unit Calculation

It is generally tricky to arrive at a conclusive number in terms of the capacity unit when the Datasphere assessment needs to be done. The capacity unit is measured based on the capacity services available.

There are many options to choose from to get the final capacity unit value. See Figure 9-1.

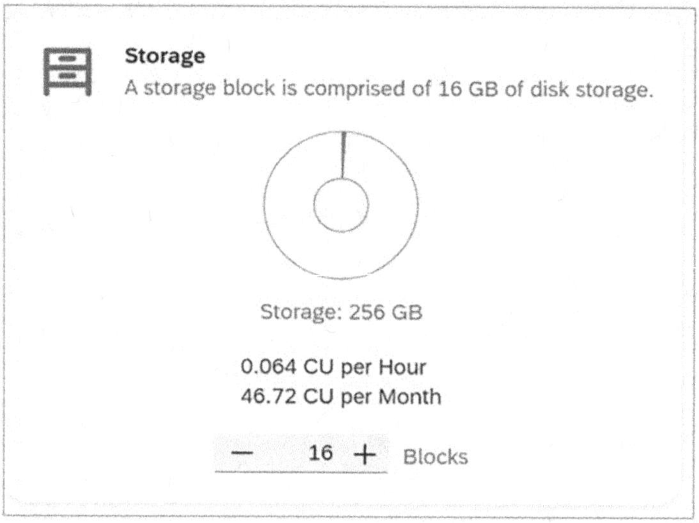


***Figure 9-1.*** *Storage calculation: Datasphere*

See Figure 9-1 explains the total storage block, and each block consists of 16 GB storage. In Figure 9-1, 16 blocks are used for a total of 256 GB of storage. If more storage capacity is required, then the number of blocks needs to be increased. See Figure 9-2.

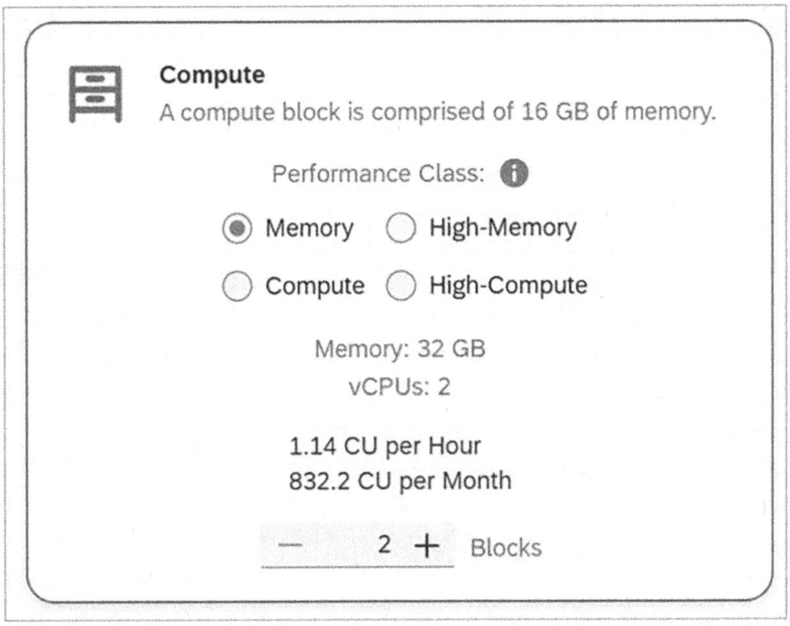


***Figure 9-2.** Compute for Datasphere*

A compute block will have four performance class options:

*Memory:*

This option requires 32 GB of memory and two vCPUs with a minimum of two blocks of compute, and each block has a capacity of 16 GB of memory.

*High-Memory*:

This option requires 3776 GB of memory and 120 vCPUs with a minimum of 236 blocks of compute, and each block has a capacity of 16 GB memory.

*Compute:*

This option requires 32 GB memory and four vCPUs with a minimum of two blocks of compute, and each block has a capacity of 16 GB memory.

*High-Compute:*

This option requires 32 GB of memory and eight vCPUs with a minimum of two blocks of compute, and each block has a capacity of 16 GB of memory.

For the increasing compute requirements, a high number of vCPUs will be required.

The BW Bridge component requires at least 128 GB of storage capacity. In Figure 9-3, it is disabled because the minimum storage is not there in the calculation screen.

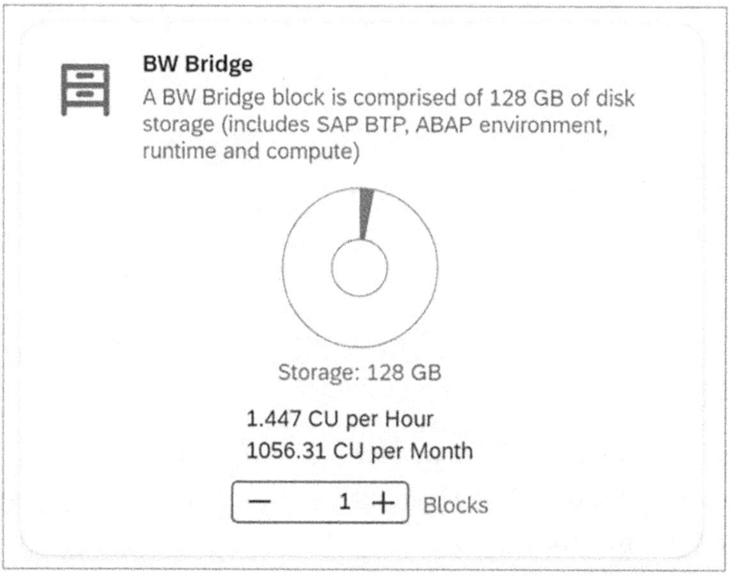


***Figure 9-3.*** *BW Bridge calculation for Datasphere*

If this is required, then first the storage space should be increased to 128 GB. In the memory section, increase the memory blocks to 8 so that the memory will be 128 GB. Then the option for BW Bridge will be enabled. Increase the blocks based on the need.

See Figure 9-4.

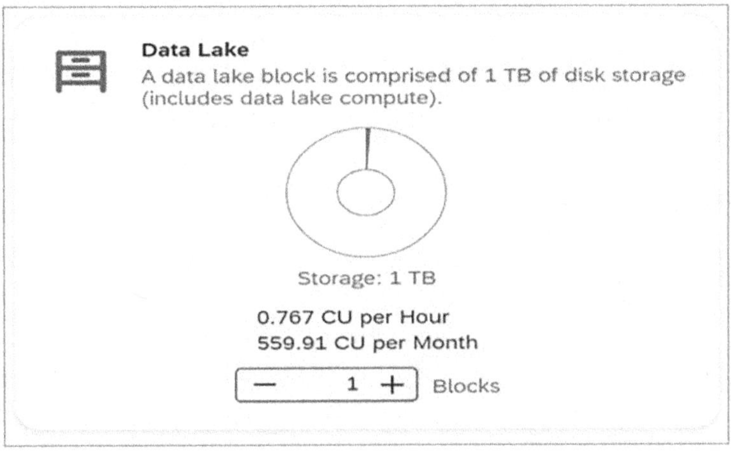


***Figure 9-4.*** *Data lake calculation for Datasphere*

A data lake comes with 1 TB storage capacity per block, and a minimum of one block is required. This includes the compute engine within the Data Lake architecture.

See Figure 9-5.

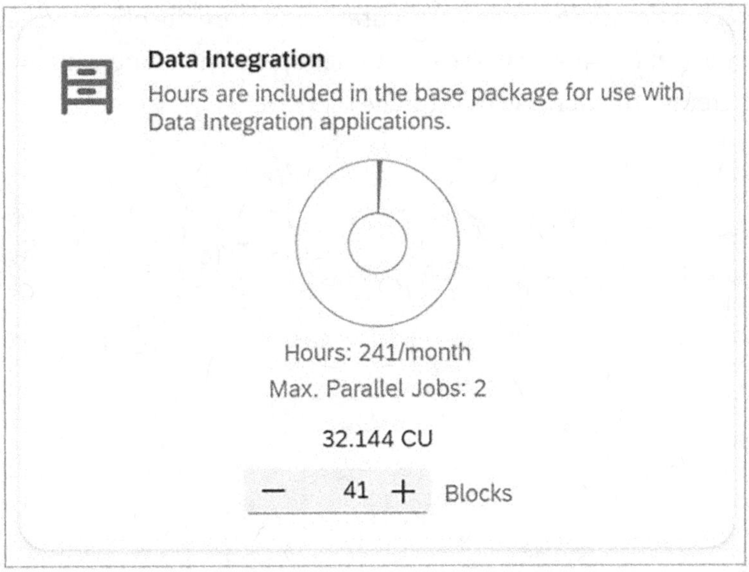


***Figure 9-5.*** *Data integration calculation for Datasphere*

By default, 200 hours/month of integration hours are included in the base package. But this can be increased based on the requirements. Here one block is the same as one extra hour of integration per month. By default, the maximum number of parallel jobs is two; it increased after every 100 additional hours/month. For example, if the integration hours is estimated as 100/month, then the number of parallel jobs will automatically increase to 3.

See Figure 9-6.

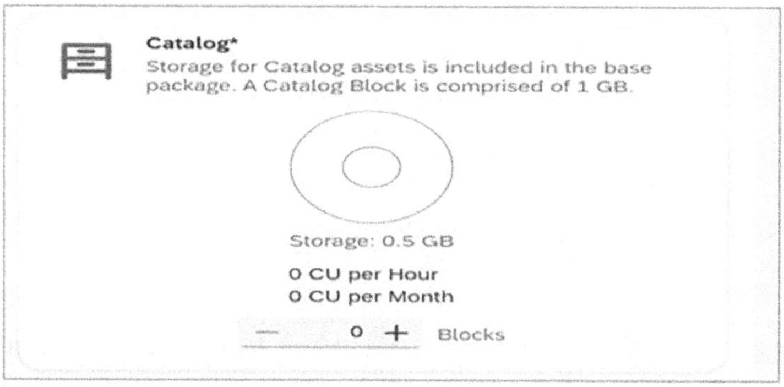


***Figure 9-6.*** *Catalog for Datasphere*

The catalog is a process to categorize, curate, and store the objects of similar business relevance at one place; 0.5 GB of storage space will come with the base plan. Every block increase will increase the storage by 1 GB.

See Figure 9-7.

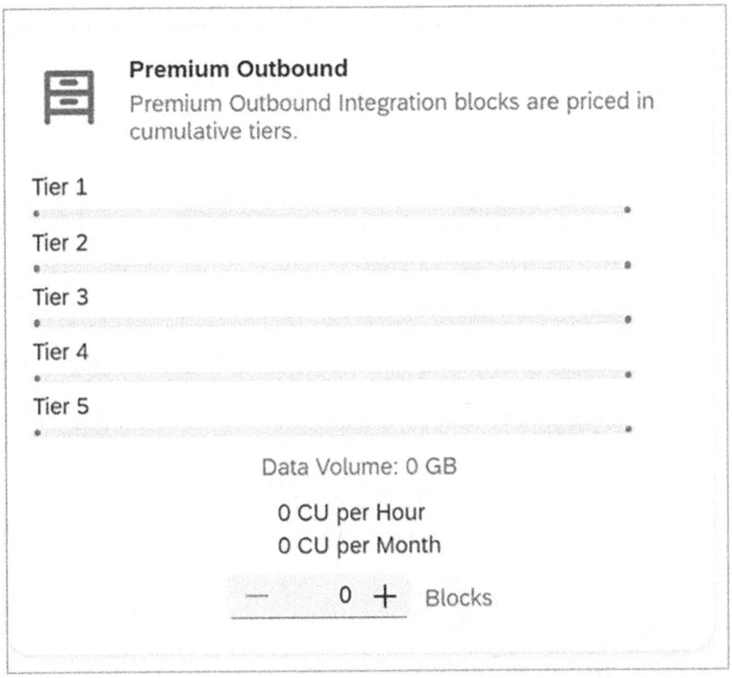


***Figure 9-7.*** *Premium outbound calculation for Datasphere*

The premium outbound service is priced based on tiers:

- Tier 1 is up to 10 blocks (i.e., 200 GB of data volume).
- Tier 2 is from 11 to 25 blocks (i.e., 300 GB of data volume).
- Tier 3 is from 26 to 50 blocks (i.e., 500 GB of data volume).
- Tier 4 is from 51 to 100 blocks (i.e., 1000 GB of data volume).
- Tier 5 is above 100 blocks of data volume.

For any non-SAP replication, we need a premium outbound service. If the outbound service quota is exceeded, the outbound service will be stopped, and further replication is no longer possible. This is the reason why the potential data volume measurement should be done as accurately as possible to avoid disruption in the service.

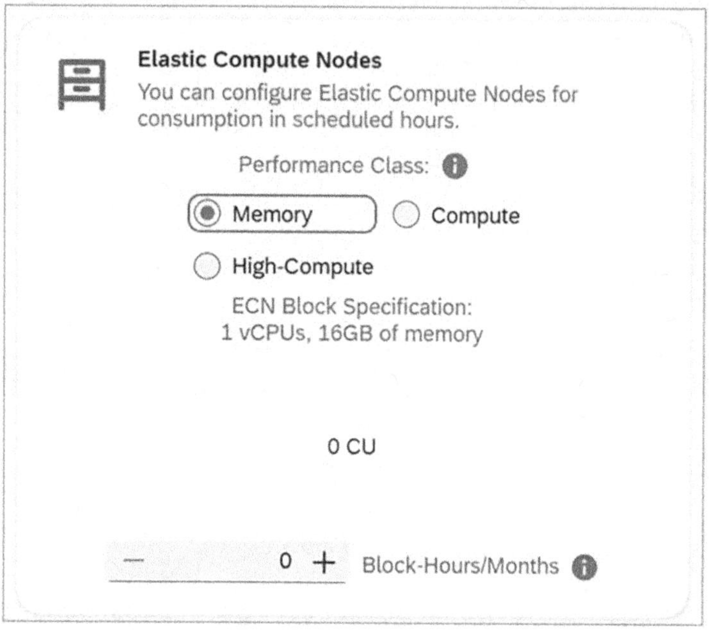


***Figure 9-8.*** *Elastic Compute nodes for Datasphere*

The minimum memory requirement for this service is 128 GB. Without this much memory, you can't make change to the blocks shown in Figure 9-8. There are three memory classes:

- Memory: One block requires one vCPU and 16 GB of memory.
- Compute: One block requires two vCPUs and 16 GB of memory.
- High-Compute: One block requires four vCPUs and 16 GB of memory.

Each block increase will increase the capacity units by 5.952. See Figure 9-9.

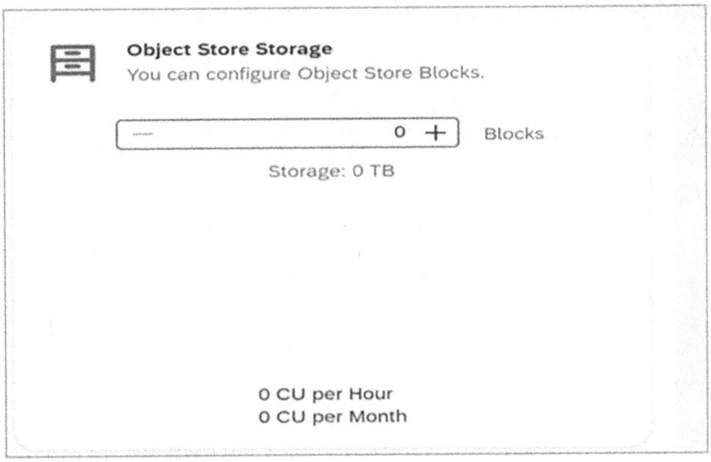


***Figure 9-9.** Object store for Datasphere*

The object store storage capacity is identified by each block equaling 1 TB of storage.

## 9.1.3 SAP Analytics Cloud Capacity Unit Calculation

Unlike Datasphere, the SAP Analytics Cloud capacity unit is calculated based on the number of users. See Figure 9-10.

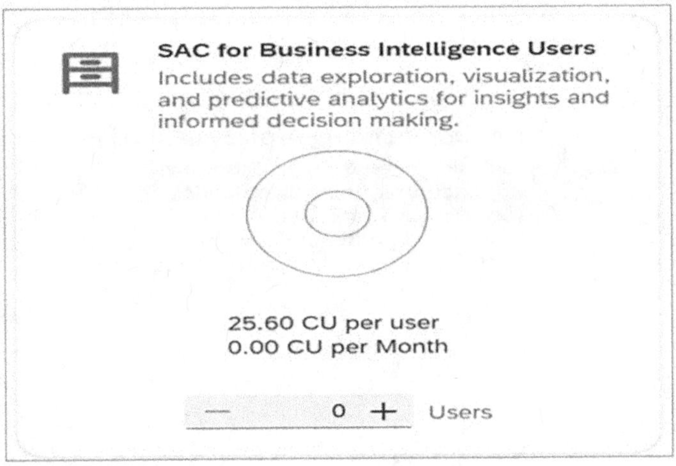


***Figure 9-10.** SAC-BI calculation*

The number of business intelligence users can perform most of the visualization tasks. The minimum number of users that can be procured is 25, with 640 capacity units per month. After that, for every increase in the number of users, the capacity unit will increase by 25.60 per month. See Figure 9-11.

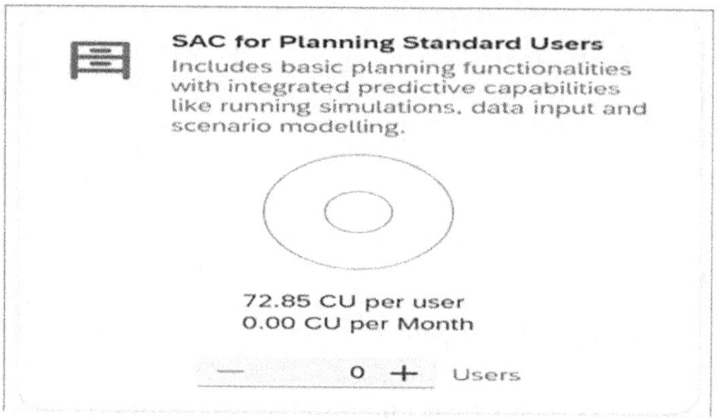


***Figure 9-11.*** *SAC planning standard calculation*

Planning Standard users can execute most of the planning tasks, but they are not able to create planning models. A minimum of 10 users need to be procured with 728.5 capacity units per month, after which every increase in the number of users will increase the capacity units by 72.85 capacity units per month.

See Figure 9-12.

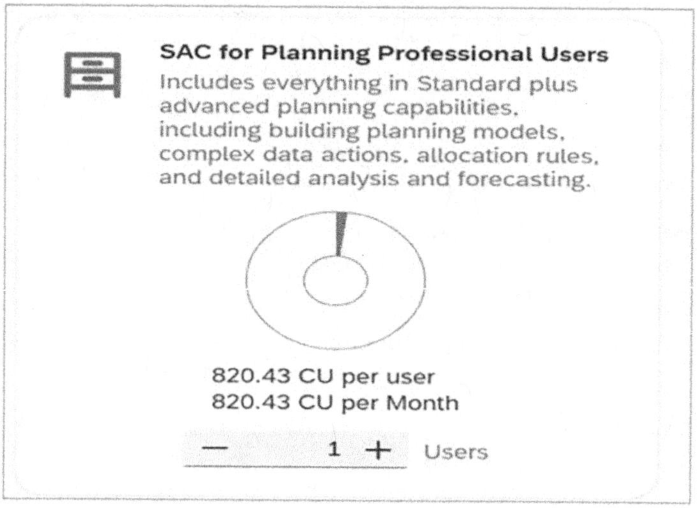


***Figure 9-12.*** *SAC planning professional calculation*

Planning Professional users can perform all the changes in planning-relevant objects, including creating and deleting them. A minimum of one user needs to be procured (along with 10 planning standard) with 820.43 capacity units per month, after which every user increase will raise the capacity units by 820.43 capacity units per month.

See Figure 9-13.

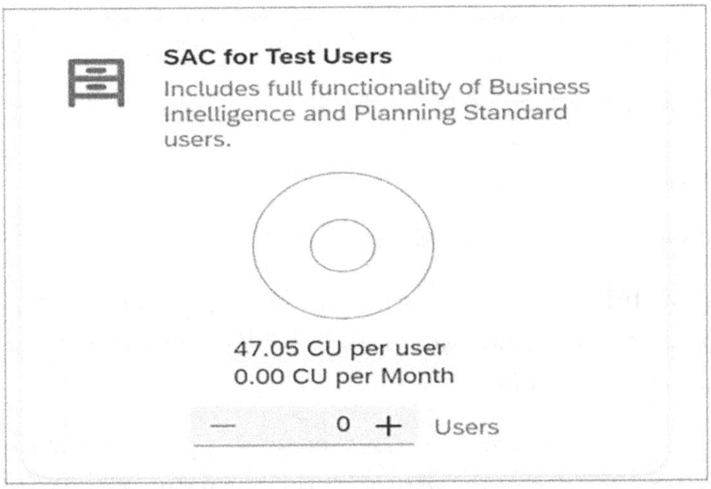


***Figure 9-13.** SAC for test user calculations*

A minimum of 20 users must be procured with 941 capacity units per month, after which every increase in the number of users will increase the capacity units by 47.05 per month. Test users will have full access to the analytics and planning services with the exception that they can't create or modify any planning models (i.e., similar to planning standard access).

## 9.1.4 SAP Databricks Capacity Unit Calculation

The SAP Databricks capacity unit calculation is different from that of the other components of Business Data Cloud. See Figure 9-14.

| Service | Quantity | | Capacity Units (Promotion)[1] | Capacity Units (Standard) |
|---|---|---|---|---|
| Automated Serverless Compute | 1 | DBU | 0.54 | 0.89 |
| Public Connectivity Data Processed | 1 | GB | 0.06 | 0.1 |
| Private Connectivity Endpoint | 1 | Hours | 0.02 | 0.03 |
| SAP Databricks Storage | 1 | DSU | 0.03 | 0.05 |
| Inter-Availability Zone Egress | 1 | GB | 0.02 | 0.02 |
| Inter-Region Egress From | 1 | GB | 0.03 | 0.04 |
| Interactive Serverless Compute | 1 | DBU | 1.07 | 1.78 |

***Figure 9-14.*** *SAP Databricks calculation*

Figure 9-14 shows the following services:

*Automated Serverless Compute:*

Each Databricks unit uses 0.54 capacity units per month during the promotional period (until April 2026) and after that 0.89 capacity units per month.

*Public Connectivity Data Processed*: For each gigabyte of data, 0.06 capacity units per month are used during the promotional period and after that it's 0.1 capacity units per month.

*Private Connectivity Endpoint*: For every hour of connectivity 0.02 capacity units per month during promotional period, after which it is 0.03 capacity units per month.

*SAP Databricks storage:* For every Databricks storage unit, 0.03 capacity units per month are used during the promotional period, after which it is 0.05 capacity units per month.

*Inter-Availability Zone Egress*: For every gigabyte, 0.02 capacity units per month are used during the promotional period, and then it's 0.02 capacity units per month.

*Inter-Region Egress From*: For each gigabyte, 0.03 capacity units per month are used during the promotional period post, and then it's 0.04 capacity units per month.

*Interactive Serverless Compute*: For each Databricks unit, 1.07 capacity units per month are used during the promotional period, and then it's 1.78 capacity units per month.

Figure 9-15 shows the following services:

*Internet Egress From:*

For each gigabyte, 0.1 capacity units per month are used during the promotional period, after which it changes to 0.16 capacity units per month.

*Model Serving*:

For each Databricks unit, 0.09 capacity units per month are used during the promotional period, after which it changes to 0.15 capacity units per month.

*Model Training:*

For each Databricks unit, 0.84 capacity units per month are used during the promotional period, after which it changes to 1.39 capacity units per month.

*Private Connectivity Data Processed:*

For each gigabyte, 0.02 capacity units per month are used during the promotional period, after which it changes to 0.02 capacity units per month.

*Serverless SQL Compute*:

For each Databricks unit, 0.97 capacity units are used per month during the promotional period, after which it changes to 1.62 capacity units per month.

*Enhanced Security and Compliance:*

If this option is enabled (optional), then 0.56 capacity units per month are used during the promotional period, after which it changes to 0.94 capacity units per month.

*SAP Object Store for SAP Databricks:*

For each terabyte of space, 0.11 capacity units per month are used during the promotional period, after which it changes to 0.11 capacity units per month.

*SAP Object Store request for SAP Databricks:*

For each API call, 0.03 capacity units per month are used during the promotional period, after which it changes to 0.03 capacity units per month.

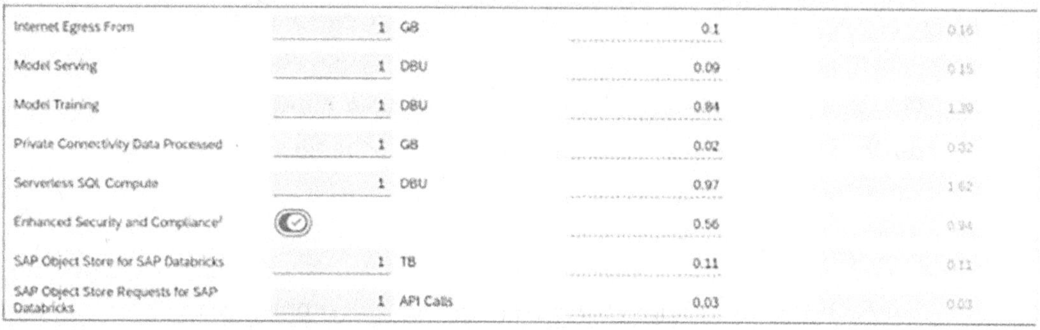

| | | | | |
|---|---|---|---|---|
| Internet Egress From | 1 | GB | 0.1 | 0.16 |
| Model Serving | 1 | DBU | 0.09 | 0.15 |
| Model Training | 1 | DBU | 0.84 | 1.39 |
| Private Connectivity Data Processed | 1 | GB | 0.02 | 0.32 |
| Serverless SQL Compute | 1 | DBU | 0.97 | 1.62 |
| Enhanced Security and Compliance[1] | | | 0.56 | 0.94 |
| SAP Object Store for SAP Databricks | 1 | TB | 0.11 | 0.11 |
| SAP Object Store Requests for SAP Databricks | 1 | API Calls | 0.03 | 0.03 |

***Figure 9-15.*** *SAP Databricks calculation (continued)*

Note that any change in the capacity unit calculation can happen at any time, and it is purely SAP AG's decision.

# 9.2 Assessment for Scoping

Analyzing the scoping is a critical activity, because the accuracy determines the success criteria of the project. An initial scoping was performed previously on the proof of concept. That was a small exercise performed on only some objects. A detailed assessment requires an understanding of the holistic view of the landscape as this assessment decides what objects will be migrated, and eventually what is left will be decommissioned.

The following are the steps for the assessment period (this can be executed as part of the project in the name of due diligence, or it can be performed as an individual activity outside the project window):

**End-to-End Architecture**

The architecture from the analytics perspective is only a subset of the entire ecosystem. During this study the following points to be investigated:

*How the data is flowing to the source systems?*

For example, Datasphere or SAP Business Warehouse may receive the data from an S/4 HANA system. But there could be a third-party system that pushes data into

S/4 HANA. For example, in some landscapes, the vendor management or sales quotes are performed using a different tool outside SAP landscape. That data flows into S/4 HANA bidirectionally to maintain consistency. Such master data is not up-to-date in S/4 HANA. Therefore, making S/4 HANA the source system won't allow Datasphere to get the full picture. In such cases, the data into Datasphere must also flow from that third-party system. A feasibility check is required to see if a connection can be possible. Sometimes middleware can push data into the Datasphere HDI container for further consumption.

*Are additional layers or products used within the existing analytics ecosystem?*

In such cases, a decision needs to be made whether to decommission those components. It may happen that the additional layer is introduced to deal with a product limitation. Those scenarios should be evaluated based on the capability of Business Data Cloud and should be eliminated if possible.

*How planning is done at present?*

Are there systems that receive the data after planning? For example, in some cases the consolidation data moves back to the S/4 HANA system. This data copy requires a push from the planning engine into the S/4 HANA system.

*Reporting tool choices*

What reports are shown using SAP products, and what ones are using non-SAP (Power BI, for example)? A decision needs to be made on whether the customer want to go ahead with this process in the future.

**Master Data Management**

Master data management is one of the most critical activities, especially for the financial planning applications. It is useful to understand if this is an IT task or it can also be performed by users directly. Although most master data flows from sources directly, there are a few (lookup tables, allocation tables, master data that exists only in OLAP, etc.) that needs a maintenance process to be established. Manual maintenance can be exposed to the users through SAP Analytics Cloud planning forms. Also, it is useful to know whether the master data is time dependent or not. In some cases, source master data tables do not store the history, and therefore pushing the data in BW or Datasphere with a time dependency includes duplicating the data at the time of loading.

In some scenarios, hierarchies are also manually maintained, which then can be decided based on the source of the hierarchy and the target architecture. If the hierarchy is created in SAP Analytics Cloud, then it can be edited there even by the superuser with right privileges. If this is something that is created and managed by Datasphere, then the change is not possible from SAP Analytics Cloud, even if it is exposed there. In such cases, only the IT team can change it based on the request. An alternative would be to get the hierarchy updated through a flat file load, which can be done from Datasphere, and the control can be given to the users (by writing a CLI command and calling it from SAP Analytics Cloud API under "Multi-action").

**Authorization Framework**

It is useful to know what level of access is given to users. You can divide this into two parts: the access on the SAP reporting tool (SAP Business Warehouse) and the access on Power BI (as an example).

Generally, SAP Business Warehouse uses analysis authorization for row-level security. This framework works by identifying the authorization-relevant objects and creating analysis authorizations by adding the value of those fields in simple (values) or complex (hierarchy nodes) ways. Then the authorizations are added to roles, which are eventually added to a group role (called *composite roles*). A similar set of users are added to those group roles to get their access assigned. In BW queries, authorization variables are used to pass the value of the authorization from the user profile into the field's input. This is how the framework generally works.

This assessment gives an opportunity to rethink the authorization process that needs to be activated for Business Data Cloud.

**Data Migration**

This topic will receive input from the sizing analysis. This will ensure that the data migrated must be able to be contained within the Datasphere tenant. If ERP was recently migrated to S/4 HANA, then the volume of the data would be less because only one item is migrated during the ERP migration.

If we think holistically, then there could be the possibility that years and years of data exists in the ERP databases and are not archived. So, there could be two routes available:

1. Data migrated from SAP Business Warehouse
2. Data migrated from SAP S/4 HANA or ECC

There are many questions that need to be answered before the Data Migration strategy is finalized:

*Question 1:* What are the functional areas for which the data needs to be migrated?

*Question 2:* Can master data be made virtual? This means there is no data to be migrated. This could create a potential performance impact that needs to be assessed.

*Question 3:* If there are very large tables like CDHDR or if CDPOS is required, then can a subset be implemented? If not, then it will have to perform a replication on regular interval.

*Question 4:* How many years of data must be available in the reports that will be used frequently? The rest of the data can be made virtual as they are not frequently accessed and the penalty in performance is acceptable.

*Question 5:* What is the data retention period for some of the data that does not have much business relevance?

*Question 6:* What is the retention period for the staging data when the data moves through multiple layers?

*Question 7:* What is the frequency of each data loading?

## 9.3 How to Plan

Planning the entire implementation is the next step after the scoping exercise is completed. This means now the project sponsor will have a decent idea about the manpower needed and the cost of database procurement with licenses. At this stage, it is necessary to produce the overall timeline for the implementation. While creating the plan, one must look at the budget and estimated days to achieve a balance between the two.

### Project Plan

A project plan should clearly show the overall timeline and intermediate milestones. There are two options:

a) Perform the complete migration as a project and decommissioning BW as a follow-up project.

b) Perform the migration and decommissioning as a single project.

Both of these approaches will have pros and cons.

If both projects are executed at the same time, it would be most cost effective to have the same team will work on them. Therefore, the knowledge will be retained within the project.

It is a drawback if the decommissioning piece will not have enough time to be designed and execute. As it is toward the end of the entire project, stakeholders may be in hurry and push to reduce the overall staffing. This will have significant impact on the quality of the delivery.

If the projects are executed one after another, then the decommissioning project will have more design, contingency, and enthusiasm to start, which will help to maintain the quality of the deliveries.

The drawback would be that the consultants who worked on the migration may not be available for this work. Generally, a gap of at least one to two months is required to plan for the next phase in terms of documentation, earlier project closure, budget approval, resource onboarding, etc. So, it might not be feasible to keep the old team alive without any significant work.

From a delivery perspective, the following phases are executed:

**Due Diligence**

Time required: One month

Goal:

- To identify the gaps in the system where the new product may not be able to address the existing functionalities
- To list all the required objects, data flows, interfaces, and reports
- To identify which objects can be decommissioned or merged with other objects
- To get all the requirements (including nice-to-have ones)

Deliverables:

- Assessment report on the system
- Business blueprint document
- Scope list
- User stories

**Design**

Time required: One to two months

Goal:

- To prepare end-to-end architectural scenarios
- To identify new objects, name, metadata, mappings
- To perform connectivity with the source and target systems
- To define an authorization framework

Deliverables:

- Architectural diagram
- Technical specification
- Mapping documents

**Development**

Time required: Three to four months (based on the system complexity)

Goal:

- To create all new objects in the new tool
- To perform unit testing

Deliverables:

- Test scripts
- Test evidence

**System Integration Testing**

Time required: Two months based on the complexity

Goal:

- To be able to test the end-to-end scenario
- To perform a complete data load from the source
- To test the outbound interfaces

Deliverables:

- SIT script
- Test evidence
- UAT test script

**User Acceptance Testing**

Time required: One to two months based on user availability

Goal:

- To help the user perform the test
- To fix bugs
- To support a real-time data scenario and user training

Deliverables:

- User handbook on the new solution and product
- Bug fixing documents
- Feedback report

**Go-live and Hypercare**

Time required: One to two months

Goal:

- To make the new product available for production scenarios
- To provide support to the user post implementation
- To monitor the aging queries and inflow of queries

Deliverables:

- Ticket monitoring report
- Go-live communication

**Decommissioning**

Time required: Three months

Goal: To retire BW and any other relevant component

Deliverables: Scope versus delivered report, old versus new functionality report

# 9.4 Post-implementation

After the successful implementation, the next step is to estimate the run cost. In most cases, the implementation partner does not provide support after the hypercare. In such cases, a careful examination of what was delivered is measured, and then only the run cost can be given.

The following questions are typically asked of the implementation partner during the support handover:

- Object list that was migrated
- Functional specification of all dataflow and objects
- Technical mapping documents
- Known error database
- Any high-priority incidents during the hyper case
- Architectural diagram
- Project kick-off and project closure documents
- Organizational structure
- Team composition of the implementation team
- Bug list during UAT and resolutions
- Ticket dump
- All process-related documents and access to the project management tools
- Enhancement requests during the hypercare
- Any open issues

**How to Assess the Effort**

The following items need to be assessed first within the team:

- Average ticket resolution rate of a consultant per month. This can be based on a combination of incidents and service requests.
- Number of tickets (priority wise) in each functional/technical area.

- Regular support process (for example, monitoring, file loading etc.).
- Average hours of enhancement needed per year.

Based on the previous assessment, the following formula can be used to arrive at a total support hours per area:

> = Number of tickets * average resolution SLA + Regular support hours + Average Enhancement Hours
>
> Number of resources can be identified based on the total effort / number of tickets that can be resolved by a consultant

Unlike an implementation project, run cost can be highlighted based on the number of resources required. In some cases, it is wise to put more resources at the beginning until the project is stabilized and eventually reduced to a lean team within six to eight months. Subsequent years, the number can be further reduced based on the following initiatives:

- Automating certain tasks that required manual efforts before
- Identifying recurring issues and providing a permanent resolution to reduce
- Providing self-service capabilities against tasks that require smaller efforts for example: password reset, role assignment, etc.
- Implementing artificial Intelligence to reduce efforts
- Making process improvements
- Replacing few senior members of the team with Junior members for less critical area
- Re-performing the check on the total ticket versus efforts spent to find out where there are under booking.
- Merging multiple teams into a bigger team

## 9.5 Test Your Knowledge

Q1: For model serving in SAP Databricks, during the promotional period, one DBU is equivalent to which of the following?

a) 0.1 CU

b) 0.2 CU

c) 0.8 CU

d) 0.9 CU

Q2: To reduce resources after the stabilization period, which of the following options can help?

a) Negotiating with customers

b) Rewriting the SoW

c) Employing contractors

d) Enabling AI

Q3: Decommissioning BW is not possible even after the migration to Business Data Cloud in all scenarios.

a) True

b) False

Q4: Which of the following licenses are possible in SAC?

a) Planning standard

b) Datasphere Advanced

c) Business Intelligence

d) Both a and b

e) Both a and c

Q5: How many test users must be procured in SAC?

a) 5

b) 10

c) 20

d) No limit

## 9.6 Summary

In this chapter, you learned about the planning process for a large implementation, including the prerequisites, step-by-step migration process, and timeline preparation.

## APPENDIX A

# Interesting Facts

As you embark on the journey to the cloud, you will find the tips and facts in this appendix will add more value to your day-to-day operations on BDC components.

**S/4 HANA transformations**

Customers moving toward S/4 HANA cloud/on-premises are interested in modernizing their analytics landscape. It gives them an opportunity to reshape their end-to-end business operations by updating the ERP and analytics ecosystem together to gain a unified view of their business processes.

**Fate of SAP BW**

SAP Business Warehouse standard support is guaranteed until 2040. There has been no announcement made about end of life, but there will be no major innovations planned on this product. With the launch of BDC, modern data warehousing shifted toward products like Datasphere. BW, however, will exist as one of the components to retain the investment that organizations have made over the past several years. Ideally, BW PCE should be used to get the best of both worlds as this will allow you to convert BW objects into a consumable data product that can be used seamlessly by the components of BDC such as SAP Databricks.

**Datasphere as pass-through solution**

Datasphere can also be simply used as a pass-through scenario without any storage in the server. For example, it can bring data from S/4 and push it to Azure Data Lake. For many customers who have a lot of SAP ERP data, it is often useful to use Datasphere to stream the data to a non-SAP environment for analytics purposes. The idea is not to store any data in Datasphere and therefore not consuming any storage space. The cost is kept as minimum, and SAP still owns the data transfer process.



© Sourav Banerjee 2025
S. Banerjee, *Modernizing SAP Business Warehouse*, https://doi.org/10.1007/979-8-8688-2192-9

**Performance during currency conversions**

The performance of a Datasphere view using the automatic currency conversion is very poor in the case of a large amount of data. Normally, a currency conversion requires conversion factors from multiple tables from the source side (for example, S/4 HANA). When the view shows the currency-converted values, internally all the remote tables are accessed multiple times (the number of converted measures times the number of tables). This can result in several performance penalties, especially when the access is virtual. It is highly recommended to persist the tables (usually a small number of entries) or replicate to a local table inside Datasphere.

**Delta management during BW Bridge migration**

During the remote migration of BW Bridge, subscription queues are automatically updated to allow the delta loading. For the data transfer, the DMIS add-on is required, which works via an SLT methodology. This is useful because organizations generally want to know if the data integrity is maintained after migration.

**BW Bridge or BW PCE?**

BW Bridge has limited functionality and is not to be confused with any other BW system. The functionalities that are not possible should be re-created using Datasphere modeling. One can think of BW Bridge as a gateway to convert to Datasphere. The aim should not be to use BW Bridge forever but to use it as a starting point, eventually moving everything to the cloud. Those who are still looking for full BW functionality can make use of BW PCE as part of BDC.

**Datasphere as storage for SAC**

During tenant linking, it is possible to specify Datasphere as the storage database for SAC planning. Seamless planning can use Datasphere as your data storage platform where most of your organization's data resides. The gives you full control of data, no duplication, and a trusted data platform. The SAC model stores the definition of the model and the metadata.

**Find planning models with Cloud connector in Datasphere**

If a cloud connector is used to integrate SAC and Datasphere, then only the alpha numeric ID of the planning models can be visible as a source within the connection. It can be found from the URL that opens the planning model. The connection typically provides access to the fact and dimension tables separately.

**Read only planning forms**

A table based on a planning model in SAC does not have to be input ready. There is an option to make the table read-only even if it is based on a planning-enabled model. This is often useful when you want the user to make some part of your data read-only based on specific criteria and sometimes give a toggle option. An input-ready form can be made read-only forcefully by writing JavaScript.

**Lock some vs. lock all**

It is possible to lock only a certain set of data within your planning model. This means that only selected data is locked, but other data in the same model can still be changeable. This is often useful when you want to protect part of the data from further changes while only a subset of the data is open for change.

**Synchronize SAC models in Datasphere**

For planning models created using data storage in Datasphere, all SAC artifacts will be read-only. This means it will not be possible to make changes to any objects from Datasphere. In such a scenario, the model can still be viewable from Datasphere. Any changes made to the SAC model can cascade to the Datasphere table by synchronizing the table, but no changes will be possible from Datasphere directly. This will ensure that no dual maintenance is required and SAC is still in control of the model definition.

**Joule for developers**

Joule can be used to generate coding in JavaScript for developers who have little or no knowledge in the area. For example, a developer or users who want to create a button to perform a certain planning task within a custom dashboard can simply ask Joule to generate the code for the operation, and Joule will generate the relevant code. This enhances the self-service capabilities and user experience on the product.

**Zero copy**

Delta sharing in an approach used by SAP Databricks within SAP Business Data Cloud. All data coming from BW or Datasphere can be directly consumed in SAP Databricks through delta sharing. This ensures that the data is shared but not copied. The sharing can be bidirectional.

**Unused Capacity Units**

Any unused capacity unit purchased for a particular month will not get carried forward to the next month and will eventually expire. This is an important point to be considered during the sizing assessment to ensure that you plan for the capacity more accurately to save run costs.

**SQL query for BDC connectivity**

The recipient can also be created in Databricks by writing a SQL query with the syntax Create Recipient. This is just an alternative way of performing Databricks operations within BDC.

**Smart Predict**

The prediction scenario in SAP Analytics Cloud is also known as "Smart Predict" and usually comes with SAC as built-in functionality. Prediction can be done using classification, regression, or time-series models. The outcome can be stored as a different dataset in SAC and later can be combined with the original dataset for robust reporting.

## APPENDIX B

# Test Your Knowledge: Answers

**Chapter 1: SAP BW and HANA Evolution**

Q1: What is the main reason to use Business Warehouse in any landscape?

a) As a middleware

b) As a data warehousing solution

c) As a reporting solution

d) For AI- and ML-related scenarios

Answer: b

Q2: Why is there a need to modernize BW?

a) Support is out to date

b) Need of pushing toward a cloud-based solution

c) Integration with other tools is not reliable or robust

d) All of the above

Answer: d

Q3: Which product is a potential replacement for integrated planning?

a) Datasphere

b) SAP BTP

c) Business Objects

d) SAP Analytics Cloud

Answer: d



© Sourav Banerjee 2025
S. Banerjee, *Modernizing SAP Business Warehouse*, https://doi.org/10.1007/979-8-8688-2192-9

Q4: Why is SAP's strategic vision to move to a cloud-based analytics solution?

a) To have customer-managed data products

b) To have SAP-managed data products

c) Both a and b

d) None of the above

Answer: b

Q5: What is the end of life for SAP Business Warehouse?

a) By the end of 2040

b) By the end of 2030

c) No date disclosed

d) None of the above

Answer: c

Q6: What is the full form of BW PCE?

a) Business Warehouse Public Cloud Enterprise

b) Business Warehouse Private Cloud Enterprise

c) Business Warehouse Public Cloud Edition

d) Business Warehouse Private Cloud Edition

Answer: d

Q7: Which one of the following is not an advantage of the HANA database?

a) In-memory architecture

b) Atomicity, consistency, isolation, and durability

c) High security firewall

d) None of the above

Answer: c

Q8: You should never write a SELECT on an intermediate table (scalar).

a) True

b) False

Answer: b

Q9: HANA always stores data in the disk memory.

a) True

b) False

Answer: b

Q10: Which of the following does not run on the HANA database?

a) SAP Datasphere

b) Business Object Data Services

c) SAP Analytical Cloud

d) All of the above

Answer: b

Q11: For conditional statements, IF-THEN-ELSE can be written within a SELECT statement.

a) True

b) False

Answer: b

Q12: HANA is always hosted on-premises.

a) True

b) False

Answer: b

Q13: The common function between SQL scripts and ABAP is that both can run operations on the entire table instead of running operations on each row.

a) True

b) False

Answer: b

## Chapter 2: Datasphere

Q1: Which one of the following is not a valid integration process between SAC and Datasphere?

a) OData Connection

b) Link Tenant

c) Cloud Connector

d) None of the above

Answer: d

Q2: BW can be decommissioned after migrating to BW Bridge.

a) True

b) False

Answer: a

Q3: The DMIS add-on is used during the shell conversion to BW Bridge.

a) True

b) False

Answer: b

Q4: Delta pointers are automatically updated after remote conversion to BW Bridge.

a) True

b) False

Answer: a

Q5: Fuzzy logic can be used within a data flow in Datasphere.

a) True

b) False

Answer: b

Q6: Which table is not required for currency conversion in Datasphere from SAP ECC or S/4 HANA?

a) TCURR

b) TCURN

c) TCURP

d) TCURF

Answer: c

Q7: ARIBA integration with Datasphere requires writing Groovy Script.

a) True

b) False

Answer: b

Q8: BW Bridge contains all the functionalities that an on-premise BW system can provide.

a) True

b) False

Answer: b

**Chapter 3: SAP Analytics Cloud (SAC)**

Q1: Tables created on planning relevant models can't be read-only.

a) True

b) False

Answer: b

Q2: A waterfall chart can only be vertical.

a) True

b) False

Answer: b

Q3: Which chart type can run without a dimension?

a) Waterfall

b) Bullet

c) Stacked area

d) Donut

Answer: d

Q4: A script in SAC is written in which language?

a) C++

b) SQL

c) JavaScript

d) Python

Answer: c

Q5: Which SAC event is triggered during the refresh of the story?

a) On Click

b) On Initialization

c) On Select

d) On Start

Answer: b

Q6: One story can have only one page.

a) True

b) False

Answer: b

Q7: Starter widgets are only used for the planning purposes.

a) True

b) False

Answer: a

Q7: A currency conversion table requires a time hierarchy in SAC.

a) True

b) False

Answer: b

**Chapter 4: SAC Planning and Datasphere**

Q1: Which one of the following is not a data exchange option between Datasphere and SAC?

a) CDI

b) OData Connection

c) Through Communication user

d) None of the above

Answer: c

Q2: Which dimension is mandatory to create a planning model?

a) Date

b) Year

c) Version

d) Both a and c

e) Both b and c

Answer: d

Q3: Which one is a prerequisite to enable planning data storage in Datasphere?

a) Both tenants use AWS.

b) Both tenants use MS Azure.

c) Datasphere has a minimum storage capacity of 200 GB.

d) Both Datasphere and SAC are using same identity provider.

Answer: d

Q4: A product switch is possible only from SAC and not from Datasphere.

a) True

b) False

Answer: b

Q5: Only a BI admin can do link tenant.

a) True

b) False

Answer: b

Q6: Data locking during planning can have the following states except which of the following?

a) Open

b) Restricted

c) Unlocked

d) Locked

Answer: c

**Chapter 5: Business Data Cloud (BDC)**

Q1: Which of the following is not a component within Business Data Cloud?

a) SAP Databricks

b) BW Bridge

c) SAP Analytics Cloud

d) Datasphere

Answer: b

Q2: Anthropic Claude Sonnet model is which of the following?

a) Hybrid reasoning model

b) AI agent

c) Used within Datasphere

d) None of the above

Answer: a

Q3: Which of the following is not a capacity service in Business Data Cloud?

a) Object store request in SAP Databricks

b) Object Store request in Datasphere

c) Object store request in SAC

d) None of the above

Answer: c

Q4: A data product generator is available in SAP BW PCE and Embedded BW.

a) True

b) False

Answer: b

Q5: What is the production backup strategy for SAP BW PCE?

a) Daily with 60 days retention

b) Daily with 90 days retention

c) Daily with 2 weeks retention

d) Daily with 30 days retention

Answer: d

Q6: A data product generator can have which of the following targets?

a) SAP Datasphere

b) SAC Model

c) Databricks Unity Catalog

d) SAP Joule

Answer: a

Q7: One Joule agent can't collaborate with other AI agents.

a) True

b) False

Answer: b

**Chapter 6: Evolution of Artificial Intelligence**

Q1: Which of the following model uses a neural network?

a) Long short-term memory network

b) IOT

c) Classification

d) Regression

Answer: a

Q2: Which of the following model overcomes some of the limitations of RNNs?

a) Long short-term memory network

b) GAN

c) All of the above

d) None of the above

Answer: a

Q3: Smart Predict can be used for which the following (choose all that apply)?

a) Transformer network

b) Classification

c) BPTT

d) Time series

Answer: b and d

Q4: An entity in the time series can't have multiple fields.

a) True

b) False

Answer: b

Q5: SAC only supports binary classification.

a) True

b) False

Answer: a

Q6: Fluctuations are patterns in a time series.

a) True

b) False

Answer: b

Q7: Which of the following metric compares the predicted value with that of the Naïve Bias Forecasting Method?

a) MAPE

b) MAE

c) MASE

d) RMSE

Answer: c

**Chapter 7: Need for Modernization**

Q1: Just Ask is relevant for a particular story.

a) True

b) False

Answer: b

Q2: Just Ask is applicable only for the acquired model and Datasphere model.

a) True

b) False

Answer: a

Q3: Data mesh is a subset of Data Warehouse.

a) True

b) False

Answer: b

Q4: Which of the following is a data mining tool?

a) SAP Analytics Cloud

b) SAP Ariba

c) SAP Concur

d) None of the above

Answer: d

Q5: Indexed SAC models are useful for creating a semantics layer.

a) True

b) False

Answer: b

Q6: Which one of the following is not a layer in a data lake architecture?

a) Landing Zone

b) Staging Zone

c) Data Exploration Zone

d) Analytics Zone

Answer: d

Q7: Which one is not a type of data lake?

a) Hybrid

b) On-premises

c) Multicloud

d) Multilayered

Answer: d

**Chapter 8: Path of Adoption**

Q1: What activity is not done during the Environment Preparation Phase?

a) Clean up old data

b) Perform a one-time load

c) Configure the tenant

d) Set up the users

Answer: c

Q2: Why is proof of concept useful in analytics modernization?

a) It can help to perform a feasibility check on an approach.

b) It can find out product limitations.

c) It can help to assess the estimation of the entire implementation.

d) All of the above.

Answer: d

Q3: All system (SAP and non-SAP) connectivity is generally a scope of POC.

a) True

b) False

Answer: b

Q4: Datasphere can be used as a pass-through solution without any replication.

a) True

b) False

Answer: a

Q5: Which one of the following should not be part of the demo kick-off session?

a) Planned agenda discussion for the entire demo period

b) Solution overview

c) Detailed design overview including the pseudologic, metadata, loading methodology, naming conventions, etc.

d) None of the above

Answer: c

Q6: A batch job schedule for updating data is generally considered out of scope from the POC.

a) True

b) False

Answer: a

Q7: It is usually beneficial to keep the POC execution period short because of the following reasons.

a) To keep the cost controlled

b) To generate quick results

c) To onboard resources quickly

d) Both a and b

Answer: d

**Chapter 9: Project Planning**

Q1: For model serving in SAP Databricks, during the promotional period, one DBU is equivalent to which of the following?

a) 0.1 CU

b) 0.2 CU

c) 0.8 CU

d) 0.9 CU

Answer: d

Q2: To reduce resources after the stabilization period, which of the following options can help?

a) Negotiating with customers

b) Rewriting the SoW

c) Employing contractors

d) Enabling AI

Answer: d

Q3: Decommissioning BW is not possible even after the migration to Business Data Cloud in all scenarios.

a) True

b) False

Answer: b

Q4: Which of the following licenses are possible in SAC?

a) Planning standard

b) Datasphere Advanced

c) Business Intelligence

d) Both a and b

e) Both a and c

Answer: d

Q5: How many test users must be procured in SAC?

a) 5

b) 10

c) 20

d) No limit

Answer: c

## APPENDIX C

# Supplemental Terms and Conditions for BDC

This appendix provides details on the system assessment to procure a Business Data Cloud subscription. The calculation will help organizations to decide what level of server needs to be procured.

## C.1 Core Capacity Unit Metric

The subscription to BDC is a service-based calculation and relies on the capacity units (ratio of the service consumed via capacity service). The usage is calculated based on capacity unit per month except for the Datasphere Capacity service and the Databricks capacity unit.

The calculation is based on multiplying the total number of capacity unit per month and the capacity unit value.

## C.2 Datasphere Capacity Unit

An SAP Datasphere capacity unit is measured using some or all the following services:

- Datasphere SaaS foundation
- Memory-optimized compute
- High-memory-optimized compute
- CPU-optimized compute
- High-CPU-optimized compute
- Memory-optimized elastic compute



© Sourav Banerjee 2025
S. Banerjee, *Modernizing SAP Business Warehouse*, https://doi.org/10.1007/979-8-8688-2192-9

- CPU-optimized elastic compute
- High-CPU-optimized elastic compute
- Spark compute
- Object store
- Object store requests
- Disk storage
- Catalog storage
- Data lake relational engine
- SAP BW Bridge
- Data integration
- Premium outbound integration

The premium outbound service is calculated based on blocks of 20 GB each. An increased outbound service may result in a higher cost. Any API usage to export data from cloud services to a third-party product is not permitted unless it is explicitly described in the functional document of the API.

The SAP BW Bridge capacity service includes an SAP BTP ABAP environment. A restriction of about 2000 OData API calls per 1 GB of compute memory per tenant per month is applied. An optional use of an on-premise SLT component for data exchange purposes is included in the Datasphere services.

## C.3 SAP BW PCE Capacity Unit

For a productive system, the base package includes the HANA DB with 256 GiB of memory and 256 GB of usable space. The application server has 64 GiB of memory.

For a nonproductive server, the package includes the HANA DB with 256 GiB of memory and 256 GB of usable space. The application server has 64 GiB of memory.

The capacity service outlined here includes SAP Web Dispatcher, both productive and nonproductive. A cloud connector is included per customer's VNET unless it is already installed using another subscription. The transport file storage capacity with this subscription is about 100 GB. Along with this, the SAP Analytics Cloud agent and SAP DP agent are included, and both will have one productive and one nonproductive server.

## C.4 SAP Analytics Cloud Capacity Unit

The SAP Analytics Cloud capacity unit is measured using the following capacity services:

- SAP Analytics Cloud for business intelligence public system
- SAP Analytics Cloud for Planning, Standard Edition, Public system
- SAP Analytics Cloud for Planning, Professional Edition, Public system
- SAP Analytics Cloud test Tenant, Public System

## C.5 SAP BW Capacity Services

The SAP Business Warehouse capacity unit is measured using the following capacity services:

- SAP BW/4 HANA Cloud, base package, Private Edition
- SAP BW/4 HANA Cloud, additional non-productive, base package, Private Edition
- SAP Business Planning and Consolidation professional edition for SAP BW/4 HANA Cloud (Planning only), Private Edition
- SAP Business planning and consolidation, Professional Edition for SAP BW/4 HANA Cloud, Private Edition
- SAP Business planning and consolidation, Standard Edition for SAP BW/4 HANA Cloud, Private Edition
- SAP Business planning and consolidation, standard Edition for SAP BW/4 HANA Cloud (Planning only), Private Edition
- SAP BW NetWeaver Cloud, base package, Private Edition
- SAP BW NetWeaver Cloud, additional non-productive, base package, Private Edition
- SAP Business planning and consolidation professional edition for SAP NetWeaver Cloud (Planning only), Private Edition

- SAP Business planning and consolidation professional edition for SAP NetWeaver Cloud, Private Edition
- SAP Business Planning and consolidation standard edition for SAP NetWeaver Cloud, Private edition
- SAP Business Planning and consolidation standard edition for SAP NetWeaver Cloud (Planning only), private edition
- SAP Cloud memory extension for productive tiers, private edition
- SAP Cloud memory extension for nonproductive tiers, private edition
- *SAP S/4 HANA* Cloud private edition application server for Linux, additional productive tenant, upgrade
- *SAP S/4 HANA* Cloud private edition application server for Linux, additional non-productive tenant, upgrade
- SAP BI JAVA server cloud, additional nonproductive, private edition (eight cores)
- SAP BI JAVA server cloud, private edition (eight cores)
- SAP additional database storage, private cloud edition
- SAP additional file storage, private cloud edition
- SAP S/4 HANA cloud private edition Application server for Linux, additional productive tenant
- SAP S/4 HANA cloud private edition application server for Linux, additional nonproductive tenant
- SAP IaaS server Linux cloud, private edition (128 GB)
- Connection package for productive tiers, private edition
- Connection package for nonproductive tiers, private edition
- SAP S/4 HANA cloud, disaster recovery, private edition

## C.6 SAP Databricks Capacity Services

The following capacity services are available for SAP Databricks:

- Enterprise SAP Automated Serverless Compute—region AP (Seoul)
- Enterprise SAP Automated Serverless Compute—region AP (Singapore)
- Enterprise SAP Automated Serverless Compute—region AP (Tokyo)
- Enterprise SAP Automated Serverless Compute—region Europe (Frankfurt)
- Enterprise SAP Automated Serverless Compute—region US East (N. Virginia)
- Enterprise SAP Public Connectivity Data Processed—region AP (Seoul)
- Enterprise SAP Public Connectivity Data Processed—region AP (Singapore)
- Enterprise SAP Public Connectivity Data Processed—region AP (Tokyo)
- Enterprise SAP Public Connectivity Data Processed—region Europe (Frankfurt)
- Enterprise SAP Public Connectivity Data Processed—region US East (N. Virginia)
- Enterprise SAP Private Connectivity End point—region AP (Seoul)
- Enterprise SAP Private Connectivity End point—region AP (Singapore)
- Enterprise SAP Private Connectivity End point—region AP (Tokyo)
- Enterprise SAP Private Connectivity End point—region Europe (Frankfurt)
- Enterprise SAP Private Connectivity End point—region US East (N. Virginia)
- Enterprise *SAP Databricks* Storage—region AP (Seoul)

- Enterprise *SAP Databricks* Storage—region AP (Singapore)
- Enterprise *SAP Databricks* Storage—region AP (Tokyo)
- Enterprise *SAP Databricks* Storage—region Europe (Frankfurt)
- Enterprise *SAP Databricks* Storage—region US East (N. Virginia)
- Enterprise SAP Inter-Availability Zone Egress
- Enterprise SAP Inter-Region Egress from—region AP (Seoul)
- Enterprise SAP Inter-Region Egress from—region AP (Singapore)
- Enterprise SAP Inter-Region Egress from—region AP (Tokyo)
- Enterprise SAP Inter-Region Egress from—region Europe (Frankfurt)
- Enterprise SAP Inter-Region Egress from—region US East (N. Virginia)
- Enterprise SAP interactive Serverless Compute—region AP (Seoul)
- Enterprise SAP interactive Serverless Compute—region AP (Singapore)
- Enterprise SAP interactive Serverless Compute—region AP (Tokyo)
- Enterprise SAP interactive Serverless Compute—region Europe (Frankfurt)
- Enterprise SAP interactive Serverless Compute—region US East (N. Virginia)
- Enterprise SAP Internet Egress from—region AP (Seoul)
- Enterprise SAP Internet Egress from—region AP (Singapore)
- Enterprise SAP Internet Egress from—region AP (Tokyo)
- Enterprise SAP Internet Egress from—region Europe (Frankfurt)
- Enterprise SAP Internet Egress from—region US East (N. Virginia)
- Enterprise SAP Model Serving—region AP (Seoul)
- Enterprise SAP Model Serving—region AP (Singapore)
- Enterprise SAP Model Serving—region AP (Tokyo)

- Enterprise SAP Model Serving—region Europe (Frankfurt)
- Enterprise SAP Model Serving—region US East (N. Virginia)
- Enterprise SAP Model training—region AP (Seoul)
- Enterprise SAP Model training—region AP (Singapore)
- Enterprise SAP Model training—region AP (Tokyo)
- Enterprise SAP Model training—region Europe (Frankfurt)
- Enterprise SAP Model training—region US East (N. Virginia)
- Enterprise SAP private connectivity Data Processed
- Enterprise SAP Serverless SQL Compute - region AP (Seoul)
- Enterprise SAP Serverless SQL Compute—region AP (Singapore)
- Enterprise SAP Serverless SQL Compute—region AP (Tokyo)
- Enterprise SAP Serverless SQL Compute—region Europe (Frankfurt)
- Enterprise SAP Serverless SQL Compute—region US East (N. Virginia)
- Enterprise SAP Enhanced Security and Compliance - for workspaces
- Enterprise SAP Anthropic model serving
- Object storage for SAP Databricks
- Object store requests for SAP Databricks

# C.7 Backup Strategy for SAP BW

The backup strategy for BW PCE edition is defined by SAP as follows:

*Production backup frequency*: Daily backup with 30 days retention period. The backup will be stored in a different data center for disaster recovery purposes

*Nonproduction backup frequency*: Weekly full backup with 14 days retention period. Backups will be stored in different data center.

*Long-term backup*: Monthly full backup with 1 year retention, quarterly full backup with 1 year retention, and yearly full backup with 5 years retention

*Retention for file system:* For production, monthly full and daily incremental with two months of retention. For nonproduction, the retention is monthly full and daily incremental with two months of retention.

## C.8 Incident Response Time

The response time for any SAP incident related to the previous sections are as follows:

*Very high*: If the issue reported has a very serious effect on the business and urgent work can't be performed. The response time is 20 minutes for a workaround and 4 hours for an action plan. Coverage is 24/7.

*High:* The effect is very serious on the server, and certain tasks could not be performed, although the production system is not down. The response time is two hours for the production server and four hours for the nonproduction server.

*Medium*: If normal business processes are affected and the problem is caused by inaccurate computing. The response time is four hours irrespective of the type of server.

*Low*: If the problem has little or no impact on the regular business process. The response time is one business day irrespective of the type of server.

# Index





© Sourav Banerjee 2025
S. Banerjee, *Modernizing SAP Business Warehouse*, https://doi.org/10.1007/979-8-8688-2192-9

## C

## D



## E, F

## P, Q

## R



## S

## T



## U, V



## W, X, Y, Z

GPSR Compliance
The European Union's (EU) General Product Safety Regulation (GPSR) is a set of rules that requires consumer products to be safe and our obligations to ensure this.

If you have any concerns about our products, you can contact us on

ProductSafety@springernature.com

In case Publisher is established outside the EU, the EU authorized representative is:

Springer Nature Customer Service Center GmbH
Europaplatz 3
69115 Heidelberg, Germany

www.ingramcontent.com/pod-product-compliance
Lightning Source LLC
LaVergne TN
LVHW060447061126
851857LV00016B/1753
* 9 7 9 8 8 6 8 8 2 1 9 1 2 *